HOT & SPICY

Also by Marlena Spieler
Naturally Good

HOT & SPICY

Unusual, Innovative Recipes from the World's Fiery Cuisines

Marlena Spieler

JEREMY P. TARCHER, INC.
Los Angeles
Distributed by St. Martin's Press
New York

Library of Congress Cataloging in Publication Data

Spieler, Marlena.
  Hot and spicy.

  Includes index.
  1. Cookery, International.   2. Spices.
3. Condiments.   I. Title.
TX 725.A1S63   1985   641.6'384   85-16853
ISBN 0-874-77370-9
ISBN 0-874-77371-7 (pbk.)

Jeremy P. Tarcher, Inc.
9110 Sunset Blvd.
Los Angeles, CA 90069

Design and illustration by Tanya Maiboroda

Manufactured in the United States of America
10   9   8   7   6   5   4   3

*To Leah and Gretchen,
with so much love*

Contents

Acknowledgments

To:

Theresa Chris, my agent and friend, for her belief in me; without her this book never would have been written.

Janice Gallagher, my editor and fellow hot-food fanatic, for her enthusiasm and understanding throughout this project.

Jeremy Tarcher, my publisher, for his personal attention to the book.

Laura Beausoleil, my typist, whose devotion to this project was as great as mine.

Ronn Weigand, my beverage consultant, for his talented and skillful pairing of drink with hot foods.

Esther Novak, whose friendship extended to her kitchen and who was always eager, or at least willing, to try the latest recipe.

My London friends: Paula Levine, David Aspin, and Joan and Malcolm Key, who opened their kitchen and studio for me to finish this book in, and Jill Vaux for her invaluable photographic assistance.

The following friends who tasted and contributed to this book: Linda Ackerman, Ardath and Neal Biskar, Sally Brown, Lori Fahn, Etty Katzeff, David and Sari Jefferies, Ethel Long, Jonathan Liechtling, Stacie Orey, Wendy Stern, Noah and Dinah Stroe, Yossi Shimron, Sandy Waks.

My grandmother, Sophia Dubowsky, for her joy of good food.

My parents, Caroline and Izzy Smith, for their support and encouragement, and my Auntie Stelli and Uncle Sy, for taking me to the House of Hot Tamales once upon a time; look what you started!

Alice Waters, Paula Wolfert, Elizabeth David, M. F. K. Fisher, and Alice B. Toklas, whose books inspired me to write this one.

Diana Kennedy and Elizabeth Lambert Ortiz, whose wonderful writings helped me fathom the often confusing world of chiles.

Thanks, Leah and Gretchen, for your understanding when the refrigerator, the kitchen, and our lives were so filled with chiles that there was room for little else.

Preface

It was a sweltering summer day in the Sacramento Valley when, at the age of five, I discovered my passion for spicy dishes. The temperature had hovered over 100 degrees for weeks. My family, too listless to eat, had nonetheless gathered for Sunday lunch. I observed the beads of condensation on the kitchen tiles; the air was warm and thick. No one really wanted to cook. "Mexican food is what we need!" interjected my uncle, who never let any adversity interfere with his appetite. Soon we were all piled into the old Dodge on our way to the House of Tamales. Even the breeze from the open car window did not cool me off—my taco, however, did. Bite after spicy bite (even at this tender age I asked for extra jalapeños), I began to feel exquisite relief. The air around me felt cool, and I became happier than I thought a person could ever feel.

Despite my family's partiality to Mexican food, I led a gastronomically sheltered childhood. So I was unprepared for the flavors and aromas of the Middle East when I shipped myself off to school in Jerusalem. This was the year of my culinary awakening. Who could ignore the sights and smells that engulfed me on the street, let alone on the plate? Wheelbarrows filled with steaming-hot fresh pita bread pushed by young boys through the crowded marketplace; spicy fried felafel sold by street vendors; fruits and vegetables piled high, ripe and pungent, on produce carts. It was a new universe, filled with foods spiced with sensuous abandon.

Since then I've expanded my hot-foods repertoire to encompass as many unusual cuisines as the world offers. When I studied French and Italian cuisine, I added a jolt of chile here and there for surprisingly wonderful results. When I visit a new city, I immediately find the local source of fresh chiles and cilantro (I travel with my own garlic and cumin). And once, when I lived on Crete where hot spices were not available for sale, I became so desperate for a fix of hot food that I made a middle-of-the-night raid on my neighbor's cayenne chile plant. She was growing it for decor and, I'm sure, was shocked by its appearance the next day. This book is a result of my peculiar passion, of my joy in searching for unusual spicy foods.

An Introduction to the Hot & Spicy

From Latin America's chile-spiked stews to the red-hot curries of India and Louisiana's volatile gumbos, hot foods burst forth with fiery flavors. Sometimes the heat gets your attention immediately, causing your eyes to tear and your hands to reach for water or soft, absorbent bread. Other times it sneaks up on you, say, after your third bite of a particularly delicious salsa, when you begin to whimper and calculate the distance to the nearest glass of beer.

Eating hot food is a gustatory thrill, a delectable blend of pleasure and pain, but it does not have to be scorching to be exciting. Many of the dishes in this book are only mildly hot.

In testing recipes, I noticed an interesting phenomenon: hot is not merely one sensation, but a whole range. There is the hot that burns immediately, tantalizing the tongue, then quickly disappearing; the hot that warms the throat and reddens the cheek; and the hot that feels benign at first but gradually leaves its legacy. There is also the hot that brings only gentle warmth. The sensations of hot foods are limited only by the cook's imagination in combining flavors.

The chile, native to tropical America, is the main source of this tasty fire, although my *Hot & Spicy* dishes use a variety of hot ingredients. Known also by its botanical name, *Capsicum frutescens,* it has been cultivated as early as 3500 B.C. It was a staple of the native Americans, along with many of the other indigenous New World foods. While the Eastern world had a richness of spices, before

3

the discovery of the New World their only hot seasonings were ginger and black pepper (which, by the way, is not related to the chile pepper). Imagine Columbus's surprise (and terror) when his crew found tiny red and green fruits that tasted hotter than anything in the known world! After Columbus's discovery, Vasco de Gama sailed around the globe, opening the way to Asia by sea for Europeans. Trade routes were established and the chile made its way to the rest of the world, especially to the warmer climates. In India it fired up curries; in Hungary it became paprika, synonymous with Hungarian food; and in Southeast Asia it generally ignited the diet.

Today, approximately 200 varieties of chiles are eaten both fresh and dried. When fresh, they come in vivid hues of primary colors—some bright red, others orange, yellow, and light to purple-tinged green. When dried, their skins shrivel and turn to earth tones: browns, brick-reds, and rusts.

The heat of the chile covers the full spectrum, from the mildness of the Anaheim or California chile to the savage bite of the Thai chile.

With hot food, you may often find yourself eating more than you intended. The reason lies in the chile's active ingredient, a volatile oil that gives the chile its distinctive bite. When this substance touches your mouth, your body starts the salvation process in an attempt to wash away the irritant. The saliva stimulates your taste buds, and as soon as the pain wears off, you find yourself saying, "I'll have just one more bit of Pasta Arabbiata, please."

Sometimes, however, you may find you've eaten too much chile in one bite. Do not reach for water! The water spreads the volatile oils throughout your mouth, actually increasing your misery. Reach, instead, for a piece of soft bread, a tortilla, or a spoonful of rice. The bland, starchy material absorbs the irritating oil, neutralizes it, and relieves your distress. In Texas they douse the fire by sprinkling salt on the side of the hand, then licking it off, much like the tequila ritual. After the bread, rice, tortilla, or salt is the time to drink water, juice, or icy beer. The beverage that puts out the fire most efficiently is milk, but I find it too filling to drink along with a meal, and there are other beverages that complement food better. In fact, you will find beverage suggestions with recipes in this book where appropriate, as well as in the chapter titled "On Pairing Foods and Beverages."

Some cuisines are very hot. In the south of India there are curries so incendiary that they sear your mouth if you're not used to them. In Mexico, raw jalapeños lie strewn atop dishes so intensely hot that you may spontaneously begin to speak Spanish. Thai and Szechuan foods routinely numb the taste buds with their molten heat. Besides these familiar cuisines, I have also included delicious sauces and dishes from cuisines not known for their spiciness. Piri-Piri, the torrid Portuguese sauce of chopped chiles, and Liutenitsa, the Bulgarian pepper relish, are both as fiery as anything from Mexico, India, or Southeast Asia.

The hottest cuisines emanate from warm, tropical climates. Since the volatile oil of the capsicum stimulates perspiration, eating chiles activates an effective air-cooling system. And the sharp, peppery flavors invigorate an appetite lagging from the sultry atmosphere. Fiery foods are also wonderful in the fall and winter seasons when their spicy heat warms and comforts from within. Think of chili con carne on a crisp winter day, or a zesty Hungarian goulash to stave off the cold.

Hot cuisines can be a blend of starchy, bland foods and sizzling accompaniments. Take Nasi Kuning, the Indonesian dish of yellow rice cooked in coconut milk, for example. Bland by itself, it is served with a variety of foods cooked with chiles and spices. Couscous is another example. This dish of fluffy, bland semolina is rescued from dullness by a liberal dousing of Harissa Sauce.

Hot foods are traditionally peasant in nature. These are robust dishes, based on culinary heritage and dependent upon the local marketplace. Hot food does not have to be limited to these classic dishes, however. Innovations have been taking place, especially in the Southwest United States and California. Creative cooks are combining classic cooking techniques with hot ingredients to produce such delicious hybrids as Goat-Cheese-Stuffed Poblanos, Cilantro Pesto, and Red Chile Pasta with Ratatouille. These recipes develop distinctive flavors along with the heat. It is in the spirit of both traditional peasant food and contemporary ideas that I have created *Hot & Spicy.*

This book is an innovative collection for those who like exciting and unusual foods, flavors that stimulate both the imagination and the palate. My recipes have been gathered from all over the world—personally, through friends, and from books. I have omitted many delicious hot dishes because they are standard cookbook inclusions. When I do include a classic dish, it is a particularly vibrant version. Some recipes are totally new ideas based on authentic ingredients and classic technique. In all cases I have searched for the unexpected: the surprise squeeze of lime, aroma of cinnamon, or jolt of chile when least expected.

Though many people protest that they can't eat hot foods, it's just a matter of acclimation. Extremely hot foods need working up to. To guide you through the recipes so that you can choose dishes that correspond to your desired heat tolerance, each recipe is designated by an illustration of one to three chiles. One chile = mild, two chiles = medium, three chiles = hot. This is only a guide, as I've found the intensity of individual chiles varies greatly. The serrano I used may be much hotter or milder than the one you use. I know of no other way to tell than by tasting a small amount.

Hot condiments are by their nature hotter than other dishes. A few of the hot condiments surpass the three-chile rating system and veer into the territory of the very, very hot. They are labeled exactly that: Very, Very Hot.

Cumin and cilantro are important seasonings in hot cuisines. I must admit my particular weakness for these flavors, which even testing for this book did not diminish. It is possible—indeed likely—that you do not share my passion for one or both. If you feel that the amount of cumin called for in any recipe is excessive for your tastes, cut back. I've given suggestions in various recipes, but you could substitute ground coriander or Curry Powder (not the store-bought variety; make your own from the recipe included in this book) for cumin or even eliminate it. Cilantro is another controversial flavor. Most people either love or loathe it. Like so many other complex and unusual flavors, it is an acquired taste, and once acquired becomes an addiction. Its deep pungency brilliantly sets off the flavors of accompanying ingredients. It is worth attempting to like it by starting with small doses and working up, since its impact on the dishes it touches is amazingly good. If, however, you still dislike even the smell, I've indicated where cilantro may be eliminated or replaced by parsley, fresh mint, or green onion.

Most cookbooks advise you to underspice rather than overspice. Don't listen to them; be bold! Take the culinary risk. Timidity in the kitchen begets insipid food. Vibrant spicing is one of the keys to delicious, inspired cooking, one of the simple joys that enriches and expands our lives.

A note on the basic ingredients:

All butter used is sweet (unsalted).

All eggs are large.

Garlic cloves are on the large side and coarsely chopped unless otherwise noted.

Olive oil should be fruity and flavorful, the kind that is usually greenish in color, and extra virgin (from the first pressing).

Vegetables are all medium-sized.

A Guide to Hot Stuff

Hot seasonings come in a huge variety. There is an endless array of chiles, fresh and dried, each size, shape, and color yielding a slightly different flavor and heat. There are prepared sauces, pastes, and spices that add glowing warmth along with aromatic flavor. Even garlic, which is better known for its more odoriferous quality, stings the tongue when raw.

Many hot ingredients are interchangeable. A basic chart of equivalency is:

1 mild dried chile pod = 1 tablespoon ground chile powder
1 small, dried red chile = ¼ to ½ teaspoon cayenne pepper
= ½ teaspoon hot pepper flakes
= 4 shakes Tabasco
= ½ teaspoon hot chile paste (such as Ají or commercial garlic-chile paste)

As for fresh chiles, the serrano is hotter but smaller than the jalapeño, so if substituting one for the other, one-half serrano probably equals one jalapeño, but keep in mind the variable heat quality of the fresh chile. When a recipe specifies Anaheim chile, any mild chile may be used; when serrano is called for, any small, hot chile is fine.

FRESH CHILES

The bite of the fresh chile is hot and assertive. They are usually available green but are sometimes sold in their ripe, red stage, when they are slightly sweeter and a bit less *picante*. Though the general rule is the larger the pepper, the milder the heat; the smaller, the hotter, this is not true for the fiery habanero or Rocoto.

Choose chiles as you would any other vegetable or fruit: Look for firmness, avoid pulpiness. Fresh chiles keep several weeks in the refrigerator if they were fresh and in good condition when you bought them and are kept dry. Following is a brief description of each of the more available varieties.

Anaheim   Also known as California chile, this is the same chile that, once dried, becomes the New Mexico or California chile. It is 4 to 6 inches long and about 1½ inches wide at the top. It is flat and generally sold green. As the skin is tough, this chile should be roasted and peeled before using. It is used commonly in the Southwest United States and is sold canned, labeled "mild green chiles."

Bird's eye or Bird pepper   Very hot and similar to Thai chiles.

Chile caballero   Similar to the habanero of Yucatan, the chile caballero is very hot. It hails from Guatemala and is usually found only there.

Cayenne   This fresh chile is medium green, 3 to 4 inches long and ⅜ inch wide. It is very hot but not very juicy, so the heat remains in the pieces of chile rather than diffusing throughout the dish it is cooked with. When ripe, dried, and ground, this becomes cayenne pepper.

Chilaca   This long, slim, dark green chile is 6 inches long and 1 inch wide. It is mild to medium in heat intensity and has a deep, rich flavor much like a poblano. Once it is dried it becomes the chile pasilla, which is known as the chile negro on the West Coast.

Güero   Called *X-cat-ik* in its native Yucatan, this pale yellow chile is 3 to 4 inches long, 1 inch wide, and hot. Sometimes the same chile is called chile largo. To confuse things further sometimes the Güero refers to a mild, sweet pepper.

I first noticed this pepper in a specialty international food shop in New York City, where it was called "Dutch chile" because it is grown in Holland for export. Since then I've found this mildish chile in marketplaces throughout Italy, France, and even staid Britain. It is 3½ to 4½ inches long and about ¾ of an inch wide at top; similar to an Italian frying pepper, but smooth and straight. Though I sometimes see it sold green, it is generally sold in its red ripe stage. Usually as mild as an Anaheim, occasionally they will be quite hot. It is the most common mild green chile I have found in Europe.

Italian frying pepper   This mild pepper resembles a small Anaheim, both in flavor and heat intensity.

Jalapeño   Mid to dark green, this very hot chile is approximately 2½ inches long and ¾ inch wide at the top. Sometimes sold red in its ripe stage, when it is slightly sweeter and less hot. The jalapeño is also available canned and pickled. See recipe for Jalapeño Boats in this section for an attractive Mexican garnish.

Habanero   This small, lantern-shaped chile is about 3 inches long and 1 inch wide, generally colored yellow to light green, but sometimes available ripe-red, and it is very hot. Eaten in Mexican salsas, stews, etc.

Mirasol   A small Peruvian chile, orange-yellow, in color. It is not too hot and used as a garnish and in relishes and salads. Also used dried.

Poblano   This richly flavored chile is colored deep green with a purple cast. It is similar in size and shape to a green bell pepper but flatter and squarer. The poblano can range in heat from very mild to hot, and I have yet to find a way of telling without tasting. They have a tough skin and should be roasted and peeled before using. If unavailable, substitute Anaheim or California. When dried, this becomes the ancho chile.

Rocoto   Also known as locoto, this very hot chile is eaten in Peru, Bolivia, and Central America, and is occasionally seen in Mexico as chile manzana. Much larger than most hot chiles—4 to 5 inches long and as thick as a man's thumb— it has distinctively colored black seeds.

Serrano   This small chile is the most easily available very hot chile. The serrano is about 1½ inches long and ¼ to ½ inch wide. Usually deep green in color, when ripe it turns blazing red and makes a delightful garnish. In addition to fresh, the serrano is available dried, canned, and pickled.

Thai   This is the hottest chile available in the United States (though I have heard stories of frighteningly hot chiles in Southeast Asia). The Thai chile is 2 to 3 inches long and thin as a needle. Use sparingly, allowing about one-half Thai chile in place of one serrano. See recipe for Thai Chile Flowers in this section for a fiery flower garnish for Southeast Asian dishes.

Wax chile   This is also called Hungarian wax pepper and looks much like a light yellow jalapeño, but is considerably milder, both in flavor and heat.

Fresh Chile Garnishes

These garnishes are more for decorative purposes than for eating. For Thai Chile Flowers, long, thin chiles are cut lengthwise several times; after being immersed in ice water, they open up into "flowers." A platter of spicy food, such as Nasi Kuning, Gado Gado, or Pad Thai, is even more beautiful and exotic when garnished with a few of these fiery flowers.

Another attractive garnish, probably the hottest thing I've ever eaten, is jalapeños hollowed out into little boats and filled with salsa. Use them to surround a platter of Arroz con Pollo or Couscous Fassi.

Thai Chile Flowers   *Very, very hot*

Thailand, Southeast Asia

Small, thin chiles (often called Thai chiles); if these are not available, use red serranos. Green may be used if red is unavailable, and a combination of red and green is even nicer.

Ice Water

FRESH CHILES

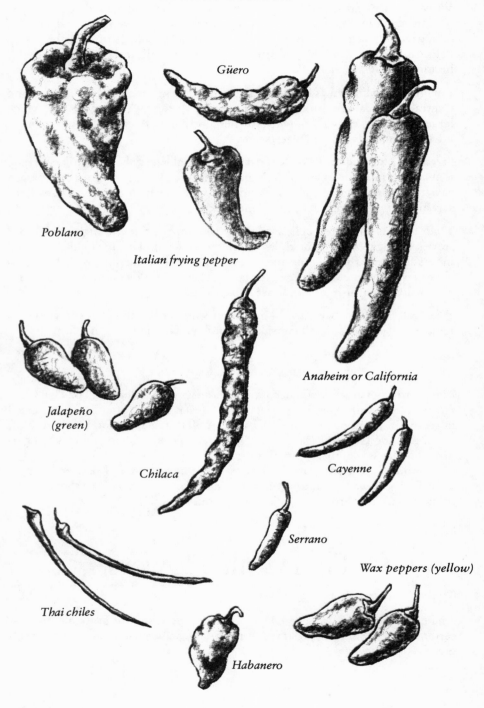

Güero

Poblano

Italian frying pepper

Jalapeño
(green)

Chilaca

Anaheim or California

Cayenne

Serrano

Thai chiles

Wax peppers (yellow)

Habanero

With a small, sharp knife, make lengthwise cuts in chiles; remove any seeds and pith that you can with tip of knife, then pop chiles into ice water and leave for 30 minutes. They will open into flower shapes. You may cut either end, retaining stem and cutting from the pointed end, or removing stem and cutting the "petals" from that end.

Advance Preparation: "Flowers" last 3 to 4 days in the refrigerator, covered with cold water.

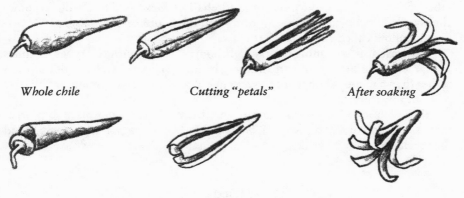

Whole chile   *Cutting "petals"*   *After soaking*

Jalapeño Boats   *Very, very hot*

   Red and/or green jalapeños
½ *cup freshly prepared salsa (from Salsas, Hot Sauces, and Condiments)*

Cut off top of jalapeño lengthwise, retaining stem to use as handle. Remove seeds and pith. Fill with a spoonful of salsa.

Cut top

Salsa

DRIED CHILES

Dried chiles come in an even more dizzying array than fresh chiles. As with the fresh, smaller usually means hotter. In choosing, look for whole chiles with no signs of insects. I have divided the following description into mild and hot chiles in an attempt to clarify a very confusing situation.

One cannot begin to describe and categorize chiles without mentioning the fact that often the name will vary from place to place. The ancho is occasionally labelled "pasilla" in California, or "morelia" in Mexico. The Pasilla is sometimes called "chile negro" in California and the Southwest. In parts of Mexico the guajullo is called "cascabel."

Because it is so confusing, try to become familiar with the types of chiles available in your area. If you are ordering by mail, send a sample, or description rather than a name. Though it can seem like a maze in the beginning, familiarity will simplify things.

Whichever chiles you do choose, store them in a cool, dry place to protect them from moisture and insects. I keep mine in plastic bags in a storage bin and they seem to last quite well.

Mild Dried Chiles

These are the chiles that are steeped and simmered for Southwestern sauces, stews, and chili or ground into mild flavoring spice. They have much flavor but little heat, and several types are often combined for a richer, more complex flavor. Since there are so many varieties of mild dried chiles, the names can be confusing, especially when they are labeled differently in different geographical locations. A basic guideline that I use separates the large mild chiles into two groups: the smooth-skinned, reddish colored ones such as New Mexico or California; and the thick-skinned, dark colored, chewy-textured chiles such as ancho or chile negro. I have found that within these two groups you can choose whichever is available and substitute one chile for another, such as New Mexico for California, or ancho for chile negro.

Ancho   This is the ripened and dried chile poblano, wrinkled and deep reddish brown. Rich in taste, it is generally soaked and pureed into sauce but may be toasted and ground into chile powder as well. This 5-inch-by-3-inch chile ranges in heat from mild to slightly *picante* and is sometimes mislabeled as pasilla.

Cascabel   Its name means "rattlesnake," because of the sound it makes when shaken. It is round and about 1 inch in diameter. Very mild, it gives a distinctive, nutty flavor to sauces and stews.

Chile negro   Long and narrow, with the thick, wrinkled dark skin of the ancho, it is the dried chilaca chile. Robust and delicious combined with other chiles or toasted and ground into chile powder. Chile negro is labelled pasilla in parts of Mexico and the Southwest.

Chimayo   The New Mexico chile or the chile de ristra, which is grown in the Chimayo Valley, is labeled Chimayo. Mild and rich. See the description under New Mexico Chile.

Guajillo   This long, slender, pointed chile is about 4 inches long and about 1 inch wide. It is thin-skinned and reddish, pinkish-brown when dried but imparts a bright orangeish tint to dishes. Tangy and flavorful, it is often combined with other chiles to give its distinctive flavor and color. It is much hotter than the other mild chiles.

Mirasol   Small, orange-yellow colored chile used in Peru to season stews, and for preparing Ají, the ubiquitous Peruvian chile sauce.

Mulato   Shaped much like an ancho, the mulato is slightly larger, darker brown, and sweeter in flavor. It is used in conjunction with the ancho or in its place.

New Mexico chile   This is the most common large dried chile. It is flavorful, with just enough heat to give interest. The New Mexico chile is also known as California chile, chile de ristra, as well as (in California) pasilla. In New Mexico it is said that the Chimayo Valley grows the tastiest chiles; throughout New Mexico these chiles, called ristras, are strung into long bunches and hung on the walls. Use these brick-colored chiles by themselves or in conjunction with the ancho or chile negro.

Pasilla   In California, pasilla refers to the ripe, dried Anaheim chile, New Mexico chile, California chile, or Chimayo chile. In other areas of the Southwest and Mexico, pasilla refers to the dried Chilaca chile. To confuse things even further, this chile is known as chile negro in California. Use in conjunction with other mild chiles.

Pulla   This chile looks much like a smaller version of the guajillo. It is 4 to 5 inches long and about ¾ inch wide and much paler in both flavor and heat. They are not readily available, but if you do find them, you might include several with other chiles in a chile-infused meat stew.

Hot Dried Chiles

There are many varieties of small hot chiles. Often they are sold simply labeled "hot peppers" or "chile peppers." In the recipes I have listed them as such, since most small dried chiles are quite hot, with similar flavor, and are interchangeable though they may vary somewhat in degree of heat. These chiles may be simmered whole in a dish, then fished out at the end for a subtle result, or crumbled and added for more fire. Following is a brief description of the small chiles you are most likely to encounter. Except for the ají, they are all red.

Ají   The Peruvian word for chile in general. Ají is also the name of a type of chile as well as a table condiment. The ají pepper is yellowish in color and not as hot as the hontaka, árbol, or pequín.

DRIED CHILES

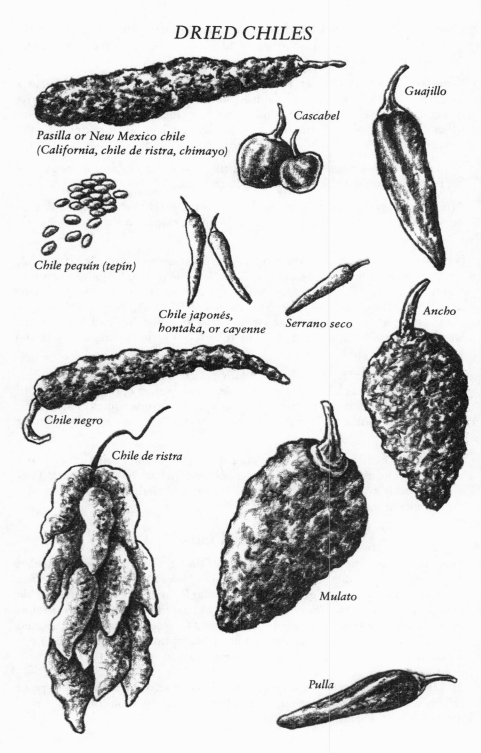

Pasilla or New Mexico chile
(California, chile de ristra, chimayo)

Cascabel

Guajillo

Chile pequín (tepín)

Chile japonés,
hontaka, or cayenne

Serrano seco

Ancho

Chile negro

Chile de ristra

Mulato

Pulla

Árbol   This small red pepper is very, very hot (but wonderful).

Cayenne   Small, hot red chiles, variable in heat.

Hontaka   Red, thin, 1 to 2 inches long, very hot. These are raised in Japan and exported to Latin America.

Japonés   Similar to hontaka; sometimes spelled Japone.

Kashmiri   Of Kashmiri origin, these are often ground into a powder; not as hot as the other small hot chiles.

Malagueta   A very hot, small chile used in Brazilian cooking.

Pequín   This is also known as *tepín*. These are small, hot, and round, about ½ inch in diameter.

Serrano seco   The dried serrano chile; it is very hot and sometimes called chile japonés.

Commercial Chile Powders

All dried chiles may be made into powder by toasting and grinding (see recipes for chile powders in this section). This powder of ground chile is delicious spooned into dishes like soups and stews, and is easier than soaking and pureeing the whole pods. When using powdered chiles, except the small, hot ones, a good guideline is 1 tablespoon powdered chile=1 large pod. Following is a brief guide to some of the chile powders and mixtures available.

Chili powder   The readily available commercial chili powders are usually mixed with other ingredients and not at all to my liking (when I want other spices, I will add my own!). I do not recommend using them unless there is no choice.

Cayenne pepper   The small, hot cayenne chile ground into powder.

Chile Caribe   Very hot pepper flakes with seeds.

New Mexico chile powder   Usually sold marked "Mild," "Medium," or "Hot," this is the ground New Mexico chile with varying amounts of cayenne or its equivalent. In the recipes in this book, however, when a recipe calls for New Mexico chile it means the toasted, ground pods of New Mexico chiles.

Hot Hungarian paprika   Sweet, flavorful Hungarian paprika with almost enough bite to rival its cousin cayenne; use as you would cayenne to fire up mild paprika.

Hot or red pepper flakes   Sold under that simple name, these are small, hot red chiles, crumbled, seeds and all. Best known for sprinkling on pizza. Also known as hot chile or red chile flakes.

Chile Powder

Yield: 1 large, mild chile pod =
1 tablespoon, 4 pods =
⅛ cup

Pure powdered chile makes a delicious addition to soups, stews, sauces, and many other dishes. Toasting the chiles not only gives a slightly roasted flavor, it also makes them easier to grind. Powdered chile is delicious added to Southwestern specialties, of course, but try it in such unorthodox combinations as New Mexican Chile Bread, a flavoring for fresh pasta dough, a spoonful added to rich, unctuous hollandaise. Keep an array of ancho, New Mexico, pasilla, etc., powders for use as desired.

1. Place chiles in a single layer on a cookie sheet. Toast in a preheated 400° F. oven until they darken slightly in color, 3 to 5 minutes. Watch carefully so they do not burn or they will be bitter. Remove and let cool. They will be hard and brittle.
2. Remove stems and crumble chiles into electric coffee grinder. (Different types of chiles will have different textures. Basically the ancho, pasilla, and negro will have a more pliable, leathery consistency; the New Mexico and California, a thinner, crisper consistency.) Small coffee grinders can handle 1 to 3 chiles at a time. Turn on and off as you would for grinding coffee, until chiles become a coarse powder.

Advance Preparation: Prepare a big batch and store in jars or airtight plastic bags.

Note: Small electric coffee grinders are excellent for grinding spices and chiles. If you use it for coffee as well, the grinder should be cleaned before and after it is used for spices. To clean, place several tablespoons raw rice in the grinder and grind as for coffee. The next batch of coffee may still retain a suspicion of spice flavor; I do not find it objectionable. If you do, clean the grinder with rice twice after use for spices. If you grind chiles and spices often, you might consider investing in a second coffee grinder expressly for this purpose.

PREPARING CHILES

Chiles must be handled with care and respect. The volatile oil of the capsicum fruit will sting if you have any cuts on your fingers, and unless you wash your hands extremely well after handling the chiles, you will get a stinging surprise later when you rub your eyes or other sensitive spot. For best protection, thin rubber gloves are perfect. The disposable ones are best, since you won't have to worry about rubbing your eyes with them the next time you wear them. When preparing chiles, remember that the flavor is in the flesh, the heat is concentrated in the membranes and seeds. Occasionally a recipe will indicate that the chile is to be seeded; if not indicated, then I intend the seeds to be included. You may omit the seeds anytime you desire a milder flavor.

Roasting and Peeling Chiles and Peppers

The skin of fresh large chiles and peppers is tough and must usually be removed before the pepper is used for cooking. This is done by roasting, then wrapping in plastic or other airtight container, leaving to "steam," then rinsing and peeling. The steaming after roasting separates the charred skin from the flesh so the chile or pepper peels easily. Roasting also imparts a slightly smoky, subtly robust flavor. Use the following method whenever a recipe calls for "chiles or peppers, roasted and peeled."

As many chiles or peppers as desired.

1. Place chiles or peppers directly on top of gas stove; turn the heat to medium and rotate peppers every so often to allow the flame to char the skin evenly. (Small chiles must be toasted in an ungreased skillet; I use a chestnut roasting pan since then the chiles have direct contact with the flame and develop that smoky flavor.)
2. Remove to a plastic bag or to a saucepan; tie the bag to seal it, or place tight lid on top of pan. Leave to "steam" for 15 to 20 minutes, then rinse chiles or peppers under cold running water and peel off skin with fingers and a small paring knife. Note: If you have an electric stove, broil the chiles or peppers under the broiler. Proceed to steam and peel.

Advance Preparation: Chiles may be roasted, peeled, and kept in freezer for use as desired; they will become a little mushy and lose a little heat, but will still be flavorful and slightly *picante*. Strips of chiles or peppers may also be kept in a marinade (see Goat-Cheese-Stuffed Poblanos or Roasted and Marinated Peppers).

When frying or pureeing hot chiles, be sure the area is ventilated; the fumes can sting your eyes and throat.

If you have gotten the chile oil in a cut or in your eyes, wash with cool water and continue washing until the pain subsides. Don't be alarmed; depending on how much you've absorbed, it may take some time for the sting to dissipate.

PICKLED AND CANNED CHILES

Chipotle Brown, wrinkled, with a smoky taste and aroma. It is the jalapeño, ripened, dried, smoked, and canned. Rich and distinctive, chipotles come in small cans. You may also use the sauce they are canned in. Chipotles make a savory condiment atop a tostada or tucked into a burrito.

Mild green chiles Whole or diced, these are Anaheim chiles, roasted and peeled. They are very mild and have little flavor but may be used when fresh ones are unavailable.

Italian pickled peppers.   Mild to medium whole chiles pickled in vinegar. Eaten in Mediterranean countries.

Jalapeño en escabeche   Jalapeño chiles pickled in vinegar. These are hot and often pickled with garlic, carrots, onions, etc. The vegetables become delicious and hot as they pickle with the jalapeño.

Serrano en escabeche   This is the serrano chile pickled similarly to the jalapeño. The pickled serrano is similar in flavor to the jalapeño but is hotter.

Pequín or tepín   These small, very hot peppers are occasionally available.

Tabasco peppers   Small, hot, yellow-colored chiles pickled in vinegar, eaten in Brazil and much of Latin America. A similar version is enjoyed in Hawaii. In the Caribbean, small hot peppers are placed in a jar and covered with sherry or vinegar. The liquid is sprinkled onto dishes as seasoning.

SAUCES AND PREPARATIONS

There is a huge array of prepared hot condiments and sauces available in ethnic groceries. The following is a selection of my favorites and ones that are used in this book. There are many others I haven't the space to mention, most notably a number of Mexican seasoning pastes. Try purchasing and tasting several until you find one you especially like.

Chile oil   Fiery peanut oil in which hot red chile flakes have be steeped. Purchase in Oriental groceries or make your own by bringing ⅛ cup small hot chiles, crumbled, and 1 cup peanut oil just to a boil; turn off heat and let cool to room temperature. Strain if you wish, or let the chiles remain for greater heat. Lasts indefinitely. Use as a condiment in the Chinese kitchen and at the table; try some dribbled over a pot-sticker (Chinese dumpling) or a Mo-Mo (Tibetan dumpling), along with a little soy sauce and vinegar.

Chile sauce   This along with enchilada sauce, I mention only because it is often available when dried chiles are not. It is thin, acidic and a poor substitute for homemade Basic Chile Sauce, but there are times, especially when you need only a small amount, that this is useful.

Garlic-chile paste   Vietnamese garlic-chile paste is my favorite, but China and other Asian countries have good ones as well. Delicious added to stir-fries, soups, anything, garlic-chile paste is a staple in my hot-foods kitchen since it is flavorful as well as hot.

Fermented chile paste with fermented beans   Pungent and hot, it turns a simple stir-fry into a distinctive, fiery dish.

Jalapeño jelly   Popular in the Southwest United States; much like chutney in its combination of sweet and hot. It's really not a very sophisticated flavor, but nonetheless good dribbled over a little cream cheese or used to glaze a roast duck or loin of pork.

Hot bean sauce This wonderful hot sauce turns any simple dish into a mysterious Chinese delicacy.

Hot chutney Sweet-sour and hot preserve of fruit, spices, chiles, and vinegar. Much-used in Anglo-Indian cookery. See, also, the entry for chutney in Other Special Ingredients.

Salsa Refers to the Mexican variety of sauces made from chiles, tomatoes, and spices. May be red or green, mild to very hot. A good commercial salsa is always handy to have in stock; it keeps well and can perk up your cuisine when you haven't time to prepare a homemade one.

Tabasco Very hot, thin, vinegary liquid made of pureed small, hot cayenne chiles. Originally made in Lousiana.

Special Ingredients

Achiote seeds A seed used in Caribbean cooking, achiote tints food with a reddish color. It has a mild flavor and is often infused with oil for easier usage, since the seeds are very hard and must be strained out.

Blue corn tortillas A regional specialty from New Mexico, where legend has it that corn was given to the world by a huge turkey that flew over the Earth and dropped an ear of blue corn from under its wing. You may find it more convenient to order from a mail-order source.

Cellophane noodles Noodles made from the starch of mung beans; brittle and whitish when dry, they are chewy and transparent when cooked.

Chutney There are two kinds of chutney, fresh and preserved. The fresh is the intense pounded mixture served in Indian cuisine, made freshly for each meal. This concoction is based on fresh chiles with other spices, coconut, herbs, etc., included. The second type of chutney is that familiar preserve of fruit and chiles; it is really more a part of British cuisine than Indian. Sweet and sour, it can be very hot as well.

Cilantro The plant grown from the coriander seed. Cilantro is also known as Chinese parsley. It has a pungent, distinctive aroma and flavor that not everyone appreciates, but those of us who do are enthusiastic indeed. It is much used in the hot-foods kitchen.

Coconut milk The liquid extracted from the pressing and squeezing of the coconut flesh, not the liquid contained inside the coconut. You may make your own (the directions will generally be available in any Indian or Southeast Asian cookbook), or you may buy the unsweetened coconut milk in a can, usually sold frozen.

If you wish to make coconut milk yourself, here's how to do it using fresh coconut. This produces the best result but is time-consuming and demanding. A shortcut simply simmers dessicated, unsweetened coconut milk in water, 2 parts water to one part coconut, then purees and strains it. While it is easier, the coconut milk is not as rich.

Choose a coconut, one that makes a noise when you shake it. That noise indicates liquid inside and is a sign of freshness. Also avoid any that have moldy "eyes" as that usually indicates an over-the-hill coconut. To open it you will need a hammer and a screwdriver or ice pick. Puncture two of the eyes using the ice pick or screwdriver and hammer. Drain the liquid; this is not the coconut milk. Throw it away or set it aside and drink it. Next, take the hammer and hit the shell hard, about a third of the way down all around the shell. There is a "faultline" here, something like the equator which runs around the shell, and when you hit the right spot, a crack will form, opening it right up.

Peel the tough skin and break or cut the coconut into 1- to 2-inch sized chunks. Place in processor and puree, slowly adding very hot water (just below boiling). You will need about half as much water as coconut flesh. When mixture is a thick, chunky liquid you are ready to extract the coconut milk. Set a strainer over a large bowl; line strainer with a cheesecloth. Pour as much of the mixture in as possible, pressing hard with a large spoon to extract as much liquid as you can. Twist the cloth and squeeze the coconut as hard as you can to continue extracting the coconut essence. Repeat until all coconut mixture is gone. As it sets, it will separate and the top will be thick like cream. They may be used separately, or stirred together before using. Coconut milk will last about 3 days refrigerated and freezes very well.

Dahl The Indian term for lentils. In India a huge variety of lentils—white, black, green, yellow, orange—are eaten. *Masoor dahl,* the reddish colored one, is my favorite for its meaty, rich flavor.

Dêndé oil Brightly orange-colored oil extracted from palm, it is used much in the cooking of Brazil, especially where the African influence is strong.

Dried shrimp Small dried shrimp much used in Southeast Asian cuisine. Purchase them in Asian groceries. Sometimes they are sold as a powder.

Egg roll wrappers Squares of delicate noodles sold for making into egg rolls but also useful for many pasta dishes, especially ravioli.

Filé powder Sometimes called gumbo filé, it is dried, pounded sassafras root. Used to thicken the gumbos which have no okra.

Filo dough Tissue-paper-thin dough sold in Middle Eastern groceries for making strudel, baklava, and that heavenly Greek spinach pastry, *spanakopitta.* Best when purchased fresh, though it freezes well and is handy to keep in the freezer any time you wish to make something elegant but easy. Filo bakes into the crispiest, flakiest pastry possible.

Fish sauce   A fermented liquid brewed from fish, much used in Southeast Asian cooking. In fact, next to the chile, it is their most distinctive flavor. Also known as Nuoc nam.

Gyoza noodles   Slightly thicker than egg roll or won-ton wrappers, Gyoza noodles are round, about 2 inches in diameter. They are used to make gyoza, a Japanese pot-sticker, or for ravioli.

Hoisin sauce   A sweet, slightly spicy bean-based sauce used in Chinese cooking as an ingredient and condiment, spread on moo-shu dishes and used in stir-fries.

Hominy   Hominy is corn that has been soaked in lye to loosen the hulls and swell the kernels. The kernels are then rinsed and boiled. It has a distinctive flavor and consistency. When ground, it is known as hominy grits, sold dried in fine, medium or coarse grind. The whole kernel is generally sold in cans, though occasionally you can find it dried.

Hot bean paste   A pungent Chinese seasoning paste of beans, garlic and chile. A spoonful enlivens any stir-fry.

Jícama   A crunchy root vegetable, light brown on the outside, creamy white on the inside. It is something like a potato, something like an apple. Generally eaten raw, sprinkled with cayenne pepper or cut up into a salad.

Kimchee   Korean pickled vegetables with chile and vinegar. Cabbage is the vegetable most often pickled in commercial kimchee, and it's redolent of garlic, blazing with chile. Try it alongside bland rice and shreds of barbecued meat.

Laos   Also known as galangal, this spice is ground from a root much like ginger both in appearance and aroma. Used in Southeast Asia and occasionally North Africa.

Lavosh   Armenian flatbread. It is sold in small, medium, or huge rounds (about 18 inches in diameter). *Lavosh* may be enjoyed as a cracker or moistened. Let stand to soften, then spread with cream cheese and other salad fillings and roll up tightly.

Masa harina   Dried corn ground finely into flour. Use for tortillas, tamales, gorditas and to thicken chile con carne.

Nopales   Cactus leaves. Used in Mexican stews, salads, egg dishes. Available in jars and fresh. If using fresh, be sure to parboil as they exude a sticky substance.

Orange flower water   A flavoring extract made from distilling the essence of orange blossoms, much as a perfumer would. Used in Middle Eastern cooking and for flavoring mixed drinks.

Ouzo The strong, liquorice-scented alcoholic beverage of Greece. Clear in color and potent, Ouzo is served in small glasses accompanied by nibbles of savory hors d'oeuvres.

Pine nuts The nut of the pine tree; also known as piñon, pignolia, or "Indian nuts." Buy the longer, thinner ones, known as Portuguese; they have a richer flavor. The Chinese ones are shorter, fatter, and have an unpleasant, turpentine-like flavor. As pine nuts are time consuming to shell, I always buy them shelled.

Rice noodles Noodles made from the flour of rice; also called rice sticks. They are sold in widths varying from no thicker than a string to ¾ inch. Generally available dried, they are also occasionally sold fresh, especially in Asian neighborhoods.

Sausages Lately there has been a rekindled interest in the ancient art of sausage-making and consequently a larger selection of more unusual, spicy sausages have become available. Here are only a few: Andoville, a hot chile spiced sausage from Louisiana; kielbasa, garlic and black pepper flavored; merguez, a lamb sausage redolent of North African spices and hot red chile.

Sereh Also known as lemon grass or citronella, this is a grass that resembles a green onion in appearance but smells distinctively of lemon. Also sold as a powder, it is used in Southeast Asia and Indonesia.

Shrimp paste (blacan or **trassi)** Pureed fermented shrimp; used in Southeast Asia and Indonesia.

Tahini A creamy paste ground from sesame seeds, used as the basis of many sauces and dips throughout the Middle East. Sweetened, it is the basis of halvah.

Tomatillo Small green tomatoes in a papery husk; not to be confused with unripe tomatoes. They have a tart flavor and are enjoyed cooked in Mexican sauces.

Tortilla Flat, pancake-like unleavened bread made of masa harina, or ground corn. Tortillas are the basic food of Mexico and popular throughout California and the Southwest. They are also made from New Mexico blue corn, or wheat flour. Wonderful when freshly made but delicious too, when purchased and warmed.

To warm tortillas, spray or sprinkle lightly with a small amount of water. Wrap up tightly in foil and place in grill or in a hot oven and heat for 5 to 10 minutes. Do not use too much water or they will become gummy; if heated too long, they will become tough.

Tortillas may also be heated on a lightly oiled skillet, after being moistened. Heat them individually or warm the whole stack over a low heat and seal the top with foil. They may be kept warm by wrapping them in a clean cloth napkin.

Udon Thick Japanese noodles, usually served in a bowl of soup. Try some with a spoonful of garlic-chile paste or a dribble of chile oil.

Spices and Spice Mixtures

There is a world of spices in the hot-foods kitchen. To describe them all would take a lengthy chapter, and many other books devote chapters to spices. Here I will briefly describe the hot spices, in addition to chile-derived spices, and offer some recipes for homemade spice mixtures.

Cumin   I love the earthy, dusty flavor of cumin. Cumin has a way of warming the throat, supporting the heat of chile. It is an indispensable spice in Mexico, India, and the Middle East. I like to mix a little with salt and sprinkle it on seafood, eggs, or lamb kabobs. Many of the recipes in this book call for a generous dose of this ground seed of the cumin plant; if you do not share my enthusiasm, you can substitute ground coriander, a much milder flavor.

Gingerroot   A pungent root, aromatic and flavorful. Ginger should be used fresh, in root form, simply chopped and added to a dish. It is used throughout Asia and much of Latin America. Also sold dried and ground for use in baked goods.

Horseradish   The large, potent root of the horseradish is available fresh, in jars, or dried. Use a little in mustards, sour cream sauces, or rich meat stews.

Mustard   The seeds of the yellow or black mustard plant, ground into a powder (the black is the hottest). Mixed with vinegar or wine and seasonings, the mustard powder becomes a favored condiment throughout much of the world. A book could be written on mustards alone: the huge variety available and recipes using them. Mustards range from mild to so hot you break into an immediate sweat. Mustards may be smooth, or coarsely ground with whole seeds; they may be sour from vinegar, or mellow from champagne or wine. Other spices such as tarragon, garlic, peppercorns, *herbs des Provençe,* and green chiles can flavor both California and French mustards. Some mustards are hot and sweet, like Russian mustard, or just hot, like Chinese mustard.

Peppercorns   The familiar black peppercorn is also sold with its outer coating removed, as a white peppercorn, or in its unripe stage, as a green peppercorn. Pink peppercorns are an entirely different berry with a distinctive warming flavor. Each peppercorn has a different taste and aroma, all with the underlying heat of basic black pepper. I am particularly fond of the four of these peppers combined, not only for aesthetics, but for the complex, interesting flavor that results. Try the peppercorns coarsely crushed and pressed into a tender steak, then sautéed for an unusual steak *au poivre;* or try green peppercorns generously spicing a sauce for duck—sublime!

Szechuan peppercorns   Not a true pepper at all, but a similar type of dried berry, peppery in flavor, with cool woodsy overtones. Used in Szechuan cuisine, where it is pounded and often used in conjunction with the small hot chile.

Wasabi powder   A Japanese horseradish powder that makes a strong condiment when mixed with water. Dip sushi into it or dab it onto deep-fried shrimp.

Curry Powder 〞

India	*Yield: ¾ cup*

In Indian cuisine, each dish is individually spiced. Sometimes only one or two spices are used, but often a mixture is used as a base. Other spices are then added, creating individual and distinctive combinations of flavors. This prepared spice mélange is called *garam masala.* It is mixed at home or commercially and labeled according to its characteristics or usage, such as "masala for fish" or "coriander masala." Western countries have taken this spice mix and prepared a standard version called curry (perhaps from the Hindu word *kari,* which means "stew").

Roasting and grinding your own mixture from whole spices will of course give the most fragrant, authentic results. As this is time-consuming and not always practical, I usually prepare curry with already ground spices. If you'd like to roast and grind the spices, simply substitute whole spices for the ground and heat in an ungreased skillet. Cook over medium heat for about 5 minutes, shaking pan once or twice to prevent burning. (Or bake the spices for 30 minutes in a 200° F. oven.) Grind in a mortar and pestle or blender (a food processor won't work), and sieve to remove any coarse bits.

Don't, however, use curry powder from a supermarket shelf; it's mostly celery seed, salt, and other adulterations that don't belong in a proper curry. I have found that it's worth the extra effort to mix my own.

The danger of relying on a curry powder, no matter how good, for all Indian dishes is that you run the risk of each dish tasting exactly like the next. If you use curry the way Indians use *garam masala,* and build upon the basic spice mix, you will have excellent results.

The following recipe calls for each spice to be ground.

> *3 tablespoons coriander*
> *1 ½ tablespoons cumin*
> *1 ½ tablespoons turmeric*
> *1 tablespoon cloves*
> *2 teaspoons cinnamon*
> *2 teaspoons nutmeg*
> *1 ½ teaspoons cardamom*
> *1 teaspoon ginger*
> *1 teaspoon black pepper*
> *1 teaspoon cayenne*
> *1 teaspoon fenugreek (optional)*
> *1 teaspoon fennel (optional)*

Mix all ingredients and store in an airtight jar.

Variation: Middle Eastern Spice Mixture: In the markets of old Jerusalem are stalls that specialize in spice mixtures, each a subtly different color and fragrance. My favorite, which I use for Sephardic dishes or instead of curry, is the following: Prepare the above recipe for Curry Powder but increase the cardamom to 1 tablespoon and the turmeric to 2½ teaspoons.

Ras Al Hanout ”

Morocco   *Yield: ½ cup*

Literally translated, Ras al Hanout means "head of the shop." Authentically, it is a huge assortment of spices, dried flowers, aromatics, resins, and even dried insects.

This exotic seasoning is used in Moroccan cuisine to flavor most everything from couscous to the lamb sausages called *merguez* to the hearty stews called *tajines.* This particular mix is not as exotic as one you would find in a Marrakesh bazaar; it is, however, flavorful and fragrant.

1   teaspoon crumbled, dried rose buds or petals
½   teaspoon fennel
½   teaspoon lavender
1   tablespoon cardamom
1   tablespoon cinnamon
2   teaspoons nutmeg
1½   teaspoons turmeric
1   teaspoon cloves
1   teaspoon cumin
1   teaspoon ginger
1   teaspoon cayenne
1   teaspoon coriander
1   teaspoon laos

1. Crush rose petals, fennel, and lavender in mortar and pestle or blender.
2. Add to rest of spices and stir well to combine. Seal in an airtight jar. This will keep its flavor for several months.

Cajun Spice Mixture "

United States   *Yield: approximately ½ cup*

Cajun cooks mix combinations of favorite spices to use in grilling, gumbos, jambalaya, and so on. This mixture is herby from oregano and thyme, flavorful from garlic and onion powder, and hot from cayenne. Rub it onto food that is to be grilled or sautéed, or mix some with a little melted butter and brush over kabobs of boned chicken breast. I like to nibble small cubes of mild cheese dipped into this spice mix or sprinkle the mixture over melted cheese sandwiches.

2   tablespoons dried oregano leaves
2   tablespoons garlic powder
2   tablespoons cayenne pepper
1   tablespoon paprika
1   tablespoon cumin
1   tablespoon dried thyme leaves
1   tablespoon onion powder
1   teaspoon freshly ground black pepper

Combine all ingredients; you can use a food processor or blender to really crush the flavors together, but it's also good simply combined and stirred.

Advance Preparation: Store in airtight jar or plastic bag. It will last several months on the shelf.

Salsas, Hot Sauces, and Condiments

Though it's unusual to begin a cookbook with sauces, I've put them early in this book because the salsas, hot sauces, and condiments in this chapter are the essence of "hot eating," and many of the recipes in the rest of the book use them. A mere spoonful of these flavorful, heat-intensive concoctions will enliven even the most ordinary foods. A bowlful of aromatic Yemenite Zhoog, chunky Pico de Gallo, or exotic Sambal Dabo Dabo Lilang on the table calls out to each diner with its ardent promise but allows each person to control his or her individual heat level. If you never prepare a single dish from the rest of the book but only add these sauce recipes to your repertoire, your whole cuisine will still be electrified.

Hot relishes are eaten all around the world, especially in the warm tropical countries where the chile flourishes and cuisine is based upon this volatile fruit. In this chapter are sauces made from small dried chiles, such as Berberé, Thai Chile Sauce, and Ají, which are so hot a dab exceeds the mild, medium, and hot ratings. There are also sauces based on fresh chiles, some quite powerful and even painful if you so choose, others just mildly *picante*. From the Yucatan comes the addition of fruit juices and achiote seeds; in the Caribbean, salty green olives or tart slices of mango are added; and dried shrimp mingle with chiles in fiery Thai Chile Sauce. Hot horseradish and herbed mustard appear here, too, for those occasions when you want spice but don't want the scorching chile.

When there's no time to make a fresh condiment, quality store-bought ones are invaluable. I like to keep an array of canned or bottled preparations on hand, each with its slightly different level of heat and flavor. A zesty Mexican salsa is the most useful addition to a cook's supplies. Always have some on hand to brighten soups, stews, omelettes, anything; add a spoonful to a few tablespoons of chopped onions for an "instant" fresh salsa. Vietnamese-style garlic-chile paste is also useful: fragrant with garlic, sizzling with chile heat, it is a good substitution for small, hot dried chiles, especially in stir-fries. Tabasco sauce and cayenne pepper, of course, should be on your shelf, ever ready to add their straight heat. Besides sauces, pickled serranos or jalapeños add great punch. They keep forever in the refrigerator, and their fiery marinade may also be used. Most purchased sauces and condiments keep for months if stored covered in the refrigerator, so each time you visit a specialty store, choose a new one to try.

Many of the recipes in this book make use of the sauces in this chapter. Often the sauces are specified by name, but at other times they are listed by intensity. For example, if a "medium hot" sauce is called for, then you would choose a medium hot sauce from this section as designated by a two-chile rating. When you're making your own sauces, prepare them within several hours of eating to be at their peak. They begin to deteriorate in flavor and potency after that but are still quite good for about one week. I almost always have a jar of one homemade salsa or another in my refrigerator to enliven whatever is on the menu that day. You can prepare a large batch and freeze some in ice cube trays, ready to pop out and defrost at your desire. Though this defrosted mixture lacks crispness, it retains its flavor and is excellent for cooking.

This chapter includes a huge variety of hot tastes and textures: salsas, condiments, and hot sauces flavored with onion, garlic, herbs, vegetables, spices, even fruit. Use these sauces not only with the recipes in this book but with all of your favorite dishes, even the ones that you never thought of adding a hot condiment to.

Basic Chile Sauce ♪

Mexico, Southwestern United States Yield: 1 quart

This is the basic method of preparation for turning large dried red chiles into the sauce that is used throughout Mexican and Southwestern cuisine—to stew chicken, meats, or seafood, or to dip tortillas in when preparing enchiladas. The combination of several types of chiles gives the sauce a complex character—the more different kinds of chiles you use, the more depth the sauce will have. You can also use just one type for a sauce that reflects the character of that particular chile (for example, ancho). For a sharper sauce, add several small, hot chiles.

5 dried New Mexico chiles
5 dried ancho chiles
3 small, hot dried chiles (optional, for a hotter sauce)
   Boiling water, to cover chiles (about 2 to 3 cups)
3 to 4 cloves garlic
2 cups chicken broth
   Juice of 1 lime
   Salt

1. Pour boiling water over chiles; cover and let soak 45 minutes or until tender (skins will remain tough, so tear one open to test). Drain and reserve broth. Remove stems and tear chiles into 1-inch pieces.
2. Puree garlic in processor or blender. Add soaked, cut chiles and ½ cup soaking water and puree to a thick, chunky consistency. With machine running, gradually add broth and puree until smooth.
3. Put sauce through sieve or strainer; discard solids. Season with lime and salt to taste.

Variation: Add 1 cup tomato sauce to sieved sauce.

Advance Preparation: Store covered in refrigerator for up to 1 week or in freezer almost indefinitely. Try freezing in ice cube trays for use anytime you need a few tablespoons of chile sauce.

Basic Chile Sauce Variations:

Variation 1: Use all ancho chiles; season with 1 teaspoon oregano and ½ teaspoon cumin. Add ¼ cup tomato sauce or paste and a tiny squeeze of lime juice.

Variation 2: In food processor or blender, chop ¼ cup pine nuts; add 1 seeded, stemmed, and sliced jalapeño (or leave seeds in for more heat), 3 ounces of feta cheese, 1 cup Basic Chile Sauce, and ½ cup chopped cilantro. Serve spooned onto Navajo Fry Bread or with boiled potatoes, topped with a little more crumbled feta cheese.

A simple dish: Cook 1 pound clams in Basic Chile Sauce until clams pop open, 10 to 15 minutes. Squeeze lime juice generously over clams and serve with Molho de Pimenta e Limao to which you've added cilantro instead of parsley

Picante Vinaigrette

Chile-Flavored Salad Dressing

United States, Mexico   *Yield: approximately ½ cup*

This vinaigrette incorporates the citrus flavors of lemon and lime with the kick of the chile. It is a lively dressing to enjoy on tossed greens when a Latin American flavor is desired. Try it on romaine leaves accompanying a lemon-and-poblano-roasted chicken surrounded by Goat-Cheese-Stuffed Poblanos.

1   *tablespoon or more green salsa (other salsas may be used,*
    but I like the tart tanginess of the green)
2   *teaspoons cider vinegar*
1   *to 2 teaspoons finely chopped cilantro (optional)*
    Juice of ½ lemon and ½ lime
3   *tablespoons oil*

1. Whisk 1 tablespoon salsa into vinegar; add cilantro and citrus juices.
2. Whisk oil into vinegar mixture. Season to taste with salt and a dash more salsa if desired.

Advance Preparation: Best when freshly made but can be stored covered in the refrigerator for up to 2 days.

Cilantro Aïoli

Garlic Mayonnaise with Cilantro and Jalapeño

France, Latin America   *Yield: 1 ½ cups*

In the bright sun of the south of France, in the region known as Provence, garlic is pounded to a paste and combined with oil and egg to make a mayonnaiselike sauce, aïoli. This golden, unctuous mixture is eaten on almost anything, meat, fish, or vegetable, and is sometimes referred to as the "butter of Provence."

One day, with cilantro and jalapeño on my mind, I put together this spunky version of aïoli. Enjoy it with lamb shanks braised in Basic Chile Sauce, grilled fish, or with crisp-tender steamed green beans and small boiled potatoes.

1   *clove garlic*
1   *egg*
½   *bunch cilantro (approximately ⅔ cup coarsely chopped)*
    Juice of 1 lemon
1   *tablespoon Dijon mustard*
½   *jalapeño*
½   *cup vegetable oil*
½   *cup fruity olive oil*
    Salt

1. Mince garlic in food processor. Add egg, cilantro, lemon juice, mustard, and jalapeño and process until smooth.
2. With machine running, slowly dribble in oils. Add salt to taste.

Advance Preparation: Store covered in refrigerator for 5 to 7 days.

Variation: Add 1 tablespoon New Mexico chile powder to mixture before oils are added.

Parsley-Tarragon Mustard ◗

France　　　　　　　　　　　　　　　　　　　　　*Yield: 1 cup*

This zesty, emerald green spread is delicious with *pot au feu* or Italian dry salami. On a sandwich, this mustard redefines the word "deli."

> 1　*clove garlic*
> 1　*bunch parsley (1 cup chopped)*
> 1　*tablespoon dried tarragon*
> 1　*teaspoon red wine vinegar*
> ¼　*mustard of choice (or combine coarse-grained and smooth)*
> 　　*Dash cayenne pepper*

1. In processor, chop garlic. Add parsley and process until finely chopped.
2. Add rest of ingredients and process until fairly smooth.

Advance Preparation: Covered in refrigerator, this will keep 2 to 3 days.

Salsa Ranchera ◗

Spicy Tomato Sauce

Mexico　　　　　　　　　　　　　　　　　　*Yield: 2 to 3 cups*

This simple tomato sauce is chunky from the tomatoes and peppers, spicy but not too hot. It is the sauce that turns unadorned poached or fried eggs into *huevos rancheros* and can also be enjoyed with roast chicken, *chiles rellenos,* omelettes, or any time a mild tomato-chile sauce is desired.

> 1 onion, chopped
> 3 cloves garlic, chopped
> 1 California or Anaheim chile, seeded and chopped
> 1 or 2 jalapeños, seeded and chopped (2 will give a much hotter sauce)
> 1 teaspoon cumin
> 1 teaspoon dried oregano
> 1 tablespoon vegetable oil
> 2 to 3 cups chopped tomatoes, fresh or canned

1. Sauté onion, garlic, chiles, and spices in oil.
2. Add tomatoes and cook until flavors meld, 5 to 10 minutes.

Advance Preparation: This can be stored covered in the refrigerator for 4 to 5 days, though it will become milder as it stands. Salsa Ranchera freezes extremely well.

Indonesian Spicy Peanut Sauce

Indonesia, Malaysia   *Yield: 1 ½ cups*

The idea of eating a spicy sauce made from peanut butter often sounds unpalatable to those uninitiated into the joys of Indonesian food. How to describe the complex taste? Hot, sweet, savory flavors all bound up in the peanut butter's smooth richness; usually one bite is enough to convince even the staunchest skeptic.

Authentically it is prepared using shelled, roasted peanuts, pounded to a paste with a mortar and pestle. Peanut butter is a shortcut but does not detract from the final result.

Spicy peanut sauce is traditionally enjoyed with the soy-marinated and grilled meat or chicken morsels known as *saté* or with Gado Gado, the Indonesian vegetable platter. Less traditional is to serve it as a dip for crudités, with an hors d'oeuvre of soy-basted crispy chicken wings, or as a sauce to accompany Kofta Kabob with rice and shredded cabbage salad.

A spoonful or two added to a stir-fry completely changes the character of a dish; try it with greens and beef.

    3   *cloves garlic*
    1   *cup peanut butter*
    2   *tablespoons to ¼ cup sugar*
    ¼   *cup water*
    ½   *teaspoon (or to taste) of Sambal Olek, Harissa, Yemenite*
        Zhoog, Marlena's Salsa, Vietnamese garlic-chile paste,
        commercial salsa, or several generous shakes of Tabasco
        sauce
    1   *tablespoon fresh lemon juice*
    1   *tablespoon soy sauce (or to taste)*

1. Chop garlic in processor.
2. Add everything else and puree until smooth. Adjust seasoning.

Advance Preparation: Keeps, covered in the refrigerator, for 3 to 5 days.

Yucatecan Red Chile Paste

Mexico   *Yield: 1 ½ cups*

This flavoring paste is used in the Yucatan to prepare the traditional dish of *puerco* or *pollo pibil*. It is rubbed onto pieces of pork or chicken, which are then wrapped in banana leaves and cooked in the traditional Yucatecan oven: a pit lined with hot stones. To prepare at home, the leaf-wrapped packages are cooked over an open grill or slow-cooked in an oven. The resulting tender, spicy meat makes fabulous tacos. Try this with fish such as red snapper; it tastes great!

   The paste may be diluted with a little pineapple juice to use as a marinade or basting liquid.

    3   *ancho chiles*
    2   *chiles negros*
    2   *New Mexico chiles*
        Boiling water to cover chiles
 1 ½ *tablespoons achiote seeds*
    1   *cup olive oil*
    6   *large cloves garlic*
        Peel and juice (½ cup juice) of ½ orange (see note)
        Peel and juice (½ cup juice) of ½ grapefruit
    1   *tablespoon black pepper*
    1   *tablespoon cumin*
    1   *teaspoon cayenne pepper*

1   *tablespoon paprika*
½   *teaspoon oregano*
½   *teaspoon salt*

1. Pour boiling water over chiles; cover and let stand 1 hour. Drain and reserve soaking water, if needed to thin the paste down during pureeing.
2. Heat achiote seeds in oil until bubbling around edge. Remove from heat and let stand for 30 minutes; strain.
3. Chop garlic in processor. Add chiles, citrus juices and peels, and spices; puree to a paste. Thin with a spoonful or two of the soaking water if it's not pureeing smoothly. Stir in achiote-tinted red oil and salt.

Advance Preparation: Store covered in refrigerator for up to 1 week.

Note: In the Yucatan, Seville oranges are used for this. They have a slightly bitter, slightly astringent quality. The addition of grapefruit to the oranges in this recipe is an approximation of the Seville.

Although this recipe calls for steeping the chiles, you may prepare it using chile powders. Use about ½ cup each of ancho and New Mexico chile powders.

Texas Barbecue Sauce

United States   *Yield: 4 to 4½ cups*

This is a simple, smoky barbecue sauce. The cayenne measurement is only a starting point; you can make this into a two- or three-chile sauce. Use as a basting sauce for grilled meats, seafood, or ribs. Coat chicken pieces with the mixture, season with a bit more garlic powder and cayenne, then oven-bake until tender. Texas Barbecue Sauce is delicious added to baked beans, along with a generous shake of black pepper and chopped raw onion.

2   *cups water or beer*
1   *cup catsup*
½   *onion, grated*
3   *tablespoons Worcestershire sauce*
2   *tablespoons brown sugar, firmly packed*
2   *tablespoons fresh lemon juice*
1   *tablespoon butter*
2   *teaspoons Liquid Smoke flavoring*
2   *teaspoons garlic powder*
1   *to 2 teaspoons prepared strong mustard*
1   *teaspoon cumin*
½   *teaspoon cayenne pepper (or to taste)*
1   *bay leaf*

Combine all ingredients and simmer 10 to 20 minutes.

Advancé Preparation: Sauce keeps several weeks in refrigerator and freezes well.

Rouille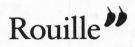

Red Chile-Olive Oil Mayonnaise

France   *Yield: ¾ cup*

In France, the hot capsicum is known as *piment enragé*, or "enraged pepper." Rouille is enjoyed in the south of France to spice up fish stews, soups, or grilled fish. A bowl is often brought to the table with the classic fish stew, bouillabaisse.

> 3   *cloves garlic*
> 1   *red serrano or jalapeño, seeded and stem removed*
>   *Pinch salt*
> ½   *red bell pepper, roasted and peeled (or substitute canned pimiento)*
> 1   *thick piece (1 to 1 ½ inches) French bread, soaked in water and squeezed dry*
> ¼   *cup fruity olive oil*

1. Puree garlic, serrano or jalapeño and salt in processor.
2. Add bell pepper and puree until smooth; add bread and puree to a smooth paste.
3. With machine on, slowly add olive oil and blend until emulsified into a slightly fluffy sauce.

Advance Preparation: Store covered in refrigerator no more than 3 or 4 days.

Cebollas en Escabeche

Pickled Onion Slices

Mexico   *Yield: approximately 1 ½ cups*

A Mexican side dish of simple pickled onion slices. Their slightly hot, flavorful crunch is a delicious accent served atop rich black-bean tostadas, or wrapped up into a soft tortilla oozing melted cheese. This is a traditional Yucatecan accompaniment to pit-roasted, banana-leaf-wrapped pork, or to any meat or fish that has been coated with Yucatecan Chile Paste and grilled. Cebollas en Escabeche are a delicious accompaniment to enchiladas or rice dishes, or try them nestled into a hearth-roasted potato at your next barbecue.

⅔ *cup distilled vinegar*
¼ *cup vegetable oil*
1 *teaspoon cumin*
1 *teaspoon oregano (Mexican, if possible)*
2 *onions, thinly sliced*
1 *jalapeño or serrano chile*
   Salt

Heat vinegar, oil, cumin, and oregano just to boiling. Pour over onions and jalapeños and let stand until cool. Salt to taste.

Advance Preparation: Delicious when freshly made, they may be refrigerated, covered, for up to a week.

Variation: Jalapeños en Escabeche may be made as above. Decrease onion to ½, increase jalapeños to 5 to 8, and add ½ carrot, thinly sliced. Yield: approximately ¾ to 1 cup.

Mixed Peppercorn Mustard "

France, United States, Germany   *Yield: ⅓ cup*

The varied peppercorns each contribute a distinctive flavor as well as heat to this mustard. Enjoy with rare roast beef or with an assortment of interesting sausages.

1 *tablespoon mixed peppercorns*
1 *teaspoon dry mustard*
2 *tablespoons olive oil*
1 *teaspoon red wine vinegar*
2 *teaspoons large-grain mustard*
2 *teaspoons medium-strength mustard (a mild Dijon or*
   light-brown American type)
   Pinch salt

1. Chop peppercorns in blender or processor with dry mustard, olive oil, and wine vinegar, stopping several times to scrape down the sides.
2. Add rest of ingredients and blend thoroughly.

Advance Preparation: Store covered in refrigerator for up to 1 week.

Salsa Verde *"*

Green Hot Sauce

Mexico   *Yield: 3 cups*

Tomatillos are also known as husk tomatoes, because of the papery skins that cover these small, tart green tomatoes. The color is not from lack of maturity; tomatillos are green when ripe. They give this salsa an unusual tanginess. Salsa Verde is delicious with roast chicken, Arroz con Pollo, vegetable soup, or tortilla chips for dipping.

> 8 *ounces fresh tomatillos (or substitute 1 8-ounce can)*
> 1 *cup chicken broth*
> 6 *fresh poblanos or Anaheim chiles*
> ½ *white onion*
> 1 *bunch cilantro*

1. Remove papery skins from tomatillos. Cut tomatillos in half and simmer in chicken broth until tender. (If using canned, simply drain and combine tomatillos with broth.)
2. Roast chiles over an open flame until skin chars. Place in plastic bag, seal, and set aside for about 10 minutes.
3. Chop onion and cilantro leaves in processor.
4. Rinse chiles in cold water; peel. Slice chiles and add to processor; puree with onion and cilantro. Add tomatillos to processor and enough of the chicken broth to make a nice salsa consistency.

Advance Preparation: This will last 4 to 5 days in refrigerator and may be frozen.

Variation: A cup of Salsa Verde may be thinned with several cups of broth to make a spicy soup base; simmer zucchini until tender and serve with freshly grated Parmesan cheese.

Pico de Gallo *"*

Chunky Fresh Chile Relish

Mexico, United States   *Yield: approximately 2 to 3 cups*

Pico de Gallo literally means "beak of the rooster," though I'm not sure why it is called this; perhaps it's because the ingredients are all cut into pieces about the size of the corn and other foods that chickens pick at with their beaks. The name is given to the chunky relishes eaten throughout Texas and parts of Mexico. It can also refer to a salad of crunchy jícama (and occasionally orange chunks) eaten in parts of Mexico. Pico de Gallo may contain a variety of fresh, uncooked components, but chiles are a constant.

This is a good basic version. Vary it at will: double or even triple the amount of jalapeños, or substitute serranos to make an even hotter relish. You may also go milder, eliminating the jalapeños completely and using mellow California or Anaheim chiles. Chopped yellow or white onion may replace the green onion, and jícama or cucumber could take the place of the radishes. The cilantro, of which I am inordinately fond, may be replaced by parsley or eliminated entirely. An unusual variation of Pico de Gallo adds one peeled, pitted, and diced avocado to the recipe.

Whichever way you prepare it, spoon it onto Mexican grilled steak strips, tortillas with melted cheese, saucy black beans, or grilled chicken.

> 2 *to 3 tomatoes, diced*
> 1 *bunch green onions (approximately 5 or 6), cleaned and thinly sliced*
> 5 *to 10 radishes, chopped*
> 1 *small bunch cilantro (or parsley), chopped (approximately ½ cup)*
> 2 *jalapeños, thinly sliced*
> *Juice of ½ lime*
> *Salt to taste*

Chop and dice all ingredients; combine and serve.

Advance Preparation: Best enjoyed within the first several hours after preparation, but remains fine for several days covered in the refrigerator.

Chimichurri »

Chopped Onion, Chile, and Parsley Relish

Argentina *Yield: 1 to 1 ½ cups*

The unusual name of this relish is an Argentine-Indian word. It's delicious with the grilled meats and beef dishes enjoyed in that land of grazing cattle.

    1 *onion, finely chopped*
    1 *bunch parsley, chopped (approximately 1 cup)*
    1 *serrano, chopped*
    2 *cloves garlic, chopped*
  ¼ *cup olive oil*
    2 *to 3 tablespoons distilled white vinegar*
       Salt to taste

Combine all ingredients.

Advance Preparation: This will keep for 3 or 4 days covered in the refrigerator.

Pebre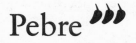

Fresh Onion, Herb, and Chile Paste Relish

Chile   *Yield: ¾ cup*

This hot Chilean sauce is eaten with meats as well as with the highly spiced stews of corn, pumpkin, rice, and beans that are so beloved in that vast land. The chile paste measurement is just a guide; for more heat, add more chile. Some pebre has hardly any chile in it, while other blends are hot enough to sauté your tongue. This version is medium hot.

    1 *onion, finely chopped*
  ½ *cup chopped cilantro or parsley (or a mixture of both)*
  ¼ *cup olive oil*
  ¼ *cup red wine vinegar*
    2 *cloves garlic, finely chopped*
    2 *teaspoons Ají, Sambal Olek, or a strong commercial sauce*
       such as Vietnamese-style garlic-chile paste
  ½ *teaspoon salt*

Combine all ingredients.

Advance Preparation: Sauce will keep in refrigerator for several days.

Salsa Fresca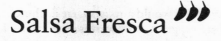

Fresh Table Sauce

Mexico *Yield: approximately 1 ½ cups*

The Mexicans make many different kinds of fresh, hot table salsas and relishes. Most are quite simple, and though all have similar ingredients, each salsa is just a little different from the others.

Serve salsa to enhance grilled foods; with thin grilled steaks and French fries, it is the Mexican version of steak and *pommes frites*. Try it with a grilled whole fish, basted in olive oil and lemon, or with a platter of tiny fish, crisply fried and still sizzling. This is also good with tacos, tortilla dishes, and omelettes. Even the humblest taco stand in Mexico will have a bowl of freshly made Salsa Fresca on its counter.

> 5 *ripe tomatoes (use canned if fresh are out of season, pale and mealy)*
> 1 *onion, chopped*
> 3 *fresh serranos or jalapeños, thinly sliced*
> 2 *tablespoons red or white wine vinegar*
> 1 *tablespoon minced cilantro or parsley*
>   *Salt to taste*

Mix all ingredients together and enjoy.

Advance Preparation: This keeps, covered in the refrigerator, for up to a week.

Variation: A very simple mild sauce may be prepared using canned, mild green chiles instead of the fresh serranos. It will last only 2 or 3 days.

Roasted Tomato Salsa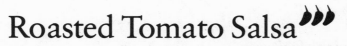

Mexico *Yield: approximately 1 ½ to 2 cups*

In Mexico, both peppers and tomatoes are often roasted before combining into salsa. The charred skin comes off easily, and the roasting gives a slightly smoky flavor and subtly different texture, which contrasts brightly with the pungent crunch of onion. Enjoy as you would any salsa, fresh chutney, or sambal, spicing up rice dishes, beans, stews, grills, and curries. Sometimes I add chopped garlic to this and eat it with pizza or calzone.

> 5 *tomatoes*
> 2 *or 3 mild California or Anaheim chiles*
> 1 *onion, chopped*
> 1 *serrano, sliced thinly*
> *Salt*

1. Roast tomatoes and mild chiles. Tomatoes may be broiled or impaled upon a fork and held over the gas flame; let skin char and tear or shrivel, then let cool and peel. To prepare chiles, see "Roasting and Peeling Chiles and Peppers."
2. Coarsely chop roasted tomatoes and chiles, then combine with onion and serrano. Add salt to taste.

Advance Preparation: Store covered in refrigerator. Best enjoyed within a day or two.

Mango Hot Condiment ▶▶▶

Trinidad   *Yield: 1 cup*

The native Carib Indians were preparing hot relishes and sauces long before the New World was "discovered." This is an exotic change from the usual tomato-based sauce. Enjoy with curried dishes, seafood, or roast pork.

> 1 *slightly unripe mango*
> 2 *fresh red jalapeños or other hot peppers (if red are*
>   *unavailable, substitute green, stemmed, seeded, and*
>   *chopped)*
> 3 *cloves garlic, chopped*
>   *Pinch of salt*
> 2 *teaspoons olive oil*

1. Peel and seed mango; dice into ½-inch cubes.
2. Combine all ingredients and serve.

Advance Preparation: Covered in refrigerator, it will keep for up to 1 week.

Liutenitsa

Mixed Hot and Sweet Pepper Relish

Bulgaria   *Yield: approximately 1 ½ cups*

This condiment of roasted, peeled, and chopped peppers is as attractive as it is delicious. A Romanian version leaves the peppers whole and adds a hefty dose of paprika to the dressing. Enjoy it accompanying grilled meats or sausages and crusty bread.

> ½ *pound sweet bell peppers*
> ½ *pound jalapeños*
> 5 *cloves garlic*
> 4 *tablespoons olive oil*
> 6 *tablespoons distilled white vinegar*
> 2 *teaspoons salt*

1. Roast, peel, and seed peppers (see "Roasting and Peeling Chiles and Peppers"). Chop garlic in processor and add bell peppers and jalapeños; chop together.
2. Add olive oil, vinegar, and salt.

Advance Preparation: Store covered in refrigerator for 3 to 4 days.

Garlic Chutney ▶▶▶

Puree of Fresh Garlic, Chiles, and Cilantro

India   *Yield: approximately ⅔ cup*

A potent paste that should be served in small dabs only, Garlic Chutney is often used in cooking instead of eaten straight. Serve with any curry dish you dare to.

> 10 *cloves garlic*
> 1 *large bunch cilantro (1 ½ cups)*
> 2 *tablespoons vegetable oil*
> 2 *jalapeños, seeded*
> ½ *teaspoon salt*
> ½ *teaspoon cayenne pepper*
>   *Squeeze of fresh lemon juice*

In food processor, puree garlic; add all other ingredients and puree to a smooth consistency.

Advance Preparation: Store in refrigerator for 1 or 2 days.

Marlena's Salsa ▸▸▸

Middle East/Mexico   *Yield: approximately 2 cups*

This hot sauce, loosely based on both Mexican salsa and Yemenite Zhoog, is always delicious no matter what the proportions. I've made it with larger amounts of tomatoes, used canned instead of fresh, and substituted parsley for the cilantro; it is indestructible.

Serve with Kofta Kabob, Tahina Dip, or Hot Hungarian Mushroom Soup. With such a great quantity of garlic, this salsa keeps vampires away!

> 6 to 10 *cloves garlic*
> 5 to 8 *jalapeños, stemmed but not seeded*
> 3 *tomatoes, quartered*
> 1 *bunch cilantro (approximately ½ cup)*
>   *Juice of 1 lemon*
> 1 to 2 *teaspoons cumin (or to taste)*
>   *Salt to taste*

1. Chop garlic in processor or blender, then add everything else.
2. Chop to desired consistency. It should be smooth and saucelike with only a little chunkiness.

Advance Preparation: This is strongest (and I think best) when freshly made but may be kept for 1½ to 2 weeks in the refrigerator.

Roasted Green Jalapeño Salsa ▸▸▸

Mexico   *Yield: approximately 1 cup*

Beware! At first this salsa is all flavor, seducing you into a bigger mouthful than you intended, and then suddenly the heat manifests itself. This is one of the hottest salsas I have tangled with. You may substitute Anaheim and/or poblanos for some or all the jalapeños to tame the salsa somewhat, or switch to serranos for a scorcher.

Serve with Borani Esfanaj and soft, chewy flour tortillas, or serve with Zuni Lamb, Green Chile, and Hominy Stew.

20 to 25 *fresh jalapeños*
5 *cloves garlic*
Juice of 1 lemon or lime
1 *teaspoon salt*
2 *tablespoons olive oil*

1. Scorch the chiles under a broiler or on a very hot skillet until their skin is charred a bit; turn and do other side. I have found that a chestnut roasting pan, the type with perforations on the bottom, is a great tool for roasting them right over the open flame of a gas stove. Once roasted they will have a slightly smoky, slightly cooked flavor and consistency.
2. Rinse chiles under cold water; remove stems and peel.
3. Chop garlic in processor. Add chiles, lime juice, and salt, then puree to a coarse consistency. Stir in olive oil.

Advance Preparation: May be stored, covered in refrigerator, for 3 or 4 days.

Molho de Pimenta e Limao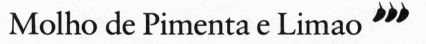

Hot Chile-Lemon Relish

Brazil   *Yield: approximately 1 cup*

On nearly every table throughout Brazil you will find a small bottle of clearish liquid packed with these tiny incendiary chiles. You can sprinkle a few drops of this firewater over your plate or, if you're either brave or foolhardy, go for a whole pepper. The lemon, onion, and parsley add zesty flavor to the fiery chopped peppers.

5 to 6 *Tabasco peppers, chopped (you may substitute pickled serranos or jalapeños)*
1 *onion, chopped*
3 *garlic cloves, chopped*
½ *teaspoon cumin (optional)*
1 to 2 *tablespoons chopped parsley*
Juice of 3 to 4 lemons

Advance Preparation: Combine all ingredients and refrigerate; will last 5 to 7 days.

Caribbean Pickled Pepper Relish 🌶🌶🌶

Caribbean Islands   *Yield: approximately ¾ cup*

A bowl of this vivid condiment adorns tables throughout the Caribbean isles. Sliced, marinated, and barbecued pork or goat, seafood stews, and grilled fish are all enhanced by this salsa. Try also with any sort of taco or *antojito* (the cornmeal- and tortilla-based dishes of Mexico such as tacos and tostadas).

  ½ *onion, chopped*
  3 *cloves garlic, chopped*
  3 *fresh jalapeños (red, green, or combination)*
  ¼ *cup white distilled vinegar*
  ½ *teaspoon salt*
  1 *tablespoon olive oil*

1. Combine onion, garlic, and chiles.
2. Heat vinegar and salt; when bubbles appear around edge, pour over onion mixture. Dribble olive oil over top.

Advance Preparation: This can be stored, covered in the refrigerator, for 3 or 4 days.

Cilantro-Mint Fresh Chutney or Sambal 🌶🌶🌶

Hot Relish of Cilantro and Mint

India, Southeast Asia   *Yield: 1½ to 2 cups*

Fresh chutneys are prepared for each meal in Indian households. They are very different from Major Grey or other preserved chutneys (although there are times when I like these as well). A pounded paste of chiles, herbs, nuts, or coconut, fresh chutney is served as a tiny dab of something refreshing and very hot on your plate. The peanuts add a Southeast Asian note to this intense relish. Enjoy with rice dishes, grilled meat or fish, Thai Cabbage Salad, or Southeast Asian curries. Cilantro-Mint Fresh Chutney is delicious dabbed onto Keema Naan or as a dipping sauce for Momo's and Khote, the Tibetan pot stickers.

3 *cloves garlic*
4 *serrano chiles*
¼ *cup roasted peanuts*
½ *bunch cilantro (approximately ⅔ cup)*
½ *bunch mint (approximately ⅔ cup)*
1 *teaspoon sugar*
  Juice of ½ lime or lemon
  Pinch of salt (omit if using salted peanuts)

1. Puree garlic in processor. Add chiles and peanuts and grind finely.
2. Add all remaining ingredients and grind to desired consistency; it should be a chunky paste.

Advance Preparation: Store covered in refrigerator for 2 to 3 days only.

Fresh Horseradish

Eastern Europe   *Yield: 1½ to 2 cups*

Fresh grated horseradish is nothing like store-bought—it is potent to the point of tears.

Sold in big, ugly chunks, horseradish root is available seasonally in many markets. This fresh preparation will not keep as long as the bottled stuff; it begins to lose strength almost immediately. Traditionally served tinted pink from beet juice with the Jewish specialty gefilte fish, it's wonderful as is or mixed with mustard and served with corned beef, cabbage, and potatoes, or with *pot au feu*. A classic sauce is a bit of the horseradish added to unsweetened whipped or sour cream.

1 *chunk fresh horseradish root (approximately ½ to 1*
  pound), peeled
  Squeeze of fresh lemon juice
  Salt
  A few drops of beet juice (optional)
  Pinch of sugar (optional)

1. Grate horseradish by hand or in food processor. The fumes are very strong; be careful not to let them get near your eyes. (If by some strange chance you own a gas mask, now is the time to use it.)
2. Mix horseradish with a little lemon juice, salt to taste, beet juice, and sugar.

Advance Preparation: Since it begins to lose its pungency immediately, fresh horseradish is best eaten the same day or within 3 days of preparation.

Sambal Ketjap 🌶🌶🌶

Sweet and Hot Soy Sauce

Indonesia   *Yield: approximately ¼ cup*

It's not as curious as you might think to find the word ketchup (ketjab, kechop, and so on) appearing throughout the menus and recipes of Southeast Asia. The word is of Malaysian origin and means "sauce." It originally referred to a fermented fish brew.

This hot and sweet soy sauce is used as a table condiment; a few drops can be shaken onto nearly anything. Enjoy with Nasi Kuning, grilled kabobs or fish, or in a curry.

> 2   *cloves garlic, chopped*
> 1   *tablespoon commercial garlic-chile paste or cayenne*
> 1   *teaspoon molasses*
> ¼   *cup soy sauce*

Stir garlic and chile paste into molasses. Slowly stir in soy sauce until well combined.

Advance Preparation: Kept covered, this can be stored in the refrigerator for up to a week.

Sambal Dabo Dabo Lilang 🌶🌶🌶

Fresh Chile, Tomato, and Onion Relish with Basil

Indonesia   *Yield: approximately 1½ cups*

This is much like the fresh salsas of Mexico, with the surprising sweet flavor of basil. Delicious with whole roast salmon, grilled duck that has been rubbed with curry spices, or Nasi Kuning and other rice dishes.

> 1   *yellow onion*
> 1   *tomato*

1 *fresh red jalapeño*
1 *green serrano*
2 *to 3 tablespoons fresh basil*
   Juice of 1 lime
   Salt to taste

Finely chop all ingredients and combine.

Advance Preparation: Best fresh, but you can store it for several days covered in the refrigerator.

Yemenite Zhoog *▶▶▶*

Hot Sauce Relish with Middle Eastern Flavor

Yemen, Israel   *Yield: approximately 1½ cups*

The inspiration for this condiment is a Yemenite friend who brought the recipe to the United States via Israel. She serves it with almost everything, but especially spooned into vegetable soups (which, combined with pita bread, form the traditional basic Yemenite diet).

This is a delicious hot sauce, green in color and pungent with spice. If the cilantro flavor is undesirable, eliminate it. The sauce will still be savory and authentic.

This relish is delicious stuffed into pita with salads and grilled meat or poultry.

5 *cloves garlic*
5 *jalapeño chiles*
1 *tomato (optional)*
1 *bunch cilantro* ⎱
1 *bunch parsley* ⎰ *(about 1 cup in all)*
2 *tablespoons olive oil*
1 *tablespoon cumin*
½ *teaspoon Curry Powder or Middle Eastern Spice Mixture*
   Squeeze of fresh lemon
   Salt to taste

Puree garlic in food processor; add chiles and chop finely. Add all remaining ingredients and process to a saucelike consistency.

Advance Preparation: This keeps, covered in the refrigerator, 1 to 1½ weeks but begins losing its potency the second day.

Variation: *Hilbeh.* Add several tablespoons of fenugreek seeds that have been soaked overnight to soften (they are very hard), drained, then pureed and strained.

Martinique Hot Sauce ►►►

Olive, Onion, and Tomato Relish

Martinique   *Yield: 1 cup*

This slightly unusual relish has the pungency of raw onion and the tang of green olives. Serve with grilled fish and seafood, rice and beans, or Pork and Poblano Sauté.

   ¼ *cup finely chopped ripe tomatoes or tomato sauce*
   1 *onion, chopped*
   1 *clove garlic, chopped*
   2 *fresh jalapeños, chopped*
   ½ *cup pimiento-stuffed green olives, sliced*
      Juice of 1 lime

Combine all ingredients.

Advance Preparation: Covered and refrigerated, this can be kept 2 to 3 days.

Thai Chile Sauce   *Very, very hot*

Thailand   *Yield: approximately 1 to 1½ cups*

This is hot, hot, hot! Be careful to taste only the teeniest bit at first; I found my first bite frightening. Enjoy a dab on stir-fried noodles, rice dishes, grilled meats and poultry, or added to a dressing for shrimp and orange salad (see Some Simple Suggestions and Menu Ideas).

   2 *tablespoons dried shrimp, crushed (or substitute shrimp*
      paste or powder)
   1 *cup small dried red chiles, seeded and stems removed*
      Boiling water to cover both shrimp and chiles

> 3 *cloves garlic*
> *Juice of 1 lime*
> 1 *tablespoon sugar (or to taste)*

1. Cover dried shrimp with boiling water and let stand 10 minutes. (Eliminate soaking if using shrimp paste or powder.)
2. In another bowl, cover chiles with boiling water and let stand 30 minutes or so to soften.
3. Drain chiles, reserving some liquid. Puree garlic in processor. Add chiles and shrimp; puree to as smooth a paste as you can, adding a little of the chile soaking liquid for smoother consistency.
4. Season with lime juice and sugar, continuing to blend until fairly smooth.

Advance Preparation: Store covered in refrigerator for several days.

Sambal Olek   *Very, very hot*

Red Chile Condiment

Indonesia   *Yield: approximately 1 cup*

Sambals are the relishes and condiments of Indonesian cuisine; their heat enlivens the rice-based diet. They come in a rainbow array: some raw, some cooked, fiery preparations combined with bits of vegetable, herb, meat, or seafood. Sambal Olek is much used in cooking; add a dab to stir-fries, stews, or salads.

> 1 *cup small dried red chiles*
> *Boiling water to cover chiles*
> *Juice of 2 limes*
> *Grated rind of ½ lime*
> *Salt*

1. Cover chiles with boiling water and let stand 30 minutes to 1 hour to soften. Drain, reserving some of the soaking liquid.
2. Puree chiles to as smooth a paste as possible, adding lime juice and rind, salt to taste, and as much soaking liquid as necessary to yield a thick sauce consistency.

Advance Preparation: Store covered in refrigerator for up to 2 weeks.

Variation: Sambal Trassi
Add 2 tablespoons shrimp paste to above recipe.

Harissa

Spiced Red Chile Paste

Morocco   *Yield: 1 ½ cups*

This high-voltage condiment from Morocco is dabbed onto anything savory—a *tajine* (stew of vegetables, eggs, fish, or meat); grilled mussels; or simply a chunk of crusty bread. It can be thinned down with several spoonfuls of broth to a sauce consistency and served as an accompaniment to couscous or to Brik à l'Oeuf.

> ½ to 1 cup small dried red chiles
>   Boiling water to cover chiles
> 1 tablespoon cumin
> 2 teaspoons curry powder
> ½ teaspoon salt
> 2 tablespoons olive oil

1. Place chiles in heatproof bowl and cover with boiling water. Let stand 30 minutes to 1 hour. Drain, reserving some of the soaking water.
2. Place chiles in blender or food processor with ¼ cup soaking water. Puree until smooth, scraping down sides of container a few times. Add spices, salt, and olive oil and blend well.

Advance Preparation: Store covered in the refrigerator for up to 2 weeks. May also be frozen or put up in canning jars.

Berberé

Chile and Spice Paste

Ethiopia   *Yield: approximately 2 cups*

Berberé is eaten all over Ethiopia as a condiment and seasoning mixture in cooking. The principal flavoring upon which Ethiopian cuisine is based, it is hot and very distinctive!

> 2 cups small dried red chiles
>   Boiling water to cover chiles

2 *teaspoons cumin*
1 *onion, chopped*
2 *cloves garlic, chopped*
1 *tablespoon ground ginger*
1 *teaspoon turmeric*
1 *teaspoon freshly ground black pepper*
1 *teaspoon salt*
   Seeds from 4 cardamom pods

1. Remove stems (and seeds as well, if you want to tame the fire) from the chiles. Cover them with boiling water and let stand until softened, 30 minutes or so.
2. Toast cumin in a dry heavy skillet until color darkens and aroma becomes more fragrant.
3. Drain chiles, reserving a bit of the liquid. Puree chiles with onion, garlic, seasonings, and a tiny bit of the soaking water.

Advance Preparation: Refrigerate, covered, for up to 2 weeks.

Variations:

Shata (Sudan)
Combine 3 tablespoons Berberé with 1 clove garlic, chopped, and 1 cup lemon juice.

Sakay (Malagasy Republic)
Combine 3 tablespoons Berberé or Ají with 1 clove garlic, chopped, 1 teaspoon ginger, and 1 tablespoon oil.

Ají
Very, very hot

Chile-Garlic Paste

Peru   *Yield: approximately 2 cups*

This sauce is prepared similarly to Thai Chile Sauce and Berberé. Like those pastes, ají is lethally hot. Take only the tiniest bit at first. This is good for spicing up the gentle potato-and-cheese dishes of Peru.

Ají, pronounced ah-HEE, is the Peruvian Indian word for chile. Though it is similar, it is not to be confused with the Romance language prefix *ail, ai,* or *aj,* which refers to the presence of garlic (of which, coincidentally, this sauce has plenty).

Ají is enjoyed in many variations and eaten with much gusto throughout Peru. Besides the small red—and flaming hot—chile, there is a lighter, orange-yellow colored pepper called mirasol. It is dried and used as a spice, chopped fresh as garnish, and often used to prepare a milder ají chile paste. If you can find mirasol or a similar chile, try preparing ají with it for a delicious milder condiment.

> 1   *cup small dried chiles*
> 2   *cups boiling water*
> 6   *to 8 cloves garlic*
> ¼   *cup olive oil*
>   *Salt*

1. Remove stems from chiles (and seeds, if you wish to tame the heat slightly). Crumble chiles coarsely, then cover with boiling water and let soak 30 minutes or so. Drain chiles, reserving some of the soaking water.
2. In processor or blender, puree garlic. Add chiles and puree into as smooth a paste as possible, adding a tiny bit of the soaking water.
3. With machine on, add olive oil and salt to taste. (Keep your face away from the opening of the processor; the fumes are strong.)

Advance Preparation: Cover and refrigerate for up to 2 weeks. May also be frozen or put up in canning jars.

Piri-Piri   *Very, very hot*

Fresh Red Jalapeño Relish

Portugal, Africa, Brazil   *Yield: ½ cup*

Piri-Piri is a peppery Portuguese condiment also enjoyed in Brazil and Mozambique. In Portuguese Africa, Piri-Piri spices up nearly all foods, and it is one of many hot condiments eaten in Brazil. In Portugal you're likely to enjoy Piri-Piri in a *tasca* (tavernlike cafe), accompanying juicy roast chicken or succulent fish. Piri-Piri (the name of the chile as well as of the sauce) is called *pili-pili* in parts of Africa. This sauce is a very straightforward relish, with Mediterranean overtones from the olive oil. It is delicious with rice and grain dishes, potato-and-cheese omelettes, or grilled meats and fish.

> 10   *fresh red jalapeños, seeded and chopped*
> ½   *cup olive oil*
> ½   *teaspoon oregano leaves, crushed*

Juice of 1 lemon or lime
Salt to taste

1. Chop jalapeños in processor.
2. Combine all ingredients and serve.

Advance Preparation: May be kept, covered in refrigerator, for 3 to 5 days.

Appetizers and Salads

An appetizer awakens the appetite and prepares the palate to receive the rest of the meal. Interesting dishes, perhaps richer than would be satisfactory in a larger main course, are delightful as appetizers or as a first course. In addition to the salads and appetizers in this chapter, try small portions of Chile-Stuffed Ravioli with Goat Cheese Sauce, or tiny skewers of Mediterranean Mini-Grill. Any type of seafood is a delicious hors d'oeuvre. Try serving three raw clams on the half-shell, each topped with a different-colored condiment: Cilantro Pesto, Marlena's Salsa, Molho de Pimenta e Limao. Bite-sized pieces of Eggplant with Keema or Moroccan Fish with Cumin Paste make unusual hors d'oeuvres as well.

Many salads in this chapter are also spreads—spicy vegetable mixtures combining the fire of chiles with the creaminess of tahini or yogurt. Try them as snacks or as an accompaniment to a soup or omelette.

Many people (myself included) prefer hors d'oeuvre-sized portions of many dishes to one large portion of one dish. It is a current trend in restaurant dining to order several first courses rather than a traditional three-course meal; in fact, there are restaurants called "Appetizer Bars," which specialize in this sort of eating. There you can order three or four small dishes of savory foods. Spicy appetizers are particularly delicious eaten this way, since they are often intensely flavored dishes, wonderful for nibbling on rather than eating in a more formal manner.

Salade Moroccaine ♪

Diced Pepper, Cucumber, and Tomato Salad

Morocco   *Serves 4 to 6*

Throughout the Middle East, delicious salads are prepared by chopping everything into equal-sized pieces and dressing the mixture with olive oil and vinegar.
Enjoy this with bread for scooping and Lamb and Eggplant Tajine.

    2 *cucumbers, peeled*
    2 *tomatoes*
    2 *red bell peppers, roasted and peeled*
    2 *green peppers, roasted and peeled*
    1 *bunch cilantro (½ cup), chopped*
    ½ *red onion, chopped*
    2 *to 3 cloves garlic, chopped*
    1 *jalapeño, sliced thinly or chopped*
    ¼ *cup olive oil*
    2 *tablespoons white distilled vinegar*
    1 *teaspoon cumin*
       Salt to taste

Finely dice cucumbers, tomatoes, and peppers. Toss with remaining ingredients.

Advance Preparation: Will keep several days, covered in refrigerator.

Tahina Dip ♪

Spiced Sesame Seed Paste

Middle East   *Yield: approximately 2 cups*

Tahini is a creamy beige sauce prepared from ground sesame seeds. It may be
purchased in tins or jars in Middle Eastern specialty shops and health-food
stores. Seasoned with garlic, lemon juice, and spices, it is favored throughout the
Middle East and often called tahina. Whichever way it is spelled and pronounced, it is enjoyed as an appetizer dip, mixed with chopped vegetables, or

thinned down with a little extra water and drizzled over meat, fish, or the chick-pea croquettes called felafel. Traditionally tahina is served spread on a shallow dish, garnished with chopped cilantro or parsley, Greek olives, and/or hot pickled peppers, and sprinkled with olive oil. Pita or crusty French bread is then dipped into it.

For a party, I like to decorate a large bowl of Tahina Dip with a design of concentric circles of spices—the ocher hue of cumin, bright yellow of turmeric, the brick and rust colors of paprika and cayenne, and a few green leaves of cilantro or parsley.

> 3 *cloves garlic*
> 1 *cup tahini (purchased, in tin or jar)*
> 1 *teaspoon cumin (or to taste)*
> ½ *to 1 teaspoon ground coriander (optional)*
> ½ *cup water*
>   *Juice of 2 lemons*
>   *Salt to taste*
>   *Pinch cayenne, several drops Tabasco sauce, or 1 teaspoon*
>   *Marlena's Salsa*
>
> *Garnish: hot pickled peppers and/or Greek olives, olive oil, cilantro or parsley, salsa or Tabasco sauce*

few drops oil (olive)

1. Chop garlic in food processor; blend in tahini and spices.
2. Add water and lemon juice; blend until smooth. Taste for seasoning.

Variation: Hummus
Mash 2 cups cooked chick-peas. Stir in 1 cup prepared Tahina Dip and the juice of ½ lemon (this is best done in food processor or blender). Serve garnished with chopped cucumber and tomato salad, a sprinkle each of olive oil and salsa of choice (Marlena's Salsa, Yemenite Zhoog, or Tabasco sauce).

Baba Ghanoush ▸

Pureed Eggplant with Tahina

Middle East   *Serves 4 to 6*

Baba Ghanoush is the Arabic name for this smoky, creamy eggplant puree; in Hebrew it is called *salat hatzilim*. Serve as you would tahina, with pita and raw vegetables for dipping, or pile it into a pita sandwich with salad and hot peppers or salsa and grilled chunks of lamb. *Shashlik* (skewers of grilled meat) can be laid on a bed of Baba Ghanoush and decorated with roasted red pepper strips, salsa, cilantro, and a dribble of tahina sauce. This is an authentic Baba Ghanoush but much spicier than most.

> 1 *medium-large eggplant (1¼ pounds)*
> 2 *to 3 cloves garlic, chopped*
> ½ *cup tahini*
>   *Juice of 1 lemon*
> 1 *to 2 teaspoons salsa of choice, homemade or commercial*
> 1 *teaspoon cumin*
>   *Salt*

1. Prick whole unpeeled eggplant with fork; roast over open flame on top of stove, turning once or twice until soft, limp, and charred. (The aroma and flavor of the slightly burnt skin are what you want; when the charred skin is peeled away, the smoky flavor remains. Eggplant will ooze liquid and make a mess of the top of your stove, but believe me, it's worth it. Whenever we have a picnic barbecue, I bring a few eggplants along to roast for Baba Ghanoush later in the week.) When cool enough to handle, peel eggplant with fingers or scoop out flesh with spoon.
2. Add garlic to eggplant and chop until chunky. Stir in tahini, lemon juice, salsa, cumin, and salt to taste.

Advance Preparation: This will last, covered in refrigerator, for 3 or 4 days.

Recommended Wine: A surprisingly wonderful combination with Baba Ghanoush is a medium- to full-bodied, rich and fruity California Cabernet Sauvignon.

Aram Sandwiches ◗

Rolled Vegetable Sandwiches in Lavosh

Armenia, United States   *Serves 4 to 6*

I like to make these with intensely flavored fillings and serve them in small, hors d'oeuvre-sized pieces. Aram Sandwiches are prepared using the flat Armenian cracker bread called *lavosh*, available in Middle Eastern and international groceries as well as at many gourmet specialty shops. Fresh *lavosh* (sometimes sold frozen) is the most pliable and gives a more delicate result; but if it is not available, crisp dried *lavosh* is just fine. Each round is softened, spread with an Herbed Cream Cheese mixture, layered with cucumbers, tomatoes, and alfalfa sprouts, then rolled up tightly. After sitting for several hours or overnight, it may be sliced into bite-sized (or two-bite-sized) rounds. The rounds look lovely on a platter, forming tiny pinwheels of red, white, and green.

Serve Aram Sandwich rounds as an hors d'oeuvre or as part of an elegant box lunch. The Herbed Cream Cheese is delicious spread on sandwiches or spooned on top of Pasta Arabbiata.

> 1   *round (about 20 inches) lavosh*
>   *Herbed Cream Cheese (recipe follows)*
> ½   *tomato, thinly sliced, sprinkled with garlic powder and salt*
> ½   *cucumber, peeled, thinly sliced, sprinkled with salt*
> ¼   *cup cilantro leaves*
> ½ to ⅔ *cup alfalfa sprouts*
> ½   *poblano chile, roasted, seeded, peeled, and cut into thin*
>   *strips; or 1 canned mild green chile*

1. Hold *lavosh* under running water, gently rinsing both sides for a few moments. Rounds will still be brittle. Wrap moistened bread in a clean dish towel or pillow case and let stand 30 minutes. (If using frozen *lavosh*, simply defrost; do not rinse.)
2. Spread lavosh with Herbed Cream Cheese. Make a row of tomato slices from side to side across the middle of the round. Next to tomatoes, arrange cucumber slices, cilantro leaves, alfalfa sprouts, and chile strips.
3. Roll *lavosh* tightly from top to bottom to form a cylinder. Wrap in foil or plastic and let stand in refrigerator 4 or 5 hours or overnight.

Herbed Cream Cheese

Yield: 1 generous cup

> 3   *cloves garlic*
> ½   *bunch cilantro (¾ cup)*
> 1   *to 2 tablespoons mild to medium commercial salsa, 1*
>   *teaspoon Marlena's Salsa, or 1 teaspoon Roasted Green*
>   *Jalapeño Salsa*
> 8   *ounces cream cheese, cut into several large chunks*
> 1   *tablespoon sour cream or yogurt*

1. In processor, chop garlic; add cilantro and continue chopping.
2. Add salsa, cream cheese and sour cream, then process until smooth.

Arabian Parsley Salad ♪

Chopped Parsley and Tahina

Middle East   *Serves 4*

The first time I tasted this thick, deep-green-flecked puree was in a cafe in the Old City of Jerusalem. It was with surprise and delight that I realized it was almost all finely chopped parsley. We often think of parsley only as a garnish, not as a vegetable to be eaten in large amounts. But why not, parsley is fresh tasting and full of Vitamin C. I sometimes combine equal amounts of chopped parsley and spinach with an herbed sausage stuffing for poultry or lamb.

Accompany this parsley salad with crusty French bread and serve as an hors d'oeuvre or as an accompaniment to grilled fish that has been rubbed with cumin, turmeric, paprika, and cayenne mixed with a little olive oil.

> 1   *cup finely chopped parsley (or ⅔ cup parsley, ⅓ cup mint or cilantro)*
> 1   *cup prepared Tahina Dip*
> ½   *teaspoon cayenne pepper*
> 1   *tablespoon each olive oil and salsa of choice for garnish*

Combine all ingredients; serve dribbled with the olive oil and salsa.

Mussels with Three-Pepper Relish ♪

United States   *Serves 4 as first course or 6 to 8 as hors d'oeuvre*

Fresh pepper relish is the perfect complement to the briny richness of seafood. This one is not too hot, and flecks of red and yellow peppers and green cilantro (or parsley) are very appealing nestled in the mussels' black shells. It's an elegant appetizer that is wonderful for a large party when you want a variety of interesting hors d'oeuvres.

2 pounds mussels in shells, washed and scrubbed of their
   beards
2 cups white wine
1 red bell pepper, roasted, peeled, and chopped
1 yellow bell pepper, roasted, peeled, and chopped
1 poblano, Anaheim, or California chile, roasted, peeled, and
   chopped
1 onion, finely chopped
½ cup finely chopped cilantro or parsley
2 cloves garlic, chopped
½ teaspoon chile paste such as Ají, Thai Chile Sauce, or
   commercial garlic-chile paste
   Juice of ½ lemon
2 tablespoons olive oil
   Salt

1. Wash mussels well. (If you think they may be excessively gritty, place them in
   1 quart cold water mixed with 3 tablespoons salt. Let stand for an hour to
   exude any sand.)
2. Drain mussels and place in shallow baking dish. Add white wine. Bake in
   preheated 375° F. oven until shells open, about 10 minutes. Let cool. Remove
   top halves of shells for easy presentation.
3. Combine peppers, onion, cilantro or parsley, garlic, chile paste, lemon juice,
   olive oil, and salt to taste.
4. Just before serving, lay out mussels in their shells and spoon a small portion
   of pepper relish onto each.

Radis Râpé ✏

Shredded Radish Salad

France   *Serves 4 as first course*

I seldom thought of radishes as more than a peppery decoration until I tasted this
salad of shredded radishes tossed in vinaigrette. The French often enjoy other
shredded vegetables as well—celeriac and carrots especially—as an hors
d'oeuvre or first course. This should be prepared with a food processor; using a
manual grater is rough on the knuckles.

Vivid green watercress is an attractive contrast to the scarlet radish.

2 *bunches red radishes (about 25)*
1 *bunch watercress (optional)*
2 *tablespoons vegetable oil*
2 *teaspoons white wine vinegar*
   Salt and pepper

1. Clean radishes, trimming off excess root.
2. Grate radishes using the grating or shredding disc of the food processor.
3. Divide watercress onto four plates. Dress shredded radishes with oil, vinegar, and salt and pepper to taste. Arrange one quarter of the mixture on each plate next to watercress.

Salata z Rzodkwi ♪

Poland   *Serves 4*

3 *to 4 black radishes if available, or 2 bunches red or white radishes*
¼ *cup sour cream*
   Lemon juice to taste
   Salt and pepper to taste

Shred radishes; combine with other ingredients. Serve as first course followed by kasha with onions and fried mushrooms.

Russian Variation: Same as Polish version but seasoned with Dijon mustard.

Hot Potato and Sausage Salad ♪

Germany, Italy   *Serves 4*

When I was testing recipes for this book, I served a buffet that included this dish as well as a number of foods with a three-chile rating. "How," I asked a guest, "did you like the potato and sausage salad?" "Thank God it was there," she replied. "After the Szechuan Chicken with Eggplant and the Hot and Sweet Cabbage Salad, I was afraid of what would come next." Another guest wept with relief.

This is tangy and earthy, with just a bit of heat emanating from the hot sausage. Serve on a bed of bitter greens, such as endive, arugula, mâche, and radicchio.

    2   *hot Italian sausages*
    6   *medium-sized boiling potatoes*
    2   *tablespoons German-style mustard*
    ¾   *cup vegetable oil*
    ½   *cup apple cider vinegar*
    ½   *bunch parsley, chopped*
    3   *green onions, chopped*
        Freshly ground black pepper
        Salt

1. Simmer sausages whole until cooked through (about 15 minutes); meanwhile, boil or steam potatoes in jackets until tender.
2. Whisk mustard until smooth, then whisk in oil, then vinegar.
3. Drain and slice sausages; toss with mustard dressing. Drain potatoes and cut into large cubes; toss into sausage mixture. Season with chopped parsley, green onions, and lots of freshly ground black pepper. Add a shake of salt if desired.

Munkaczina ʼ

Spiced Orange and Onion Salad

Saudi Arabia, Turkey   *Serves 4*

Spiced Orange and Onion Salad is a refreshing addition to a Middle Eastern, North African, or South American meal. The oranges' sweet-tartness balances perfectly with the fresh pungency of the onion and the salty black olive flesh, accentuated by the gentle jolt of cayenne. Variations of this salad may accompany a couscous meal in Morocco, *feijoado completa* (the Brazilian national dish of spicy black beans, rice, and grilled meats), or Turkish kabobs of swordfish basted with olive oil and lemon.

    3   *oranges*
    1   *red onion*
    8   *black Greek-style olives*
    3   *tablespoons olive oil*
    2   *tablespoons white wine vinegar, raspberry vinegar, or*
        lemon juice
    ¼   *teaspoon cayenne*

1. Peel oranges and onion. Slice each into ¼-inch crosswise slices and arrange on a platter or serving plate. Stud with olives.
2. Dribble with oil and vinegar, then sprinkle with cayenne.

Rudjak ❜

Fruit-Chile Compote

Southeast Asia   *Serves 4*

Though the idea of a "hot" fruit salad might seem strange, it is refreshing, even to the skeptical palate. Throughout India, Africa, and Asia, fruit is often paired with chile for a startling but pleasing combination. Enjoy with Nasi Kuning, curried stews, or as part of a spicy buffet.

- 2 *bananas*
- 1 *firm-ripe pear*
- ½ *pineapple*
- ½ *red bell pepper, chopped*
- 1 *orange*
- ½ *pink grapefruit*
- 3 *tablespoons sugar*
- 1 *tablespoon white vinegar or lemon juice*
- 1 *teaspoon garlic-chile paste or ½ teaspoon hot chile flakes*

1. Cut all fruits and bell pepper into ¾-inch chunks.
2. Mix other ingredients for dressing and pour over fruit. Chill until ready to serve.

Moroccan Carrots ❜

Steamed, Marinated Carrots

Morocco   *Serves 4*

The garlic-olive oil dressing complements the sweetness of the carrots. Try as part of a salad buffet accompanying couscous and Kofta Kabob, or just keep a jar in the refrigerator to snack on. A delicious enrichment for cooking as well: add to pasta salad, vegetable soup, spicy stews.

    1 *pound carrots, peeled and sliced ¼-inch thick*
    3 *cloves garlic, chopped*
    ¼ *cup olive oil*
    ¼ *cup white distilled or wine vinegar*
    ½ *teaspoon cumin (or to taste)*
    ¼ *teaspoon cinnamon*
    ½ *teaspoon cayenne pepper (or to taste)*
    ¼ *to ½ teaspoon salt*
    2 *tablespoons chopped parsley*

Steam carrots until crisp-tender. Toss with remaining ingredients and serve at room temperature.

Advance Preparation: Store, covered in refrigerator, for about 1 week.

Borani Esfanaj ”

Spinach-Yogurt Salad or Dip

Iran   *Serves 4*

This spinach and yogurt dish is Persian in origin. The yogurt is redolent with both musky and sweet spices complementing the slightly tart taste of the spinach. Borani Esfanaj is enjoyed as an appetizer, side dish, or dip to spread on bread. Though untraditional, the hot pepper flavoring adds zip. Accompany with French bread or pita; or, for a more tactile experience, tear off pieces of warm, soft flour tortillas and scoop up the savory mixture.

    1 *onion, chopped*
    4 *cloves garlic, chopped*
    1 *to 2 tablespoons butter*
    ½ *to 1 teaspoon turmeric*
    ½ *to 1 teaspoon cayenne pepper (or a generous dash Tabasco sauce)*
    ½ *teaspoon curry powder*
    1 *teaspoon cumin*
    ¼ *teaspoon cinnamon*

> 1 *package frozen chopped spinach, defrosted, or 2 bunches*
>   *fresh spinach, cooked and chopped*
> 1 *cup plain yogurt*
>   *Salt*

1. Sauté onion and garlic in butter until soft. Add spices and cook a few minutes to rid them of any rawness.
2. Mix in spinach, yogurt, and salt to taste.

Recommended Wine: Drink a slightly sweet Gewürtztraminer or California Riesling (German Rieslings fade at the spicy assertion of this dish).

Roasted and Marinated Peppers ❯❯

Italy   *Serves 4 to 6*

These vivid red, green, and yellow strands are tangy and savory on a sandwich, as a salad, or as an accompaniment to meats, cold cuts, or pasta. Try a few spoonfuls cooked into a soup or stew. The poblanos make this a spicier version of the classic Italian peppers, adding more flavor and heat than the sweeter green bell pepper.

> 2 *poblanos*
> 2 *red bell peppers*
> 2 *yellow bell peppers*
> ½ *cup olive oil*
> ¼ *cup white distilled vinegar*
> 3 *cloves garlic, chopped*
>   *Salt*
>   *Cayenne pepper*

1. Roast and peel the chiles and peppers (see "Roasting and Peeling Chiles and Peppers"). Stem, seed, and cut into strips.
2. Marinate in mixture of olive oil, vinegar, garlic, and salt and cayenne to taste.

Advance Preparation: These can be kept for up to a week in the refrigerator— probably longer, but we've always eaten them by then.

Mo-Mos and Khotes 》》

Steamed Meat/Curried Vegetable Dumplings

Tibet

Mo-Mos and Khotes are the national dishes of Tibet, much like our hamburger or Britain's fish and chips. Mo-Mos are filled with meat and chopped greens and are traditionally enjoyed dipped into soy sauce, shredded ginger, vinegar, and hot chile oil. Khotes are filled with a curried vegetable mixture and are dipped into Achar, a relish made of tomatoes, onions, and chiles. Both are fabulous dipped in Cilantro-Mint Fresh Chutney.

The Tibetan friend who gave me this recipe said that the beverage of choice in Tibet is a raw white-lightning rice drink called chang. "Chang," she emphasizes, to go with the Mo-Mos, you will enjoy the authentic combination. I suggest an icy beer or my recommended wine in the event the corner wine shop is out of chang.

Serve as a pasta course or snack.

Dough

Yield: 12 to 15 dumplings

- 2   *cups all-purpose flour*
- ¾   *cup hot water (bring to boil and let cool a moment)*
    Mo-Mo or Khote Filling (recipes follow)
- 1   *bunch of kale to line steamer*
    Dipping sauce for Mo-Mos or Achar (recipes follow)

1. Pour hot water over flour; mix with fork. When cool enough to handle, finish mixing with your hands until dough holds together. Wrap in plastic and refrigerate until chilled through.
2. Work one piece of dough at a time: pinch off a walnut-sized chunk, shape into a ball, knead several times, then roll flat on a floured board.
3. Place dough circle in the palm of your hand; in the middle of the dough, place about 1 tablespoon filling. Bring up edges and seal at top with little gathers. Leave a tiny hole at top for steam to escape during cooking.
4. Line steamer or bottom of skillet with kale leaves. Top with a layer of dumplings and steam over boiling water 15 to 20 minutes. If using a skillet, use just enough water to cushion the Mo-Mos; replenish water as needed. Serve immediately, pairing Mo-Mos with soy sauce, ginger, and vinegar. May also be served with Achar or Cilantro-Mint Fresh Chutney.

Mo-Mo Filling

Yield: enough for 12 to 15 Mo-Mos

8 ounces lean ground lamb or beef
½ onion, finely chopped
1 cup chopped raw kale
½ cup cilantro, chopped
3 cloves garlic, chopped
1 tablespoon chopped fresh ginger
1½ teaspoons Curry Powder
1 tablespoon sherry, vermouth, or brandy
2 teaspoons flour
2 teaspoons soy sauce
½ teaspoon cayenne pepper or hot chile paste such as Aji

Combine all ingredients.

Khote Filling

Yield: enough for 12 to 15 Khotes

2 tablespoons butter
1 onion, chopped
3 cloves garlic, chopped
2 to 3 jalapeños, sliced
1 teaspoon cumin
1½ teaspoons Curry Powder
½ teaspoon dry ground ginger
½ teaspoon turmeric
1½ cups raw broccoli, chopped
½ red bell pepper, chopped
2 baking potatoes, peeled, quartered, and boiled, then
    mashed (or use 1½ cups leftover mashed potatoes)
¼ cup chopped cilantro (optional)
2 tablespoons yogurt
  Juice of ½ lime
  Salt
  Cayenne pepper

1. Melt butter in skillet. Add onion and garlic and cook over low heat until onion is limp. Add chiles and spices and cook a minute or two longer.
2. Add broccoli and red bell pepper. Cook until they are crisp-tender; then add mashed potatoes, cilantro, yogurt, lime, and salt and cayenne to taste.

Dipping Sauce for Mo-Mos

Yield: 3 tablespoons

1 tablespoon soy sauce
1 tablespoon vinegar
1 tablespoon chile oil
1 piece of fresh ginger (about ½ inch long), shredded.

Combine all ingredients.

Achar

Yield: 1 cup

½ onion, chopped
2 cloves garlic, chopped
1 tablespoon vegetable oil
1 teaspoon Curry Powder
2 to 3 jalapeños, thinly sliced
2 to 3 tomatoes, chopped
  Salt
  Lime juice

Sauté onion and garlic in oil until onion is soft. Add Curry Powder, tomatoes, and chiles and simmer over low heat until tomatoes are cooked through and mixture has a saucelike consistency. Season with salt and lime to taste.

Recommended Wine: Surprisingly, a medium- to full-bodied California Cabernet Sauvignon is wonderful with this. A crisp, slightly sweet German Riesling is pleasant as well. If served with Cilantro-Mint Fresh Chutney, choose the Riesling or a Gewürztraminer.

Moroccan Spiced Olives

Morocco   *Yield: 1 cup*

Olives are often served as part of the Middle Eastern appetizer assortment called *mezze* or *mazza* that is brought to your table with your wine, ouzo, or arak.

Anything can turn up as part of a *mezze* selection: octopus dressed in olive oil and lemon, chunks of feta cheese or salami on small pieces of bread, or a plate of creamy, tart hummus. Olives—brined, salted, or marinated—are almost always on one of the little plates.

Middle Eastern marketplaces feature huge vats and crocks of differently spiced olives in myriad array. Some are fleshy, some juicy, others bitter and dense, and each is in a subtly different marinade. The marinade in this recipe is good for almost any type of olive; it is especially delicious with green brined olives or fleshy Greek-style ones (it even improves California-style ripe olives).

> 1 *cup olives purchased from a deli or Middle Eastern grocery (green brine-cured, Kalamata, Greek-style, or shriveled black dry-cured)*
> ¼ *cup olive oil*
> 4 *cloves garlic, chopped*
> 1 *teaspoon fresh rosemary leaves, lightly crushed*
> 1½ *teaspoons Ají, Harissa, Berberé, or commercial chile-garlic paste*
> 1 *tablespoon wine vinegar*

1. Drain olives of any brine.
2. Gently heat olive oil over low heat. Remove from heat and add garlic, rosemary, chile-garlic paste, and vinegar.
3. Pour marinade over olives and let stand at least 2 hours (the flavor gets hotter the longer it stands).

Advance Preparation: Lasts almost forever, covered and refrigerated.

Variation: A Mediterranean-inspired hors d'oeuvre.

> 4 *ounces Montrachet or Lezay goat cheese*
> 1 *to 2 cloves garlic, chopped*
> 1 *teaspoon finely chopped cilantro (optional)*
> 1 *teaspoon medium salsa (or to taste)*
> ½ *teaspoon thyme*
> 1 *teaspoon olive oil*
> *Approximately ½ a French baguette, cut into ½- to ¾-inch slices*
> *Moroccan Spiced Olives*

1. Mash goat cheese with a fork. Add garlic, cilantro, salsa, thyme, and olive oil.
2. Spread goat cheese mixture on bread slices; top each with half a pitted marinated olive.

Recommended Wine: Enjoy with a glass of a medium-bodied Cabernet Sauvignon with noticeable character, one from California, Chile, or Spain.

Salata Meshwiya ❯❯

Tuna and Vegetable Salad

Tunisia   *Serves 4*

Good, reliable tuna fish is a delicious partner for hot food. Its hearty flavor is particularly compatible with fresh chiles and tomatoes in this salad from Tunisia. The addition of green beans, potatoes, olives, and hard-cooked eggs makes this a spicy version of the French *Salade Niçoise*. Serve Salata Meshwiya as a luncheon dish on a sweltery summer day or as a first course followed by Kofta Kabob or Couscous Fassi.

  4 *large curly lettuce leaves*
  4 *boiling potatoes, boiled or steamed until tender, then peeled and cut into wedges*
  2 *tomatoes, cut into wedges*
  1 *poblano or green bell pepper, roasted, peeled, and cut into strips*
  1 *red bell pepper, roasted, peeled, and cut into strips*
¼ *pound (approximately) green beans, cut into 2-inch lengths, cooked al dente*
  1 *to 2 cans tuna (6½ ounces each), drained*
  2 *hard-cooked eggs, peeled and quartered*
  8 *Greek-style olives*
    Wedges of lemon
    Olive oil
  2 *tablespoons chopped parsley*
  1 *cup medium-hot salsa, homemade or store-bought*

1. Place a leaf of lettuce on each plate. Arrange several pieces of potato, tomato, peppers, and green beans on top of the lettuce. Place a portion of tuna in the middle.
2. Garnish with egg, olives, and lemon wedges. Dribble olive oil over all and sprinkle with chopped parsley. Pass salsa separately.

Variation: In Mexico, tuna is served simply dressed with salsa and lemon wedges; a less ambitious dish, but also delicious. Try it on a hot summer day when you can barely lift a fork. Place a portion of drained tuna on a bed of curly lettuce. Accompany with hot salsa, fresh cilantro or parsley, and a wedge of lemon to squeeze over it all.

Carrots and Zucchini en Escabeche ""

Pickled Carrots and Zucchini

Mexico *Yield: approximately 2½ cups*

Crunchy-tender zucchini and carrots, lightly pickled with spicy brine. Try as an appetizer or side dish, or stuffed into a tortilla with other tasty bits: shredded meats, melted cheese, saucy beans. *Escabeche* means "pickled" in Spanish. Other vegetables also make excellent *escabeche,* as do chicken and fish, which are often prepared in this manner to make a lively first course.

> 2 *carrots, cut into sticks*
> 2 *zucchini, cut into same size as carrots*
> ¼ *cup white distilled vinegar*
> 1 *tablespoon vegetable oil*
> 3 *cloves garlic, chopped*
> 1 *to 2 jalapeños, sliced (or 1 tablespoon hot salsa)*
> ½ *teaspoon oregano*
> *Salt to taste*

1. Steam carrots for 5 minutes or until almost tender; add zucchini and continue cooking for a few minutes longer, until both vegetables are just tender.
2. Toss vegetables with all remaining ingredients.

Advance Preparation: May be kept several days, covered in refrigerator.

Mast Va Bademjam ▶▶▶

Eggplant Caviar with Yogurt

Iran   *Serves 4 to 6*

Mast means "yogurt" in the Persian language Farsi, and *bademjam* means "eggplant." In this dish, the eggplant is roasted whole, the tender flesh mashed with raw onion, garlic, chile paste, yogurt, and fried onions.

A plate containing a selection of fresh whole herbs appears at almost every Iranian meal: green onions, cilantro, mint, parsley, and radishes. These are nibbled throughout the meal or sprinkled on each diner's plate. You might think of accompanying this eggplant caviar with such an herb platter. Follow with Morrocan Fish with Cumin Paste and Ethiopian Spiced Spinach.

  1   medium-large eggplant (1 ¼ pounds)
  3   tablespoons vegetable oil
  ¼   onion, minced
  ½   to 1 cup plain yogurt
  1   clove garlic, minced
  1   to 2 teaspoons fresh lemon juice
  1   teaspoon commercial hot salsa, garlic-chile paste, or
      cayenne pepper
      Salt
  1   onion, thinly sliced lengthwise
  2   to 3 tablespoons butter

1. Preheat oven to 350° F. Pierce eggplant with fork several times, rub with 2 tablespoons oil, then place in baking dish and bake until tender, about 1 hour (it will look limp and deflated).
2. Cut eggplant open and scrape out flesh. Discard skin. Mash flesh with fork or processor. Add minced onion, yogurt, garlic, lemon juice, chile paste or other hot seasoning, and salt to taste.
3. Fry onion slices in butter and add to eggplant mixture. Serve with crusty bread.

Thai Cabbage Salad ▶▶▶

Thailand   *Serves 4 to 6*

Raw vegetables are eaten in great abundance in Thailand. In this version of coleslaw, crunchy shreds of cabbage are combined with a hot-sweet-sour dressing. The sturdy and humble cabbage is a good partner for these assertive Thai flavors.

⅓ *cup vegetable oil*
⅓ *cup white distilled vinegar*
3 *tablespoons sugar*
3 *tablespoons soy sauce*
1 *cup chopped cilantro*
1 *to 2 tablespoons red salsa or 1 teaspoon chile-garlic paste*
4 *cloves garlic, chopped*
2 *serrano chiles, thinly sliced*
1 *head green cabbage, shredded or very thinly sliced*
½ *cucumber, peeled and diced*
½ *carrot, shredded*
1 *cup dry-roasted peanuts, coarsely chopped*
5 *green onions, chopped*
½ *red bell pepper or Thai Chile Flowers for garnish*

1. Combine oil, vinegar, sugar, soy sauce, cilantro, salsa, garlic, and chiles.
2. Pour mixture over cabbage, cucumber, and carrot.
3. Toss with chopped peanuts, green onions, and garnish with red bell peppers or Thai Chile Flowers.

Advance Preparation: Salad may be prepared up to a day ahead but peanuts may be added only at the last minute to preserve their crunchiness.

Goat-Cheese-
Stuffed Poblanos ▶▶▶

California, Central America

Goat cheese (chèvre) has been eaten in Europe probably since the time goats were domesticated. Until recently, however, goat cheese was not very popular here. Over the past several years, enthusiasm for goat cheese has grown, especially in California. It's served in restaurants on everything from salads to pizza and calzone, and it's being produced in small dairies that take pride in the crafting of this cheese.

I hope goat cheese will not be dismissed as last season's "chic," the way many delicious (and less so) foods have been. It has a creamy but not heavy quality, a tart and distinctive flavor, delicious as is or delicately melted. (Try a few ounces combined with garlic or Moroccan Spiced Olives tossed with linguine. Try the Chèvre and Poblano Calzone also.)

This is a simple, contemporary version of *chiles rellenos*. It is easy to prepare, and the combination of tangy goat cheese and rich poblano chile is wonderful. I love to bake these with a roast chicken during the chicken's last 10 or 15 minutes in the oven. I then serve the chiles as a first course on a bed of shredded romaine lettuce with a spoonful of Picanté Vinaigrette and/or drippings from the chicken dribbled on top. This is one of the most delicious things I have ever tasted, but beware! Poblanos taste mild at first, but leave a legacy in your throat.

For each serving allow:

1 *to 2 poblano chiles, roasted and peeled*
⅓ *cup California or French goat cheese such as Montrachet*
   Dash salsa of choice
1 *tablespoon olive oil or chicken drippings*

1. Mash goat cheese with fork. Add a small amount of salsa to taste.
2. Stuff each pepper with about 3 tablespoons of cheese mixture. Arrange in baking dish and dribble with olive oil or chicken drippings.
3. Bake at 350° F. until cheese melts. Accompany with crusty bread or serve atop a large (10- or 12-inch), warm flour tortilla. Roll up and enjoy.

Variations:
1. Marinate roasted, peeled poblanos for 1 or 2 days in a dressing of olive oil, red wine vinegar, chopped garlic, crumbled oregano, cayenne pepper, and 1 bay leaf. This will mellow the heat somewhat. Proceed to stuff the chiles with goat cheese. Or do as they do in Mexico, stuff them with guacamole and enjoy them cold as a salad.

Simlah Mirch
2. Stuffed peppers are eaten worldwide. This is a version from India. Stuff the roasted, peeled poblanos with the filling from Curried Stuffed Potatoes; dribble with 1 tablespoon oil and bake in 350° F. preheated oven to heat through, about 10 to 15 minutes. Serve accompanied by Turmeric Raita (yogurt which has been seasoned with a little garlic and turmeric).

Udang Rica-Rica

Shrimp with Sweet, Sour, and Hot Sauce

Indonesia   *Yield: 4 servings*

Deep-frying shrimp in their shells seals in the juices and results in the flesh being particularly succulent. They're not at all greasy, since the shells protect them from the hot-oil bath.

Follow with Gado Gado or Spicy Black Beans with steamed rice.

> *Oil for frying (2 inches deep)*
> 12 *to 16 shrimp in shells*
> ½ *teaspoon sereh (powdered lemon grass)*
> 1 ½ *tablespoons soy sauce*
> 1 *tablespoon sugar*
> 2 *tablespoons white or rice vinegar*
> 1 *teaspoon commercial garlic-chile paste or Sambal Olek*

1. Heat oil until hot (a good way to test for deep-frying temperature is to throw a cube of bread into the hot oil; if it turns golden immediately, the oil is hot enough). Fry shrimp for only 2 to 3 minutes, then remove from hot oil with slotted spoon and set aside.
2. Combine sereh, soy sauce, sugar, vinegar, and chile paste in small pan. Heat until boiling, then reduce heat and add shrimp for a minute or two to reheat. Serve immediately.

Advance Preparation: Shrimp may be fried several hours ahead of time and reheated a few minutes before serving.

Ekra

Russian Eggplant Caviar

Russia   *Serves 4*

"Another eggplant puree?" you might ask. Well, I've never tasted an eggplant puree I did not consider worth eating. This slightly sweet, slightly hot version was introduced to me by Soviet emigré friends. The authentic Russian way to prepare it is without the chile pepper, but I think it tastes better hot, and that is why it is included in this book.

Accompany with crusty bread and follow with steamed green beans and Russian meatballs strongly flavored with onion and black pepper.

> 1 *medium eggplant (approximately 1 ¼ pounds)*
> 6 *tablespoons vegetable oil*
> 2 *green bell peppers (if sweet red peppers are in season, use 1 red pepper, 1 green pepper)*
> 1 *red onion, chopped*
> 4 *cloves garlic, chopped*
> ½ *tomato, chopped*
> ½ *cup tomato paste*
> 1 *tablespoon sugar*
> 2 *to 3 teaspoons commercial garlic-chile paste or ½ to 1 ½ teaspoons cayenne pepper*
> 1 *teaspoon paprika*
>   *Squeeze of fresh lemon*
>   *Salt to taste*

1. Preheat oven to 350° F. Prick eggplant all over with fork and rub with 2 tablespoons oil. Place in baking dish or on foil and bake until eggplant is limp, about 1 hour. Remove from oven and let cool.
2. Roast and peel peppers, removing stem and seeds as well. (About 6 oz. of canned mild green chiles may be used instead of the roasted bell peppers; omit chile paste or cayenne.)
3. Chop peppers and eggplant in processor.
4. Sauté onion and garlic in ¼ cup oil until golden; add eggplant mixture and remaining ingredients. Cook until flavors meld and mixture thickens, about 5 to 10 minutes.

Hot and Sweet Cabbage Salad ▶▶▶

United States   *Serves 4 to 6*

This cabbage salad is hot, sour, sweet, and refreshing. Its robust yet sophisticated flavor belies the simple ingredients and preparation. The cabbage's vibrant red color makes this dish an attractive addition to any table, especially a buffet, and it's great for picnics, since there's no mayonnaise to spoil in the heat. I'm going to make this next Thanksgiving to enjoy with our turkey.

  1 *medium-sized head red cabbage*
  ¾ *cup vegetable oil*
  ¾ *cup white distilled vinegar*
  ½ *cup sugar*
  2 *tablespoons red salsa of choice, or 1 to 2 serranos, minced*
    Garlic powder and salt to taste

1. Slice cabbage very thinly—a food processor is best for this.
2. Mix remaining ingredients and pour over cabbage. Toss thoroughly. Serve immediately or chill until ready to serve.

Horef ▶▶▶

Sautéed Chile and Tomato Appetizer

Israel   *Serves 4*

Horef is roughly translated as "hot pepper." This dish of simmered peppers, chiles, and tomatoes is served as an appetizer, salad, or relish. Spread it on bread or eat it with roast chicken and pilaf; delicious, too, in a sandwich with cumin-spiced meatballs.

  2 *green bell peppers, stemmed, seeded, and cut into slices ¼*
    inch thick, 1 inch long
  3 *California or Anaheim chiles, stemmed, seeded, and cut*
    into ¼-inch slices
  2 *jalapeños, stemmed, seeded, and chopped*
  5 *to 7 cloves garlic, coarsely chopped*
    Several tablespoons olive oil
  3 *tomatoes, quartered or coarsely chopped*
  1 *teaspoon Curry Powder*
    Squeeze of fresh lemon juice
    Salt

Sauté bell peppers, chiles, and garlic in olive oil for a few minutes until soft. Add tomatoes and Curry Powder; simmer until mixture is thick and vegetables tender. Season with lemon juice and salt to taste.

Advance Preparation: Store covered in refrigerator for 2 or 3 days.

Soups

Almost any soup can benefit from a spoonful of salsa or other condiment. A hot addition will perk it up, accentuate the flavors, and excite the palate. Even chicken soup takes to this kind of seasoning; or try a spoonful of garlic-chile paste stirred into Chinese noodle soup. For a simple, hearty soup, poach meatballs or shrimp in chicken broth, add a spoonful of rice or noodles, then splash it with salsa. Try also shaking cayenne pepper generously into pureed lentil soup.

All types of soups are delicious "hot." Clear broths, such as Spiced Zucchini-Lime Soup or Vietnamese Noodle Soup-Salad, have their flavors clarified by the heat. Thick potages such as Piquant Pea Soup or Pureed Potato Soup With Poblano Chile need the accent of heat to lift them from blandness, and in chunky soups such as Hot Hungarian Mushroom or Middle Eastern Black-Eyed Pea Soup, the hotness emphasizes each individual ingredient.

When you've eaten a hot soup that's spiced just right, you feel satisfied not full.

Vietnamese Noodle Soup-Salad ♪

South Vietnam   *Serves 4*

Flavored with pungent fish sauce, tart lime, and hot seasonings, this light and fresh-tasting dish is representative of the cuisine of Vietnam. All over the country, rich clear broths based on meat, fowl, or fish are enjoyed with a variety of ingredients added at the last minute. In the north the national dish is *pho,* a soup of this type based on beef. Some of the additions cook briefly in the bubbling broth, others are added at the table. The result: each bowlful is a mosaic of tastes and textures, all floating in a piquant broth. I love the combination of the cilantro and mint, the crunchiness of the nuts, and the cool astringency of the cucumber chunks.

> 8 *ounces thin rice noodles (rice sticks)*
> 2 *green onions, chopped*
> 2 *tomatoes, chopped*
> 1 *tablespoon vegetable oil*
> 4 *cups chicken or beef broth*
> 1 *tablespoon fish sauce*
> 1 *teaspoon hot salsa (or garlic-chile paste or Tabasco sauce to taste)*
> 6 *to 7 lettuce leaves, shredded*
> 4 *ounces mung bean sprouts*
> 1 *cucumber, peeled and diced (seeded if you wish)*
> ½ *cup cilantro*
> ½ *cup fresh mint leaves*
> ½ *cup dry-roasted peanuts, coarsely chopped*
> 1 *lime, cut into wedges*

1. Soak rice noodles in warm water to cover for 30 minutes. Drain and set aside. Some brands need cooking, some don't; if noodles are tough, boil for 2 or 3 minutes.
2. Sauté green onions and tomatoes in vegetable oil. Add broth, fish sauce, and salsa or chile paste. Simmer for 5 minutes to combine flavors, then add noodles.
3. Assemble soup-salads by serving each person a bowl of noodles and broth. Arrange lettuce, sprouts, cucumber, herbs, and chopped peanuts on a platter and let each diner add what he or she likes to the soup. Offer lime wedges to squeeze over soup, and extra hot seasoning if desired.

Spiced Zucchini-Lime Soup

Middle East, Mexico, Balkans   *Serves 4*

This soup is spicy, light, and extremely low in calories. Don't let its simplicity fool you into thinking it's ordinary, however. The tart and spicy broth exudes an exotic fragrance of cinnamon; this is a zucchini soup like no other. It is loosely based on the highly seasoned vegetable soups that are doused with lots of lemon or lime and enjoyed throughout Mexico, the Balkans, and the Middle East. You might follow this with Couscous Fassi or Arroz con Pollo.

4   *cups chicken broth*
4   *zucchini (1 pound), diced*
3   *cloves garlic, chopped*
1   *cinnamon stick*
1   *tablespoon medium-hot salsa (homemade or commercial)*
1   *lime, cut into wedges*
    Cilantro leaves for garnish
    Additional salsa for garnish

1. Combine everything except lime wedges and garnishes in saucepan.
2. Bring to boil and simmer 5 to 10 minutes, or until zucchini is tender.
3. Serve garnished with lime wedges, cilantro, and extra salsa.

Middle Eastern
Black-Eyed Pea Soup ♪

Middle East   *Serves 4*

When I think of black-eyed peas, what comes to mind first is soul food, greens and potlikker nestled next to the legumes, or "hoppin' John," that Southern mélange of rice and black-eyed peas: homey and hearty, but scarcely exotic. That is why when a friend from the Middle East told me about this soup, I was enchanted. The soup is simple, yet the combination of black-eyed peas with such flavorings as turmeric and cilantro is intriguing and satisfying.

Enjoy with flour tortillas or crusty French bread, and accompany with Borani Esfanaj for lunch or supper.

4   *ounces dried black-eyed peas*
1   *tablespoon olive oil*
1   *onion, chopped*
4   *cloves garlic, chopped*
1   *jalapeño, thinly sliced*
1   *teaspoon cumin*
1   *teaspoon turmeric*
1   *cup chopped tomatoes (canned is fine)*

    2 *cups chicken, beef, or vegetable broth*
   ½ *cup chopped cilantro*
       Juice of ½ lemon

1. In saucepan, cover black-eyed peas with water and bring to boil. Boil for 5 minutes, then turn off heat, cover and let stand 2 hours. Drain, add fresh water to cover, and simmer for 30 to 40 minutes or until tender. Drain and set aside. You will have about 1½ cups black-eyed peas.
2. Heat olive oil in skillet and add onion, garlic, and jalapeño. Cook until onion is soft, then add cumin, turmeric, tomatoes, broth, reserved beans, and cilantro. Simmer for 20 to 30 minutes. Add lemon juice, then serve.

Advance Preparation: Soup is even better prepared the day before.

Pureed Potato Soup with Poblano Chile

Europe, Latin America   *Serves 4*

This rich soup is based on the hearty potato soups of Europe with the Latin American accent of chile. The creamy pureed potatoes combine well with the assertive flavors of poblano and garlic. Mediterranean Mini-Grill or a juicy roast chicken served with Piri-Piri would be a delicious entrée served with a tartly dressed salad of mixed greens.

    1 *onion, chopped*
    3 *tablespoons butter*
    2 *tablespoons all-purpose flour*
    4 *large baking potatoes, peeled and diced*
   10 *cloves garlic, peeled but left whole*
    1 *poblano chile, roasted, peeled, and sliced*
    1 *tablespoon paprika (hot paprika, if available)*
    1 *teaspoon cumin*
    3 *cups chicken broth*
    1 *cup half-and-half*
   ½ *pint sour cream*
       Sprinkle cayenne or paprika
    2 *tablespoons cilantro*

1. Sauté onion lightly in butter until limp; do not brown. Stir in flour and cook briefly. Add potatoes, garlic, poblano, paprika, and cumin and cook a few minutes.
2. Stir in broth and simmer until vegetables are tender.
3. Remove vegetables from broth and place in food processor. Puree with half-and-half. Return mixture to broth and stir to blend. Serve hot, garnished with a dollop of sour cream, a sprinkling of cayenne or paprika, and a few leaves of cilantro.

Thick Noodles
and Lamb in Broth ✎

Russia   *Serves 4*

This soup of thick, hand-rolled noodles, lamb, and green onions bathed in chile-accented broth hails from the Uzbeck Republic of the U.S.S.R. The noodles are so delicious, you might make a batch sometime to enjoy with Braised Lamb and Vine Leaves in Tomato Sauce or Gulasz Wieprzowy. Uzbeck cuisine is descendant from both the villages and nomadic tribes that have populated this Central Asian region for centuries. Goat's- and sheep's-milk cheeses, rice cooked with vegetables, meat, and spices, abundant produce, and a dazzling array of sugar-sweet melons highlight the fare, as does a proclivity for garlic and small, hot red chiles.

  ⅓ cup water
  2 tablespoons vegetable oil
  1 teaspoon salt
1½ to 2 cups flour
  1 egg
  *½ to ⅔ pound, shoulder lamb chops, boned and cut into
      strips ½ inch wide*
  4 cloves garlic, chopped
  1 large tomato, chopped
  3 to 4 green onions, chopped
  ½ carrot, thinly sliced
  ½ onion, thinly sliced
  2 small dried chiles
  2 cups chicken broth
  2 cups beef broth

2 *tablespoons soy sauce*
1 *bay leaf*
   Cayenne pepper to taste

1. For the noodles: Boil ⅓ cup water; pour water, 1 tablespoon vegetable oil, and salt over 1½ cups flour and mix with a fork. When well mixed, add the egg and mix until it is blended in. Cover with plastic wrap and set aside for 30 to 40 minutes.
2. Sprinkle the remaining flour over board. Divide the dough into three portions. Working one portion at a time, knead onto the floured surface (dough will be sticky) and roll out to ½-inch thick. Cut with a knife into strips ¼ to ½ inch wide. Toss with flour and set aside. Continue until all dough is used up; you may need extra flour.
3. Boil noodles in approximately 2 quarts of water, for 3 to 5 minutes or until slightly chewy, dumplinglike in consistency. Drain, then rinse and set aside while you make the soup.
4. Heat remaining tablespoon of oil in 1½- to 2-quart saucepan. Sauté lamb and garlic for a few minutes, then add tomato, two-thirds of the green onions, carrot slices, onion slices, dried chiles, chicken and beef broths, soy sauce, and bay leaf. Simmer for 30 to 45 minutes. Serve over reserved noodles, and season to taste with cayenne pepper. (You may remove the dried chiles from the soup before serving; they are very hot and could be a nasty surprise. The rest of the soup is mellow and just warm.) Sprinkle each bowl of soup with some of the remaining chopped green onions.

Advance Preparation: Noodles and soup may be prepared several hours to a day ahead of time and heated together to serve.

Caldo del Pescado⸴

Broth with Assorted Seafood

Mexico   *Serves 4*

This is a Mexican bouillabaisse, enlivened not with the Provençal garlic mayonnaise, aïoli, nor with its red-pepper-flavored cousin, Rouille, but with salsa or Cilantro Aïoli. As with bouillabaisse, the flavor of this soup depends upon the variety of fish and shellfish used, as well as the richness of the stock. In Mexico I was amazed at the variety of fish available, as well as at their freshness and flavor.

It's worth making a double recipe of the fish stock to have extra. Just double, or even triple the ingredients. It's fabulous to have on hand; freeze and use in gumbos, chowders, or for bouillabaisse.

Fish Stock

2 pounds fresh fish bones, scrap, heads, etc.
½ onion, coarsely chopped
2 cloves garlic, coarsely chopped
½ stalk celery, coarsely chopped
½ cup cilantro or parsley (or combination), chopped
1 bay leaf
¼ teaspoon oregano leaves (preferably Mexican)
6 cups water
Salt to taste

Fish Soup

1 onion, chopped
4 cloves garlic, chopped
1½ tablespoons olive oil
½ pound tomatoes, chopped, or 1 8-ounce can, chopped
2 boiling potatoes, peeled and diced
1 tablespoon salsa such as Marlena's Salsa
6 to 10 clams
12 to 16 medium-sized shrimp in their shells
5 to 7 raw oysters, shucked (jarred if raw oysters are not available)
2 to 3 squid, cleaned and sliced
1 fish fillet or steak, about 6 to 8 ounces
1 avocado, peeled, pitted, and cubed
1 or 2 limes, cut into wedges
1 or 2 green jalapeños, thinly sliced, for garnish
2 green onions, chopped
¼ cup cilantro or parsley for garnish
Salsa as desired

1. Combine all ingredients for fish stock and cover with 6 cups water. Simmer over medium-low heat for 30 minutes, skimming off any scum that may rise to the surface. (Unlike meat stock, fish stock is not simmered for hours.) Strain, discarding the solids. Salt to taste.
2. Sauté onion and garlic in olive oil until onion is soft. Add tomatoes, potatoes, and 6 cups fish stock. Simmer until potato is cooked (about 10 minutes), then add salsa.

3. Add clams and cook 5 minutes. Add remaining seafood and simmer until fish is opaque and clams open up. Don't overcook!
4. Serve a selection of fish chunks, shellfish, and vegetables with a little broth in each bowl, garnished with cubes of avocado, wedges of lime, jalapeño slices, green onions, and cilantro or parsley. Offer extra salsa.

Advance Preparation: Make the stock and cook vegetables in it ahead of time; cook the fish and seafood at the last minute.

Sopa de Ajo*"*

Garlic Soup

Spain   *Serves 4*

The Spanish have many versions of garlic soup. This one is fragrant with simmered garlic and hot from dried chiles and a dash of cayenne. I find it a pick-me-up not only for the body but also for the soul.

Serve followed by Spicy Baked Pork with Clams and Cilantro-Serrano Puree or Red Chile Pasta with Ratatouille.

> 2 *cups cubed French bread*
> ½ *cup olive oil*
> 1 *clove garlic, chopped*
> 1 *head garlic, cloves separated and peeled but left whole*
> 2 *tablespoons fresh sage leaves (or ½ to 1 tablespoon dried leaf sage)*
> 3 *small dried red chiles*
> 4 *cups chicken broth*
> 2 *eggs*
> ½ *cup Parmesan cheese, plus extra, if desired, for sprinkling*
> 1 *tablespoon dry sherry*
>   *Cayenne pepper to taste*

1. Sauté bread cubes in olive oil until golden. Toss with chopped garlic. Set aside.
2. Place whole garlic cloves, sage, small dried chiles, and broth in saucepan. Bring to boil and simmer 15 minutes or until garlic is soft and sweet-flavored.
3. Beat eggs and add ½ cup Parmesan cheese. Slowly stir into soup mixture. Simmer for a few minutes over low heat to thicken soup slightly; stir in sherry. Serve immediately, topped with the reserved croutons, sprinkled with cayenne pepper to taste, and with Parmesan cheese, if desired.

Hot Hungarian Mushroom Soup"

Hungary   *Serves 4 to 6*

Mushroom soups can be insipid, but this one sure isn't! Besides the mushroom flavor, it offers both sweet and hot pepper, chunks of potato, and the aroma of onion and garlic.

Hungarian food is a rich amalgam characterized by peppers, hot or sweet, fresh, pickled, or dried and ground (as in paprika). Wild mushrooms gathered from the fields and forests add their woodsy fragrance to the cuisine. These heady flavors are mellowed by cream, sometimes sweet but often soured. While hot flavors are not a part of every dish, the Hungarians do like to use hot paprika or hot peppers occasionally. This soup is Hungarian in spirit if not in authenticity (of course, salsa is not Hungarian, but it is good in this soup).

A big bowl of Hot Hungarian Mushroom Soup, accompanied by black bread and cucumber salad, makes a warming lunch or supper.

¼   *pound mushrooms, thinly sliced*
¼   *cup butter*
1   *onion, chopped*
3   *to 4 cloves garlic, chopped*
2   *tablespoons Hungarian sweet paprika (or 1 tablespoon sweet paprika and 1 tablespoon hot paprika)*
2   *tablespoons flour*
4   *cups chicken broth*
3   *to 4 small red or white boiling potatoes, cut into ¾-inch cubes*
½   *cup sliced or chopped red bell peppers, pickled in vinegar*
1   *tablespoon tomato paste*
1   *tablespoon medium to medium-hot salsa*
½   *pint sour cream, to garnish*
     Extra salsa (optional)

1. Sauté mushrooms in 2 tablespoons butter (do them in several batches; if too many are cooked at once, they will steam instead of sautéing and will become soggy). Set aside.
2. In saucepan, sauté onion, garlic, and paprika in remaining butter until onion is limp.
3. Sprinkle on flour and stir until slightly darkened in color, then turn off heat and stir in chicken broth. Continue to stir until most of the lumps are gone

(don't worry about getting it absolutely smooth; with everything else in the soup, a few lumps will not be noticed).

4. Add potato chunks, peppers, tomato paste, and salsa and cook until potatoes are tender. Return mushrooms and any accumulated liquid to pot and adjust seasoning. Top each serving with a dollop of sour cream and extra salsa, if desired.

Pureed Pumpkin Soup ❱❱

Latin America, Native American   *Serves 4 to 6*

It's a shame that pumpkins disappear from the market after Halloween. Pumpkin is enjoyed as a vegetable in many parts of the world, especially North Africa and Latin America, where it is valued for its rich, earthy flavor. When pumpkin is unavailable, substitute banana squash; it will still be delicious. If you've a yard, grow pumpkin yourself, so you will always have it on hand to include in your pilaf, couscous, vegetable curries, and so on. Early in the season, when the pumpkins are still tiny and green and their outer skin is tender, they are delicious simply sliced and stir-fried with a little soy sauce.

This soup is inspired by the American Indians' fondness for pumpkin combined with Latin American spicing. Enjoy as a first course preceding Yucatecan Marinated Grilled Chicken.

   2 *shallots, chopped*
   4 *cloves garlic, chopped*
   4 *to 5 green onions, thinly sliced*
   1 *tablespoon butter*
   1 *tablespoon flour*
  ¾ *cup tomato sauce (or 1 cup chopped tomatoes)*
   1 *pound pumpkin or banana squash, peeled and cut into 2-inch chunks*
   1 *tablespoon New Mexico or ancho chile powder*
  ½ *teaspoon cumin*
  ½ *teaspoon cayenne pepper*
  ½ *teaspoon oregano*
   1 *teaspoon Piri-Piri or other salsa*
2½ *cups chicken broth*
  ¾ *cup milk*
      Salt
   1 *cup sour cream, for garnish*
      Thai Chile Flowers, or fresh red jalapeño slices, or a dribble of salsa

1. Sauté shallots, garlic, and half the green onions in butter. Sprinkle on the flour. Cook a few minutes, then add tomatoes, pumpkin, chile powder, cumin, cayenne, oregano, salsa, and chicken broth. Cook over a medium-low heat until pumpkin is tender.
2. Puree in blender or food processor, gradually adding milk to mixture. Season with salt to taste. Garnish with sour cream, the remaining green onions, and Thai Chile Flowers.

Shish Barak”

Noodles Stuffed
with Lamb and Pine Nuts in Broth

Middle East   *Serves 4*

Shish Barak is the Middle Eastern version of ravioli, or perhaps won-ton. Noodle dough is stuffed with a mixture of spiced lamb and toasted pine nuts, then simmered in broth. Sometimes these are cooked in water, drained, and served as a pasta, garnished with cilantro, mint, yogurt, and hot sauce. While this recipe uses egg roll wrappers (because they are so easily available, easy to use, and make a delicate noodle), you may also use tender homemade noodles. Try Red Chile Pasta encasing the filling.

    ½   *cup pine nuts*
    1   *onion, chopped*
    4   *to 5 cloves garlic, chopped*
    12 *ounces ground lamb*
    1   *egg*
    1   *teaspoon cinnamon*
    ½   *to 1 teaspoon cumin*
    1   *tablespoon tomato paste*
    ½   *cup cilantro or mint (or combination), chopped finely*
    1   *to 2 teaspoons hot salsa of choice*
    ½   *teaspoon salt or to taste*
    12 *to 15 egg roll wrappers or sheets of noodle dough, 4 to 5*
        inches square
    4   *cups beef broth*
    2   *to 3 green onions, sliced*
        Salsa of choice
        Lemon wedges

1. Toast pine nuts in an ungreased skillet until golden brown; set aside.
2. Combine onion and garlic with meat. Add egg, cinnamon, cumin, tomato paste, ¼ cup cilantro or mint, salsa, salt and pine nuts.
3. Lay out egg roll wrapper or noodle square and place 1 or 2 tablespoons of filling in center. Wet edges with fingers or pastry brush. Fold over into triangle and seal edges. Arrange on lightly floured baking sheet or platter to dry.
4. Heat broth to boiling; toss in Shish Barak. Cook only a few minutes, until noodles are tender and the meat is cooked through. Serve immediately in broth garnished with green onions, the remaining cilantro and/or mint, salsa, and lemon wedges.

Piquant Pea Soup *"*

Netherlands, Mediterranean   *Serves 4*

I always made pea soup in the traditional manner, with sweet herbs like marjoram and hearty meats such as bacon or sausage, until one winter when I was living in a village on the Greek island of Crete. One chilly day I yearned mightily for split-pea soup. There was no bacon, nor were there sweet herbs, but there was fragrant cumin seed, and pungent wild sage growing on a hillside. This is the soup I made that day, which was so good I've never made it any other way since.

> 1 *onion, diced*
> 1 *carrot, diced*
> 1 *turnip, peeled and diced*
> 1 *baking or boiling potato, peeled and diced*
> 3 *or 4 tablespoons olive oil*
> 1½ *cups dried green split peas*
> 6 *cups chicken broth*
> 3 *cloves garlic*
> 1 *bay leaf*
> 2 *teaspoons cumin*
> ½ *to 1 teaspoon cayenne pepper (or to taste)*
> ½ *to 1 teaspoon dried sage*
> *Salsa (optional)*
> *Salt (optional)*

1. Sauté vegetables in olive oil. Add split peas, broth, and seasonings.
2. Bring to boil, then simmer 1½ to 2 hours or until peas are tender and soup is the consistency of a coarse puree.
3. Taste for seasoning; if too bland, stir in a little more cayenne or some hot salsa. Add salt to taste if needed.

Harira "

Thick Bean, Lentil, and Vegetable Soup

Morocco   *Serves 4*

Harira is a thick, creamy soup eaten in Morocco to break the fast of Ramadan, the holiest holiday of the Islam year. Harira is prepared in probably every household, and differently in each one. This mysterious brown concoction of tender lamb chunks, bits and pieces of beans, aromatics, and herbs is tart with lemon, thickened with egg, and filled out by the thinnest of noodles. While Middle Eastern cuisine is not known for being particularly hot, many dishes, this soup especially, take very well to spicing up. Enjoy as a full meal, accompanied by a salad of cucumber, tomatoes, and feta cheese, along with a plate of Moroccan Spiced Olives.

8 ounces lamb stew meat, cut into chunks
1 onion, chopped
3 cloves garlic, chopped
1 tablespoon olive oil
3 to 4 tomatoes, chopped (canned is fine)
2 celery stalks, including leaves, chopped
1 teaspoon turmeric
1 teaspoon cumin
½ to 1 teaspoon Ras Al Hanout (optional)
½ teaspoon dried ground ginger
½ teaspoon cinnamon
¼ teaspoon cardamom powder
6 cups chicken or beef broth
1 cup cooked or canned chick-peas
¼ cup dried brown lentils
½ cup chopped cilantro or parsley
4 ounces thin pasta (fresh if possible)
2 eggs
 Juice of 2 lemons
¼ cup medium-mild salsa, or 2 teaspoons Harissa or
 commercial garlic-chile paste

1. Sauté lamb with onion and garlic in olive oil until lightly browned; add tomatoes, celery, and spices and cook 5 minutes longer.
2. Add broth and cook for 1½ to 2 hours, or until meat is tender. Add chickpeas, lentils, and cilantro and cook for 40 minutes. Add pasta and cook until pasta is done.
3. Beat eggs with lemon juice; stir in salsa or Harissa. Blend into hot soup and cook a minute longer; serve immediately.

Grains and Pasta

Pasta and grains are the filling foods that form the background for the rich, spicy flavors of sauces, soups, and stews. Without their bland counterpoint, how could we even consider eating bitingly hot dishes? These traditionally mild dishes are enlivened by fiery accompaniments. Indonesian Nasi Kuning or Couscous Fassi are transformed into spicy delights with just a few spoonfuls of Sambal Olek or Harissa.

Corn takes readily to hot seasonings, and many spicy corn recipes are available elsewhere, especially in Mexican and Southwestern cookbooks. I've concentrated instead on the lesser known and less available dishes. Do try the Venezuelan Hallaca: made of ground hominy, it's a new look at corn. And, for a simple treat, try slathering steamed or roasted corn with the chile-butter mixture from New Mexican Chile Bread. You don't need a recipe to enjoy warm corn tortillas topped with melted cheese, seafood, or eggs, doused with salsa; in fact, corn tortillas and salsa create one of the most perfect culinary unions I know.

Rice is also delicious with any spicy dish or condiment, and Abala—steamed, banana-leaf-wrapped packages of curried rice puree—is an outstanding example of this. And while one seldom thinks of barley as a spicy, exciting dish, Janice's New Orleans Style Barley will convince you that this grain was created to be spiced. It combines humble ingredients to produce a sophisticated taste.

We usually think of pasta bathed in tomato sauce or cream, but there are many hot pasta dishes here. I kept testing and inventing new combinations, and each was so good that I had to include them all. Chile-Stuffed Ravioli With Goat Cheese Sauce, and Ravioli Filled With Red Chile and Potato Puree are two dishes you won't find elsewhere. Spicy pastas are popular in the Orient, where they include not only chiles but also various bean-based sauces and pastas for heat, and cucumber and herbs to douse the fire. These are wonderful, startling flavors for those who may be used to olive oil and garlic. And if you're in the mood for Italian pasta, try the Pasta Arabbiata; it's almost as delicious as a trip to Italy.

Red Chile Pasta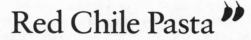

Italy, United States   *Yield: approximately 1 pound*

The proportions of egg and flour here are rather generous on the egg side. It makes a tender, delicate pasta. Experiment with the amount of cayenne—3 tablespoons make a pretty *picante* pasta. You might start with a smaller amount. Serve with Cumin-Scented Cream Sauce or Ratatouille, or try it tossed with Picadillo (the filling for our Empanado) and roasted poblano strips.

> 3 *cups all-purpose flour*
> 2 *to 3 tablespoons cayenne pepper*
> 5 *eggs*

1. Place flour and cayenne in bowl. Make a well in center and add eggs. Beat the eggs with a fork, gradually incorporating flour to form a mass of dough. Wrap tightly with plastic wrap and let rest in refrigerator for at least 30 minutes.
2. Pull off a piece of dough about the size of a large walnut. Flatten with hands to ¼ inch thick. Run through the rollers of pasta machine set at the largest opening. Fold dough in half and run it through once again to knead.
3. Run dough through the rollers on successivly smaller openings until you've run it through the thinnest. Cut dough in cutters of machine or with a knife. Toss with a little flour to prevent sticking.

Advance Preparation: Lay sheet of pasta on top of wax paper; cover with another sheet of wax paper. Repeat several times, then roll up and store for up to 2 days. Cut just before boiling.

Pasta may also be rolled, cut, and tossed with flour several hours before cooking.

Variation: Decrease eggs to 3 and substitute 4 to 6 roasted, peeled, and pureed poblanos for the cayenne pepper.

Red Chile Pasta in Cumin-Scented Cream Sauce ◗

Italy, United States   *Serves 4*

Fresh pasta, prepared with pureed vegetables or aromatics mixed into the dough, is quite chic these days. My favorite is fresh basil leaves added for a delicate pesto-flavored pasta. I've tasted delicious pasta made from ancho chile powder, jalapeño puree, and powdered ginger. Too often, though it is the novelty of the idea, rather than the taste, that is exciting. This is not the case here; this dish combines chile-spiked pasta, delicate cumin-scented cream, and a robust accent of shredded dry Monterey Jack cheese for a subtly spicy, harmonious dish.

> 1 ½ *tablespoons butter*
> 4 *cloves garlic, chopped*
> 2 *green onions, chopped*
> ½ *to 1 jalapeño, seeded and sliced*
> ½ *to 1 teaspoon cumin*
> 1 *cup half-and-half or heavy cream*
> 1 *pound fresh Red Chile Pasta*
> 12 *ounces dry Monterey Jack cheese, grated (if unavailable, use freshly grated Parmesan or Emmental)*
>   *Salt*
> 1 ½ *tablespoons chopped green onion or cilantro, for garnish*
>   *Generous sprinkle of cayenne pepper, for garnish*

1. Melt butter over medium heat until foamy; add garlic, green onions, jalapeño, and cumin; do not let brown. Add half-and-half or cream and cook over medium heat for a few minutes.
2. Bring large pot of water to boil; cook pasta in it until tender but not mushy, only 2 to 3 minutes. Drain.
3. Stir one-half to two-thirds of the cheese into sauce and toss with hot, cooked pasta; salt to taste.
4. Serve immediately, garnished with remaining cheese, green onion or cilantro, and cayenne pepper to taste.

Recommended Wine: Serve with a slightly sweet, crisp German Riesling or a California Gewürztraminer. Don't drink this dish with a Cabernet, for though it tastes fine at first, it flames up unpleasantly in the throat later.

Red Chile Pasta with Ratatouille ⟩

France, Italy, United States   *Serves 4*

Beautiful Mediterranean vegetables combine with orange-hued strands of Red Chile Pasta in this unusual cold pasta, which looks as splendid as it tastes. Do not be tempted to save time by cooking all the vegetables together; the separate cooking preserves each vegetable's integrity, otherwise it would taste ordinary with all the flavors blended together. Top with crunchy sunflower seeds, the unexpected tang of green olives, and the crisp flavor of cilantro or parsley. Enjoy as a summer luncheon dish or pack up and take on a picnic.

¼   *cup olive oil*
 1   *onion, thinly sliced lengthwise*
 4   *cloves garlic, coarsely chopped*
 2   *zucchini, sliced first in half, then into lengthwise slices ⅛ inch thick*
 ½   *large eggplant, sliced ¼ to ½ inch thick, then cut each slice into 3 pieces*
 ½   *green bell pepper, cut into ¼-inch slices*
 2   *red jalapeños (or substitute green)*
 1   *teaspoon cumin*
 1   *teaspoon turmeric*
 ½   *teaspoon Curry Powder (optional)*
 1   *cup chopped tomatoes*
 ½   *cup tomato sauce*
 3   *to 4 cups water*
 ¾   *pound fresh Red Chile Pasta*
 3   *tablespoons toasted, shelled sunflower seeds*
 ¼   *cup pimiento-stuffed green olives, sliced*
 2   *tablespoons cilantro, chopped (optional)*
 1   *lemon, cut into wedges*

1. Heat oil in skillet over medium heat. Add onion and garlic, cook until soft, then remove with slotted spoon and set aside. Add zucchini, cook briefly, then remove with slotted spoon and set aside. Repeat with eggplant, adding more oil if necessary, then proceed to the peppers combined with the jalapeños, cumin, turmeric, and Curry Powder. Add tomatoes, cook briefly with peppers and spices, then add tomato sauce and return all vegetables to to-

mato mixture. (This makes a delicious Ratatouille with the unexpected bite of jalapeño and fragrance of spices. Make a double batch and enjoy the leftovers for tomorrow's lunch or to serve along with roast lamb or chicken.)

2. Bring 3 to 4 cups of water to boil; cook pasta until tender, 3 to 4 minutes. Rinse and drain.
3. Toss pasta with vegetable mixture and garnish with sunflower seeds, green olives, cilantro, and lemon wedges. Serve at room temperature.

Advance Preparation: Vegetable mixture can be made up to a day in advance. Pasta can be cooked and dish assembled several hours ahead of time.

Couscous Fassi ❯

Couscous with Assorted Vegetables

Morocco   *Serves 6*

Couscous is the Moroccan national dish. Prepared in endless variations, it is enjoyed throughout Morocco, Tunisia, and parts of Central Africa and the Middle East. In Sicily couscous is eaten with a ginger-infused fish stew, and as far away as Brazil there is a derivative dish prepared from cornmeal, called *cuzcuzu.*

This couscous is prepared in the manner of Fez, containing chick-peas, sweet raisins, and peppery Harissa. The number seven is considered lucky in Fez, and couscous there often uses that many vegetables. To be honest, I generally cast superstition aside and use nine or ten vegetables for a lucious couscous. I've never noticed any lack of good luck, either.

The chunks of vegetables and whole chiles in this edible collage are so tasty cloaked in their spicy broth that I never want to detract by adding meat, as would be done in North Africa. Often, however, I add a meat course to the feast—Lamb and Eggplant Tajine, Tajine Msir Zeetoon, or cumin-scented lamb kabobs.

Couscous is authentically prepared by steaming the grains twice in a couscousiere (a steam-pot especially designed for preparing couscous); the grains are spread out between steamings to plump up and separate. This recipe is much simplifed and, using the couscous available in the United States, the results are agreeable. I've also included directions for traditional preparation.

In Morocco, couscous is served as one course in the copious celebration feast called a *diffa,* but it makes a substantial main course as well. Accompany with the broth from the vegetables, tart yogurt garnished with mint, and a bowl of Harissa Sauce. Munkaczina is an enjoyable salad accompaniment, as is Radis Râpé.

The eating utensil in Morocco is the hand, specifically the right hand. Consider this as more than just a novel idea to try as a lark; the food actually tastes better without the intrusion of metal utensils. Though a bit messy, eating with the fingers is very sensual and allows you to experience the true flavors of the food.

1   onion, chopped
4   cloves garlic, chopped
1   tablespoon cumin
½   teaspoon each: cinnamon, turmeric, powdered cloves,
    ground coriander, and dried ginger
2   to 3 tablespoons olive oil
3   tomatoes, chopped
6   cups vegetable or chicken broth
1   small sweet potato or ½ pound pumpkin, peeled and cut
    into 1-inch chunks
1   carrot, cut into ½-inch slices
2   small new potatoes, quartered
1   turnip, peeled and cut into 1-inch chunks
½   head green cabbage (about ½ pound), cut into 1-inch
    chunks
¼   pound green beans, trimmed and cut into 2-inch lengths
2   zucchini (approximately ½ pound), cut into ¾-inch slices
3   to 5 whole California or Anaheim chiles (these are for
    decor, not necessary for eating)
1   cup cooked, drained chick-peas (canned is O.K.)
2   cups couscous
⅔   cup raisins
3   tablespoons butter
1   or 2 tablespoons orange flower water or rose water
    Harissa Sauce (recipe follows)

1. Sauté onion, garlic, and spices in olive oil until onion is soft. Add tomatoes, broth, sweet potatoes, carrot slices, and potatoes. Simmer 15 or 20 minutes, until vegetables are tender.
2. Add remaining vegetables including chiles and chick-peas; simmer another 15 or 20 minutes, until all vegetables are tender but not mushy. Remove from heat.
3. Heat 2 cups of the broth from the vegetables to boiling. Pour this over couscous. Add raisins, cover, and let stand 10 minutes. Add butter and fluff up with fork. (For traditional preparation, see end of recipe.)
4. Serve the couscous mounded on a platter; sprinkle with rose water or orange flower water and surround with the cooked vegetables. Pass broth from the vegetables and a bowl of Harissa Sauce separately.

Harissa Sauce

1 cup broth from vegetables
1 teaspoon hot chile paste such as Harissa, Sambal Olek, or
   commercial garlic-chile paste
1 tablespoon lemon juice
1 tablespoon olive oil
1 teaspoon cumin
1 tablespoon chopped cilantro

Stir hot chile paste, lemon juice, olive oil, and cumin into broth and heat to boiling. Remove from heat and sprinkle with cilantro.

Traditional Preparation of Couscous

1. Rinse 2 cups couscous with 6 cups water. Drain and let stand 10 to 20 minutes to swell the grains. Using your hands, work through the couscous to break up any lumps.
2. Line a steamer with cheesecloth; place couscous in steamer and cook (uncovered) over simmering water for 20 minutes.
3. Spread couscous out in shallow pan or cookie sheet and sprinkle with 1 cup cold water. Work the grains with your hands once more. The couscous may be prepared up to this point in advance and set aside until you are ready for the final steaming.
4. Place couscous in cheesecloth-lined steamer and place over simmering vegetables and broth. Steam over this simmering mixture for 15 to 20 minutes. Serve as described previously.

Ravioli Filled with Red Chile and Potato Puree

Poland, Mexico	Serves 4 to 6 as a first course or side dish, 3 to 4 as a main course

Innovative cooks are stuffing ravioli with all manner of interesting fillings heretofore unimagined by more traditional pasta cooks. The inspiration for this recipe was the Polish potato-filled dumpling called *pierogen*. I've spiced up the creamy potato filling with both the richness of mild dried red chile and the bite of fresh jalapeño. This two-chile puree is surrounded by an oh-so-delicate noodle dough, extravagantly dripping both butter and sour cream. Serve 2 to 3 as a main course, or serve as a first course, followed by Pork and Poblano Sauté.

> 2 *to 3 New Mexico or California chiles*
> *Boiling water to cover chiles*
> 2 *to 3 medium baking potatoes, peeled and quartered*
> ¼ *cup butter*
> 4 *to 5 cloves garlic, chopped*
> 1 *to 2 jalapeños, seeded and chopped*
> 4 *to 5 ounces Jarlsberg or other Gruyère-type cheese*
> *Salt*
> 16 *egg roll wrappers, gyoza noodles, or squares of homemade pasta*
> ¼ *cup sour cream*
> *Cayenne*

1. Cover dried chiles with boiling water and let soak for about 1 hour.
2. Boil potatoes until tender; drain and mash.
3. Melt butter; measure out 1 tablespoon and set aside. Add garlic and jalapeño to butter in pan and cook a minute or two over low heat; do not brown. Add to potato mixture.
4. Remove stems and seeds from chiles; puree in processor with just enough of the soaking liquid to make a thick paste. Add 2 to 3 tablespoons of this paste to potato mixture (reserve any leftover chile puree to use in a soup, stew, or chili).
5. Add cheese and season with salt to taste.
6. Place about 1 tablespoon filling in center of each noodle. Brush edges with water and seal together, enclosing filling. Let sit 20 to 30 minutes to further seal edges.
7. Bring large pot of water to boil. Add ravioli and cook until just tender, about 3 to 4 minutes. Drain and serve immediately, topped with the remaining tablespoon of butter and with a dollop of sour cream. Garnish with a sprinkle of cayenne.

Advance Preparation: Ravioli may be filled several hours to a day in advance; cook at the last minute before serving.

Variation: Goat Cheese Ravioli
As stuffing, use the filling from Goat-Cheese Stuffed Poblanos, and include about ¼ cup roasted, peeled, and chopped poblanos. Sauce with the mild sauce from Sautéed Chicken Paillards With Red Pepper Sauce, the sauce from Pasta Arabbiata, or a little butter, a grating of dry Monterey Jack cheese, and a sprinkle of cayenne.

Chile-Stuffed Ravioli with Goat Cheese Sauce ❯

Italy, United States   *Serves 4*

This unusual ravioli is filled with leftover meat from Estofado, Texas Chili con Carne, or any meat braised in Basic Red Chile Sauce. The plump stuffed noodles are topped with a silken goat cheese sauce that perfectly complements the deep richness and slight bite of the chile filling. You may use purchased egg roll wrappers for a delicate result and extremely quick and easy preparation.

Filling

2 *to 3 cloves garlic, chopped*
1 *cup leftover chili meat, with just enough sauce to keep mixture bound together*
1 *tablespoon medium salsa or ½ teaspoon garlic-chile paste (or to taste)*
16 *egg roll wrappers, gyoza noodles, or homemade pasta squares*

Sauce

2 *tablespoons butter (¼ stick)*
¼ *cup half-and-half*
4 *ounces goat cheese (I use chive-flavored Montrachet, but unflavored Montrachet or Lezay is fine; add ½ clove chopped garlic or 1 tablespoon chopped chives for flavoring)*
8 *to 12 whole chives, each about 5 to 6 inches long*

1. For filling, chop garlic in processor; add meat and salsa and continue chopping until meat is smooth enough for a filling, but not pureed.
2. Place about 1 tablespoon filling in center of each noodle. Brush noodle edges with water and seal.
3. For sauce, melt butter with half-and-half. Remove from heat and crumble in goat cheese. Stir until smooth and thickened.

4. Heat pot of water to boiling; add ravioli and cook until just tender, only 3 to 4 minutes.
5. Drain ravioli and serve immediately, topped with the goat cheese sauce. A garnish of several whole chives would be elegant.

Advance Preparation: The ravioli may be prepared several hours or a day in advance and refrigerated until ready to use. Cook the ravioli and make the sauce just before serving.

Ja Jeung Mein ,

Cold Chinese Noodles
with Hot Tofu-Hoisin Sauce

Northern China   *Serves 4*

This is a variation of a dish popular in Northern China. Usually made with chopped pork, it is not unlike spaghetti Bolognese. In this version I've used tofu instead of pork; I like the tofu's lightness. The sauce is sweet and spicy, the cucumbers and cilantro add a refreshing taste, and the peanut garnish is a crunchy accent to the comfortingly bland noodles.

1 *pound fresh noodles (¼-inch-wide Chinese type; if unavailable, use fresh fettuccine)*
1 *tablespoon sesame oil*
1 *tablespoon vegetable oil*
1 *piece (about 3-by-5 inches) tofu, cut into small cubes*
3 *to 4 cloves garlic, chopped*
1 *cup chicken broth*
¾ *cup hoisin sauce*
2 *teaspoons sugar*
1 ½ *to 2 teaspoons Vietnamese garlic-chile paste, or 1 teaspoon chile oil, or 2 teaspoons hot salsa*
Dash of soy sauce
Dash of distilled white vinegar
4 *to 5 green onions, chopped*
1 *cucumber, peeled and cut into matchstick pieces*
Cilantro leaves to garnish
¼ *cup unsalted roasted peanuts, coarsely crushed, to garnish*

1. Boil noodles until tender, only 4 to 5 minutes. Rinse with cold water, then drain. Toss with sesame oil and set aside.
2. Heat vegetable oil in wok. Brown tofu, then add garlic, broth, hoisin, sugar, chile paste, soy sauce, and vinegar. Stir and cook until thickened a bit. Add green onions.
3. Serve hot sauce over cold noodles, topped with cucumber, cilantro, and peanut garnish.

Nasi Kuning

Garnished Turmeric Rice Platter

Indonesia   *Serves 4*

The turmeric yellow tint of this dish signifies happiness, and Nasi Kuning is often served at weddings, birth celebrations, and other festivities.

Traditionally this is molded into a cone shape. I mold it into a round shape in a stainless-steel bowl; it retains heat well and unmolds easily. Present the mound of yellow rice on a bed of green leaves. Authentically, banana leaves or palm fronds are used, but rich green chard or spinach leaves are equally fine. Next, surround and garnish the rice with a variety of delicious morsels, each of contrasting color, flavor, and texture. The final result will resemble an edible sunburst.

Nasi Kuning is a terrific dish for entertaining because it's so much fun to eat—you keep discovering new bits and tastes. Serve with Rendang or Chicken With Chiles in Peanut Sauce and accompany with Rudjak and Sambal Olek. Without the garnishes, the simple turmeric rice may be served as an accompaniment to a more complex dish.

1 *onion, chopped*
3 *cloves garlic, chopped*
1 *tablespoon oil*
½ *to 1 tablespoon turmeric*
2 *cups rice*
3 *cups coconut milk (see Other Special Ingredients)*

Garnishes:
1 *to 2 bunches spinach or chard leaves (for lining platter)*
½ *cucumber, peeled and cut into 1-inch chunks*
Celery and/or cilantro leaves
½ *cup dry-roasted peanuts*
Thai Chile Flowers
Omelette Strips (recipe follows)

Spiced Cabbage (recipe follows)
Fried Onion Flakes (recipe follows)
Fried Bean Curd Cubes (recipe follows)

1. Sauté onion and garlic in oil until onion is soft; add turmeric and cook a minute longer.
2. Stir in rice and sauté a few minutes. Add coconut milk. Bring to boil, cover, and simmer over low heat 20 to 30 minutes or until liquid is absorbed and rice is tender but not mushy.
3. Butter a 3-quart stainless steel bowl; pack with cooked rice, cover, and keep in a warm place (such as a low oven) while you finish assembling the garnishes.

Omelette Strips

2 *eggs, beaten*
2 *tablespoons butter*

1. Heat about one-third of the butter in flat pan.
2. Pour in one-third of the egg mixture, turning so that it forms a flat, pancake-like omelette. Turn over and cook other side; remove to plate and cut into ½-inch strips.
3. Repeat until egg mixture is used up.

Spiced Cabbage

6 *cloves garlic, chopped*
2 *tablespoons vegetable oil*
2 *teaspoons turmeric*
1 *head cabbage*
½ *cup coconut milk*
  Salt to taste

1. Sauté garlic in oil until softened; do not brown or it will become bitter. Add turmeric, then cabbage.
2. Pour in coconut milk and cook until cabbage softens.

Fried Onion Flakes

Though this garnish is authentically made with fresh onions, commercial onion flakes give fine results. Fry ⅓ cup onion flakes in 1 tablespoon oil until flakes are golden brown.

Fried Bean Curd Cubes

1 *piece tofu (3-by-5 inches)*
  Oil for deep-frying, 2 inches deep
¼ *cup cornstarch*

1. Cut tofu into cubes 1 by 1½ inches; drain excess water on towel.
2. Heat oil for deep-frying. Coat tofu cubes with cornstarch, then fry cubes in hot oil until light brown. They will be crusty on the outside and almost creamy within, thanks to the cornstarch coating.

Black-Bean-Filled South-of-the-Border Pot-Stickers ❯

China/Mexico   *Serves 4 as first course*
                                                    or 2 as main course

Pot-stickers are Chinese dumplings that are first fried, then briefly cooked in water until the liquid evaporates. They're generally filled with a ground meat mixture and, when tender, dipped into shredded ginger and vinegar.

This unorthodox version stuffs the noodles with creamy mashed beans and cheese, then tops them with Pico de Gallo and sour cream. They are much like burritos but smaller, lighter, and more delicate. Serve as a first course followed by tiny young vegetables simply steamed and seasoned with garlic-chile butter, and grilled fish accompanied by Salsa Verde.

1 *cup mashed black beans (Spicy Black Beans or canned)*
1 *tablespoon salsa of choice*
½ *to 1 teaspoon cumin*
½ *cup diced Monterey Jack cheese*
12 *gyoza noodles or egg roll wrappers*
3 *tablespoons olive oil*
  Pico de Gallo
½ *pint sour cream*

1. Mix beans with salsa, cumin, and cheese.
2. Place a tablespoon or so of beans in center of each gyoza or egg roll wrapper.
3. Seal by brushing edges with water and pinching together. If using egg roll wrappers, you will have a triangular package; the gyoza noodles will give more of a crescent moon shape. (I prefer the gyoza because it's thicker, but the egg roll wrappers are fine, too.)

4. Heat oil in skillet. When hot, add pot-stickers and brown on both sides. Pour ¼ to ½ cup water over the browned dumplings in skillet; they will sizzle loudly for a moment. Cook, turning once or twice, until water is evaporated.
5. Serve with Pico de Gallo and a bit of sour cream.

Advance Preparation: Pot-stickers may be assembled as much as a day in advance, then cooked right before serving.

Variation: Use pink or pinto refried beans (canned is fine) instead of black beans.

Jollof Rice ➴

Rice with Meat and Vegetable Sauce

West Africa   *Serves 4*

Originally from the Wollof tribe of Gambia, this saucy rice dish has myriad variations throughout West Africa.

Jollof Rice consists of a thick, tomato-y sauce (which may include any combination of meat, vegetables, and fish) ladled over rice that has been cooked in a portion of the sauce.

This version calls for eggplant and steak strips; other typical additions are cabbage, peas, salt pork, pigs' feet, or salted fish. In Ghana, Jollof Rice is sprinkled with chopped green onions and garnished with boiled pumpkin.

½ *eggplant, cut into ¾-inch cubes*
¼ *cup oil*
1 *onion, chopped*
3 *cloves garlic, chopped*
3 *serranos, chopped*
½ *bunch spinach leaves, coarsely chopped (or substitute ½ package frozen)*
6 *ounces sirloin steak, cut into slices or strips ¼ inch thick*
1 *tablespoon Curry Powder*
½ *to 1 teaspoon thyme*
½ *teaspoon cinnamon*
1 *cup chopped tomatoes*
2 *cups tomato sauce*
½ *yam, peeled and cut into ½-inch cubes*
1 *piece of ginger, ⅛ inch thick, chopped*
1 *cup rice*
1 *cup chicken or beef broth*
   Salt

1. Sauté eggplant cubes in 3 tablespoons of oil until lightly browned; set aside.
2. Sauté half the onion, 2 cloves of garlic, and 2 serranos until onion is limp; add spinach and cook until wilted. Set aside.
3. Sauté steak briefly; return onion and vegetables to pan with steak. Sprinkle with 2 teaspoons Curry Powder, the thyme, and cinnamon. Cook a few minutes longer, then stir in tomatoes and tomato sauce. Simmer for 5 to 10 minutes.
4. In remaining tablespoon of oil, sauté remaining onion, garlic, chile, yam, and ginger until the onion is soft. Sprinkle on remaining teaspoon Curry Powder. Stir in rice, then broth and 1½ cups prepared sauce. Cover and simmer until tender. Salt to taste. When rice is tender, serve on a platter with eggplant-steak sauce ladled over it.

Advance Preparation: Sauce may be prepared several hours or a day ahead of time.

Variation: Add ½ pound raw shrimp to rice mixture before it's covered and cooked.

Gratin of Pasta, Cheddar Cheese, and Poblanos »»

United States, France, Mexico   *Serves 4*

Cheddar cheese sauce clings to *al dente* shell-shaped pasta in this gratin. Enlivened not only by poblano strips but by salsa as well, this is far removed from the bland macaroni-and-cheese dishes most of us remember. Hearty and savory, it's perfect for a winter day. You could accompany it with German-style wursts and a salad of mixed greens (which could include some frizzy-leafed chicory, tender mâche, or bracing radicchio).

> 12 *ounces small shell-shaped pasta (white or green)*
> 1 *tablespoon butter*
> 1 *tablespoon flour*
> 1 *cup milk*
> 1 *poblano chile, roasted, seeded, and cut into strips*
> 1 *tablespoon medium-hot salsa*
> 1 *tablespoon sour cream*
> 1 *teaspoon Dijon mustard*
> 2 *or 3 cloves garlic, chopped*
>   *Freshly ground black pepper*

Hot Paprika
2 *cups shredded cheddar cheese*
2 *tablespoons butter, cut into small pieces*

1. Cook pasta *al dente* (or use leftover pasta).
2. Melt butter in saucepan. When foamy, sprinkle in flour, stir, and let cook a few minutes over low heat. Remove from heat and whisk in milk. Return to heat and whisk until smooth.
3. Mix in chile, salsa, sour cream, mustard, garlic, pepper to taste (be generous), and paprika to taste. Add 1½ cups cheese and toss well.
4. Transfer to buttered baking dish and sprinkle with remaining cheese. Dot with 2 tablespoons butter and bake in preheated 375° F. oven until bubbly and lightly browned, about 15 to 20 minutes. Serve hot.

Hot Bean Noodles 〞

China   *Serves 4*

Translucent, chewy mung bean noodles are stir-fried with a julienne of carrot and zucchini, then tossed with a sauce pungent from hot bean paste in this satisfying dish.

Since it is as delicious at room temperature as it is hot, I often serve it as part of a salad buffet with Hatzilim Pilpel and Arabian Parsley Salad, or as an accompaniment to a simple but interesting sandwich.

1 *package mung bean noodles (8 ounces)*
1 *to 2 tablespoons vegetable oil*
1 *carrot, julienne-cut*
2 *cloves garlic, chopped*
1 *piece fresh ginger root (½ inch), chopped*
2 *zucchini, julienne-cut*
3 *tablespoons hot bean paste*
2 *tablespoons chicken or vegetable broth*
1 *teaspoon soy sauce*
1 *teaspoon cornstarch*
1 *teaspoon sugar*
   Cilantro for garnish (optional)

1. Soak noodles in cold water for 10 minutes to soften; drain.
2. Bring 4 cups water to boil; add drained noodles and cook over medium heat for 4 to 5 minutes, or until noodles are soft and transparent.

3. Heat 1 teaspoon oil in wok. Add carrot, garlic, and ginger and stir-fry for a minute. Add the zucchini and cook a minute or two longer. Remove and set aside.
4. Mix bean paste, broth, soy sauce, cornstarch, and sugar. Add remaining oil to wok, then add the noodles, broth mixture, and remaining vegetables. Cook a moment or two, until sauce thickens. Garnish with cilantro. Serve warm or at room temperature.

Advance Preparation: Vegetables may be chopped, noodles soaked and boiled, for up to 4 or 5 hours ahead of time.

Janice's New Orleans Style Barley »

United States   *Serves 4*

Savory and hot, this is delicious enough to dispel any nasty childhood memories of boring barley. The first time I prepared it, I nibbled and nibbled until I had eaten my share of supper before I served my guests. This barley is hot from dried chiles and perfumed with woodsy mushrooms and thyme; it's a Cajun treatment of an old Eastern European classic. Serve alongside a simple roast or as a satisfying vegetarian main course.

> 1 *cup barley*
> 4 *cups beef or vegetable broth*
> 2 *ounces dried mushrooms (Italian porcini, preferably)*
>   *Warm water to cover mushrooms*
> 1½ *tablespoons olive oil*
> ½ *onion, chopped*
> 3 *cloves garlic, chopped*
> ½ *green pepper, chopped*
> ½ *tomato, chopped*
> 4 *to 6 small hot dried red chiles, crumbled*
> ½ *teaspoon thyme*
>   *Salt and freshly ground black pepper*

1. Place barley in saucepan; add broth. Bring to boil, reduce heat, and simmer until tender (about 40 minutes).
2. Soak mushrooms in warm water to cover for 10 minutes.

3. Heat oil in skillet; sauté onion, garlic, pepper, tomato, and chiles until vegetables are soft. Add mixture to barley, along with soaked mushrooms, soaking liquid, and thyme. Season to taste with salt and freshly ground black pepper. Serve immediately.

Advance Preparation: May be made several hours to a day ahead of time. Prepare barley as directed above; pour into baking dish, cover with foil, and reheat in 350° F. oven for 30 minutes or until heated through. Refrigerate if you prepare it more than 2 hours or so ahead of time, and allow extra time to reheat.

Spaghetti with Goat Cheese, Italian Sausage, and Olives »

California   *Serves 4*

Goat cheese, pasta, olives, and chile: if there ever was a more delicious combination, I haven't tasted it. I was surprised at the affinity goat cheese has for both hot dried chiles and fresh green ones; I thought the subtlety of the cheese would be overwhelmed, but that is emphatically not the case (hence the abundance of goat cheese—chile recipes in this book!).

This dish has the benefit of being quickly and easily put together. Enjoy with a medium- to full-bodied Cabernet Sauvignon.

  4 *hot Italian sausages (about 8 ounces total)*
 ½ *teaspoon thyme*
  3 *cloves garlic, chopped*
  1 *teaspoon hot chile flakes*
 ⅔ *pound (10 to 12 ounces) spaghetti (preferably Italian)*
  2 *tablespoons olive oil*
 ¾ *cup Greek or Niçoise-style olives, pitted*
 12 *ounces Montrachet, Lezay, or California Goat Cheese, crumbled*
 ¼ *cup fresh sweet basil, chopped (optional)*

1. Remove casing from sausages and break into ½- to 1-inch-sized pieces. Sauté until lightly browned. Remove from heat and add thyme, garlic, and hot chile flakes. Set aside.
2. Cook spaghetti *al dente*. Drain and toss with olive oil, sausage-garlic-hot chile mixture, olives, goat cheese, and basil. Serve immediately.

Arroz con Pollo ""

Rice with Chicken and Vegetables

Spain, Mexico   *Serves 4*

Arroz con Pollo is a combination of the Old World and New, typical of Spanish dishes transplanted to Mexico's spicy kitchens. This makes a fabulous one-dish party meal. Accompany with a selection of several salsas—mild, medium, and hot—and warm corn tortillas or crusty bread. A simple salad of mixed greens dressed with fruity olive oil and lemon juice is the only other dish you really need. Once I served this with a salad of romaine, butter lettuce, radicchio, and fresh basil leaves, topped with rounds of Montrachet goat cheese that had been marinated in olive oil and herbs, coated with bread crumbs, and baked; sublime!

Do not be put off by the long list of ingredients; it's a lovely peasant dish, simple to put together. Traditionally the chicken is sautéed, but baking it separately makes the skin crisper and the dish less oily, as well as being easier to prepare.

    5 cloves garlic, coarsely chopped
    2 tablespoons mild to medium salsa (commercial or
       homemade)
 1½ teaspoons dried oregano
    2 teaspoons cumin
    1 teaspoon salt
    1 chicken, about 2½ pounds, cut into 8 pieces
    1 to 2 chorizo sausages, casings removed
    1 onion, chopped
   ½ red bell pepper, chopped
   ½ green bell pepper, chopped
   ½ carrot, chopped
 1½ cups rice
    1 cup chopped tomatoes (canned, with juice, is fine)
 2½ cups chicken broth
   ½ cup green beans, cut into 1- to 1½-inch lengths (frozen is
       O.K.)
   ½ cup shelled peas (frozen is O.K.)
   ½ cup pimiento-stuffed green olives
    2 tablespoons medium salsa or 2 teaspoons hot salsa

1. Combine garlic, mild salsa, 1 teaspoon oregano, 1 teaspoon cumin, and salt; pour over chicken. Bake in preheated 325° F. oven for 40 minutes or until chicken juices run clear.
2. Meanwhile, prepare rice: sauté chorizo and onion for several minutes, mashing chorizo with fork, cooking spoon, or spatula; cook until onion is limp. Add peppers, carrot, remaining cumin and oregano; sauté for a minute or two longer.
3. Stir in rice. Add tomatoes and broth. (If using fresh green beans and peas, add them now.) Cover and simmer 15 to 20 minutes, until tender.
4. Add olives, medium or hot salsa, and chicken with its juices. (If using frozen green beans and peas, add them now and cook a few minutes to heat up.) Taste for seasoning. Serve immediately, or pile into a casserole and heat in oven when ready to serve.

Variations:
1. For a vegetarian version, eliminate the chicken and use vegetable broth instead of chicken broth.
2. Toss in cooked red beans to provide protein, color, and a wonderful, earthy flavor.
3. This dish may be turned into paella by the addition of raw clams in their shells, whole raw shrimp, slices of sautéed squid, and a large pinch of saffron. Dissolve saffron in a tablespoon of warm water and pour over casserole; strew shellfish all about the top, cover, and bake in preheated 375° F. oven for 15 to 20 minutes, or until the clams open up. You may need to add a little extra broth to keep the rice from drying out.

Pad Thai ⟩⟩⟩

Stir-Fried Rice Noodles with Vegetables, Seafood, and Meat

Thailand   *Serves 4*

The Thai have a long-held passion for hot foods. It's hard to imagine Thai food before the chile was imported, but it was fiery even then, with liberal doses of crushed black peppercorns. Pad Thai exemplifies the flavors of Thai cuisine: spiked with searing chiles, doused with the distinctive fragrance of fish sauce, fresh with herbs, and crunchy from chopped peanuts or dried shrimp. The sweet, sour, and hot sauce is intensely flavorful yet light enough to enhance, not overpower, the whole dish.

Like its cousin chow mein, Pad Thai can contain all sorts of ingredients. It is on nearly every Thai restaurant menu and varies wildly in seasonings (and, alas, in quality). Seafood such as crab, shrimp, or squid is often included, as are shreds of roast or stir-fried chicken or pork.

The noodles used in Pad Thai are made from rice. Chewy, fragrant, and lighter than wheat noodles, they come dried in a variety of thicknesses and are available in Asian groceries. Occasionally you may find them fresh. Another wonderful dish prepared with rice noodles is Mee Krob. Similar to Pad Thai in ingredients, Mee Krob is based on rice noodles no thicker than a string, stir-fried and puffed into crunchy billows.

The following recipe is pretty hot; you may decrease the amount of serranos to 1 or 2. The tofu, pork, and shrimp are all labeled optional: choose one or all (or more) as you desire.

12 *ounces rice noodles or vermicelli (¼ inch wide)*
 2 *tablespoons vegetable oil*
 6 *cloves garlic, chopped*
 3 *to 5 serrano chiles, thinly sliced*
 3- *by-5-inch rectangle of firm tofu (optional), diced*
 2 *ounces lean pork, thinly sliced (optional)*
 2 *tablespoons fish sauce (Nuoc Nam) or 1 tablespoon light soy sauce*
 2 *tablespoons distilled white vinegar*
1½ *tablespoons ketchup*
 1 *tablespoon sugar*
 2 *eggs, beaten*
 3 *to 4 shrimp, shelled, deveined, and halved*
    Handful of raw bean sprouts
 2 *green onions, chopped*
 4 *to 6 Thai Chile Flowers*
 ½ *cup cilantro*
 ⅓ *cup coarsely chopped peanuts*

1. Soak noodles in water to cover for 10 minutes. Drain noodles and add to pot of boiling water. Cook for 3 to 5 minutes. Drain and rinse with cold water.
2. Heat 1 tablespoon oil in wok or skillet. Add garlic, chiles, tofu, and pork and sauté until pork is browned. Add fish sauce, vinegar, ketchup, and sugar.
3. Add noodles to skillet; toss with sauce mixture.
4. Push noodles to one side. Add remaining tablespoon oil to pan and heat well. Add eggs, scrambling them to firmness, then shrimp, cooking only until pink. Add bean sprouts and cook a moment longer.
5. Turn out onto platter and garnish with green onions, chile flowers, cilantro, and chopped peanuts.

Variation 1:

> 12 *ounces rice noodles (¼ inch wide)*
> 2 *tablespoons vegetable oil*
> 6 *ounces pork or beef, thinly sliced*
> 3 *cloves garlic, chopped*
> 2 *serrano chiles, thinly sliced*
>   *Fish sauce or soy sauce*
> ½ *cucumber, peeled and diced*
> ¼ *to ½ cup chopped cilantro*
> ¼ *to ½ cup coarsely chopped peanuts*
> 1 *lime, cut into wedges*

1. Soak and cook noodles as in preceding recipe.
2. Heat oil in wok or skillet; stir-fry meat with garlic and chiles; season to taste with fish sauce or soy sauce.
3. Serve atop the freshly cooked rice noodles; garnish with cucumber, cilantro, peanuts, and squeeze of lime. Offer Thai Chile Sauce for extra heat.

Variation 2: Mee Krob

Use the same ingredients as for Pad Thai, but choose the thinnest noodles instead of the ¼-inch ones. Do not soak noodles. Deep-fry them in 2 cups oil heated in wok. Drain on paper towels and set aside. Prepare sauce, egg, bean sprouts, shrimp, etc., and pour over crunchy noodles. Garnish and serve immediately.

Abala

Steamed Packages of Curry-Spiced Rice Puree

West Africa   *Serves 4*

Variations of steamed, wrapped rice puree are enjoyed throughout West Africa, especially in Ghana, Nigeria, and Sierra Leone. Called Abala, this is much like Mexican tamales and Venezuelan Hallacas. Whereas Abala is based on rice, tamales and Hallacas are prepared from corn (tamales from masa harina and Hallacas from a soaked corn preparation much like the hominy which is available here). While both may be prepared unfilled, to accompany a highly seasoned stew, they are often filled with chile-braised meat, olives, chiles and/or raisins.

    Authentically, Abala is wrapped in banana leaves; corn husks or aluminum foil are both good alternatives. I sometimes wrap them first in banana leaves, then in foil; this imparts the subtle fragrance of the banana leaf but seals it more effectively. Instead of steaming in individual packages, Abala is sometimes steamed in a large stainless-steel bowl. Other ingredients are occasionally added: chopped onion, tomatoes, shrimp or crawfish. Authentically, small hot peppers would be used instead of the chile paste and Curry Powder, but I find the latter more flavorful. Serve these unique-tasting packages with a dab of mint chutney and a cooling spoonful of yogurt; accompany with a curry of chicken and broccoli or a plump roast chicken.

> 3 ¾ *cups chicken broth*
> ¾ *cup Cream of Rice*
> 1 ½ *teaspoons Ají, Berberé, or store-bought garlic-chile paste*
> 2 *to 2 ½ tablespoons butter or chicken fat*
> 1 *to 1 ½ teaspoons Curry Powder*
> ½ *to ¾ teaspoon cumin*
> 2 *green onions, chopped*
> 2 *cloves garlic, chopped*
> 2 *tablespoons cilantro, chopped*
> 8 *pieces of banana leaf, cut into 7-by-5-inch rectangles*
> 8 *pieces of foil, 8-by-10 inches*

1. Bring broth to boil; stir in Cream of Rice and cook 30 seconds. Remove from heat. (It will be very thick.)
2. Add chile paste, butter, Curry Powder, cumin, green onions, garlic, and cilantro.
3. Heat banana leaves lightly over an ungreased skillet or open flame to make them more pliable. Place about 2 tablespoons Cream of Rice mixture in center of each rectangle. Fold into a package, then place package inside foil rectangle; wrap, sealing ends tightly.
4. Steam packages for 40 to 50 minutes; serve immediately.

Advance Preparation: Mixture may be made ahead of time and steamed at the last minute, or it may be steamed ahead of time as well and reheated before serving.

Variation: Venezuelan Hallaca

Filling

> 2 *medium-sized cans hominy (about 8 ounces each)*
> ⅓ *cup (⅔ stick) butter or shortening*
> 1 *teaspoon New Mexico or ancho chile powder*

1 *teaspoon salt*
Banana leaves or foil, as for Abala

1. In food processor, puree hominy into moist meal. Add butter, chile powder, and salt, and combine well.
2. Fill and steam as for Abala. Serve with salsa of choice. You may also add a spoonful of any chile-braised meat, a few olives and raisins, and a strip of chile to each Hallaca along with the hominy mixture.

Vietnamese Noodles with Peanut Sauce and Salad ▶▶▶

Vietnam   *Serves 4*

The Southeast Asian culinary way is to combine savory cooked foods with bits of fresh herbs, raw vegetables, nuts, and so on. Traditionally this dish would be prepared with pork and seasoned with fish sauce. My version is delicious though a bit unorthodox. Vietnamese Noodles with Peanut Sauce and Salad is a study in contrasts: the bland, cool softness of the noodles; the spicy, salty peanut mixture; the freshness of the lettuce; and the assertiveness of the herbs.

This is great participation food; you can't help but get into conversation when everyone is reaching at once for lettuce leaves and fillings.

8 *ounces fettuccine-sized fresh Chinese noodles, or Japanese udon*
3 *cloves garlic, chopped*
1 *tablespoon oil*
8 *ounces ground lamb*
1 *jar (8 ounces) hot bean paste*
½ *cup water or chicken broth*
1 *tablespoon sugar*
1 *teaspoon medium-hot salsa*
1 *cup unsalted roasted peanuts, coarsely chopped*
Romaine or butter lettuce leaves
Fresh mint leaves
Fresh cilantro leaves
2 *to 3 green onions, thinly sliced and wilted (to wilt, pour a small amount of boiling water over onions; let stand a minute, then drain)*

1. Boil noodles until tender (fresh noodles take only a few minutes). Rinse with cold water and set aside.
2. Sauté garlic briefly in oil. Add lamb, stirring to brown meat. Drain fat.
3. Stir in hot bean paste, water or broth, sugar, and salsa; simmer 5 minutes or until slightly thickened. (Do not be alarmed if it seems too soupy; it will thicken.) Stir in peanuts.
4. Arrange the lettuce and herbs on a platter; place the noodles, sauce, and green onions in separate bowls.
5. To serve, have each person take a leaf of lettuce and place on it some noodles, then the peanut mixture, a few leaves each of mint and cilantro, and a small spoonful of wilted green onions. Roll up and enjoy!

Variation: For a vegetarian dish, use diced firm tofu in place of meat.

Pasta Arabbiata ▶▶▶

Penne with Chile-Tomato Sauce

Italy   *Serves 4*

Arrabbiata means "enraged" in Italian, presumably because of the fiery fury imparted by the chiles. This recipe was brought back from Italy by my friend Theresa Chris, who returned from an August in Florence to regale me with images of ripe fruit bursting with sweetness, days dripping with sunshine, and, of course, pasta, pasta, pasta.

Though hot is not a dominant flavor in Italian cuisine, every so often chile-heat will appear in a dish with typical Mediterranean enthusiasm. In addition to pasta, seafood dishes are occasionally spiced with fervor.

Penne (or the thinner pennini), the pasta used in this recipe, is diagonally cut, tubular, and hearty enough to splash with a robust sauce. I've made Pasta Arabbiata with other shapes of pasta but found that the Arrabiata sauce overwhelms the more delicate strand shapes. In addition, the penne provides hiding places for the delicious sauce to cling to.

Enjoy Pasta Arabbiata as a main dish preceded by Mussels with Three-Pepper Relish, or serve it as a first course and follow with Mediterranean Mini-Grill.

> 1 *pound imported penne*
> 5 *to 7 cloves garlic, chopped*
> 2 *tablespoons olive oil*
> 1 *teaspoon red pepper flakes (or hot chile paste such as Aji)*
> 1 *cup tomato sauce*

Salt (optional)
2 *tablespoons butter*
¼ *cup chopped fresh parsley, for garnish*

1. Boil pasta *al dente*; meanwhile, make the sauce.
2. Sauté but do not brown garlic in olive oil. Add hot pepper flakes or chile paste. Stir in tomato sauce and boil until pasta is ready to serve. The sauce will be approximately half its original volume. Add salt if desired.
3. Drain pasta; toss with butter. Transfer to platter or bowl. Pour sauce over pasta and toss well. Garnish with chopped parsley. Any leftover Pasta Arabbiata is fabulous the next day cold, with a dab of the Herbed Cream Cheese filling from Aram Sandwiches.

Variation, albeit unorthodox: Toss sauced pasta with shredded Monterey Jack cheese just before serving; top with a spoonful of Cilantro Pesto (recipe follows).

Cilantro Pesto

Yield: approximately 1 cup

3 *cloves garlic*
1 *bunch cilantro (approximately 1 cup)*
2 *to 3 ounces Parmesan cheese, cut into small pieces (not shredded)*
2 *to 3 tablespoons olive oil*

Puree garlic in processor. Add cilantro, cheese, and oil; puree until smooth.

Vegetables and Legumes

Many people think of eating hot flavors only with meat, fish, and heavier fare, not of spicing up vegetables. All traditionally hot cuisines, however, enjoy vegetables in abundance, whether served alone or combined with bits of meat, chicken, or fish. Try Green Beans, Malawi-Style, in a peanut-accented tomato sauce, or Hatzilim Pilpel, in which the meaty eggplant simmers with chiles, onions, and tomatoes. Bahmi is a curry of okra that will convert even the most religious okra-hater, and Gado Gado offers a selection of cooked and raw vegetables served with a spicy peanut dipping sauce.

Legumes—dried beans, peas, and lentils—are also wonderful when vigorously seasoned. Spicy Black Beans are savory and delicious in South-of-the-Border Pot-Stickers (see preceding section) or Moors and Christians. A more complex dish is Sambaar, spicy vegetables simmered in a sauce of Indian red lentils or yellow split peas. Or simply boil pinto beans and season with salsa, ready to roll up in a tortilla.

And don't forget that there are vegetable dishes in other chapters throughout this book. In Appetizers and Salads, try the Ekra or the Borani Esfanaj as well as the unusual Goat Cheese-Stuffed Poblanos. In the Grains and Pasta chapter, Couscous Fassi is resplendent with vegetables. Red Chile Pasta is topped with a spicier than usual Ratatouille, and ravioli are filled with red chile and potato puree. Even the fish, poultry, and meat chapters have dishes that highlight vegetables. Try the Burmese Pork, Potato, and Pea Curry; Daube des Langoustes aux Haricots Rouges (an elegant dish of lobster and kidney beans); or Szechuan Chicken with Eggplant.

Papas a la Huancaina

Peruvian Potatoes with Cheese Sauce

Peru   *Serves 4*

Papas a la Huancaina is a very popular Peruvian dish. Whereas only one or two types of potatoes, besides sweet potatoes and yams, are readily available in the United States, a huge array of tubers are commonly eaten in Peru. This recipe would authentically be served with the yellow-fleshed potatoes that are occasionally available here, and sometimes labelled Finnish potatoes. Use them if you can find them, but boiling potatoes are fine also. The traditional accompaniment to this dish is corn on the cob.

   1 *cup shredded Monterey Jack, Muenster, or Havarti cheese*
 ⅔ *cup sour cream*
 ½ *teaspoon turmeric*
 ½ *to 1 teaspoon cayenne pepper (or other hot pepper*
     seasoning)
     Salt and freshly ground black pepper
   8 *small boiling potatoes, cooked and cut into wedges (may*
     be freshly cooked and hot, warm, or room temperature)
   2 *hard-cooked eggs, quartered*
   8 *black Greek-style olives, pitted (optional)*
   1 *fresh red jalapeño or serrano, seeded and cut into thin*
     strips

1. Stir together cheese, sour cream, turmeric, and cayenne over low heat or simmering water until cheese is melted. Season with salt and pepper to taste.
2. Pour sauce immediately over potatoes; garnish with hard-cooked eggs, olives, and chile strips.

Aguacate Picante

Diced Avocado in Tomato-Chile Sauce

Colombia   *Serves 4*

The creamy, rich flesh of the avocado is enhanced by sharp flavors, as in this lively dish, which makes a nice change from the ubiquitous guacamole. Serve with crusty French bread and follow with Pork and Poblano Sauté.

    2   *or 3 cloves garlic, chopped*
   ½   *green pepper, roasted, peeled, and chopped*
    1   *onion, chopped*
    2   *serranos, thinly sliced*
 1 ½   *tablespoons olive oil*
   ⅓   *cup tomato sauce*
   ⅓   *cup vinegar*
    2   *ripe avocados, peeled, seeded, and cubed*
    2   *pieces crisp fried bacon, crumbled (or wedge of lime)*

1. Sauté garlic, green pepper, onion, and serranos in olive oil until vegetables are soft.
2. Add tomato sauce and vinegar; cook until most of the liquid is evaporated, about 10 minutes. Toss sauce with cubed avocados.
3. The authentic seasoning is crumbled crisp bacon, but a wedge of lime may be squeezed on instead.

Gado Gado

Mixed Vegetable Salad

Indonesia   *Serves 4*

There are many variations of this vegetable platter, each with its own distinctive flavors indigenous to its region. In West Java it is known as *lotek* and is accompanied by rice steamed in palm fronds. Central Java's sweet tooth is satisfied by the large amount of sugar in the accompanying peanut sauce. In Bali, where they like their flavors vivid, the peanut dressing is fired up with garlic, ginger, turmeric, laos, bay leaf, and lots of hot chile.

Wherever you eat Gado Gado (or gado² as the Indonesians write it), you will find a selection of raw and cooked vegetables with a spicy peanut sauce to pour over them or dip them into; a beautiful balance of colors, textures, and tastes.

    2   *medium boiling potatoes*
   ½   *pound green beans*
   ¼   *pound mung bean sprouts*
   ¼   *cabbage, shredded*
    1   *piece tofu about 3-by-5 inches, cut into ¾-inch cubes*
        Oil for deep frying, 2 inches deep
    1   *carrot, grated*

   1 cucumber, unpeeled but scored, sliced ½ inch thick
   1 bunch raw spinach leaves (about 8), cut into thin shreds
   2 hard-cooked eggs, peeled and cut into wedges
   4 to 8 small Thai Chile Flowers, to garnish
   1 recipe Indonesian Spicy Peanut Sauce

1. Boil or steam potatoes. Peel and cut into ½-inch cubes.
2. Boil or steam green beans, bean sprouts, and cabbage separately for only about 2 minutes each; you want the vegetables to be just slightly cooked, still crisp.
3. Deep-fry tofu; drain and set aside.
4. Arrange each cooked and raw vegetable separately on a platter, along with egg wedges and tofu cubes. Garnish with Thai Chile Flowers. Serve with Indonesian Spicy Peanut Sauce at room temperature or thinned out with a few spoonfuls of water and heated to lukewarm.

Chile-Potato Gratin

France   *Serves 4*

This homey casserole of potatoes and cheese is a variation of a French potato gratin. It is not really hot but has a subtle warm flavor from jalapeño and cumin. Serve it with a lemony relish such as Molho de Pimenta e Limao; the lemon balances the richness of the gratin. Crisp-tender green beans would be a nice accompaniment.

     Butter to butter baking dish
   2 pounds (approximately) boiling potatoes
   3 cloves garlic, chopped
   1 teaspoon cumin
   2 red jalapeños, seeded and chopped
1½ to 2 cups shredded Monterey Jack cheese
     Salt to taste
   1 cup cream
   2 tablespoons butter, cut into bits
  ¼ cup freshly grated Parmesan cheese

1. Butter a 2-quart (approximately) baking or soufflé dish or casserole.
2. Cut potatoes into ¼-inch slices. Place in bowl containing several cups water. Let stand 15 to 30 minutes.

3. Drain potatoes and dry on paper towels. Arrange one-third of the potatoes in bottom of baking dish. Top with one-third of the garlic, one-third of the cumin, one-third of the jalapeños, and one-third of the Jack cheese and salt to taste; repeat in layers until all are used up.
4. Pour cream over mixture and let it sink in. Dot with butter and sprinkle with Parmesan. Bake in preheated 375° F. oven 40 minutes to 1 hour, until top is crusty, liquid has been absorbed, and potatoes are tender. Serve immediately.

Sambaar

Mixed Vegetables Cooked in Lentil Sauce

India   *Serves 4*

In Southern India, vegetables and lentils are often stewed together into a spicy mélange called Sambaar. Masoor dahl is a small lentil that is coral-colored when dried and becomes a yellow puree when cooked. Yellow split peas may be used instead. Serve Sambaar with any rice or pilaf; add a dab of garlic chutney to heat things up, a spoonful of yogurt to cool them down. Although not authentic, empanadas would be an interesting hors d'oeuvre or accompaniment.

> ½ cup Masoor dahl (Indian red lentils) or yellow split peas, picked over to remove any small pebbles
> 2½ cups chicken, beef, or vegetable broth
> 1 onion, chopped
> 3 cloves garlic, chopped
> 1 piece ginger, ½ inch thick, chopped
> 1 California or Anaheim chile, seeded and sliced ½ inch thick
> 2 tablespoons vegetable oil
> ½ teaspoon each cumin, coriander, and turmeric
> 1 teaspoon Curry Powder
> ½ cauliflower, separated into florets
> 2 carrots, diced
> ½ eggplant, diced
> ½ cabbage, thinly sliced
> Juice of ½ lemon or lime
> 1 tablespoon hot salsa of choice, or ¾ teaspoon cayenne, or 1 teaspoon chile paste.

1. Cook Masoor dahl with 2 cups of broth until tender, about 30 to 40 minutes. (If using yellow split peas, cook 50 to 70 minutes.)

2. Sauté onion, garlic, ginger and chiles in oil; add spices and vegetables and continue cooking for 5 minutes longer; cover. Add remaining ½ cup broth; simmer for 15 minutes or until vegetables are tender.
3. Add cooked dahl, squeeze of lemon, and salsa or chile paste. Cook a few minutes to combine flavors.

Eggplant with Keema ❯

Sautéed Eggplant Slices Topped with Spiced Meat

Kenya   *Serves 4*

Sautéed eggplant slices topped with spiced meat (Keema) is an Indian-influenced dish from Kenya. The yogurt and cilantro topping was my idea; I've been assured cilantro is not generally eaten in Kenya. Fresh mint leaves would be another fresh, herby accent, though also unorthodox. The combination of rich, bland eggplant, spicy meat, tangy yogurt, and fresh cilantro or mint creates a lovely edible harmony. Good hot, they're also delicious at room temperature. Serve accompanied by Borani Esfanaj, a hot sauce such as Piri-Piri, and crusty bread.

> 1   *medium-sized eggplant*
> ¼   *cup oil (approximately; use vegetable oil or, for a*
>   *Mediterranean accent, olive oil)*
> 8   *ounces ground lamb or beef*
> ½   *onion, chopped*
> 2   *to 3 cloves garlic, chopped*
> 1   *teaspoon paprika*
> 1   *to 1½ teaspoons cumin*
> ½   *teaspoon Curry Powder*
> ½   *cup yogurt (approximately)*
> ½   *to 1 teaspoon Harissa or commercial garlic-chile paste*
>   *Salt*
> ¼   *cup cilantro (or substitute mint or parsley), chopped*

1. Slice eggplant ¼ to ½ inch thick (see note).
2. Heat oil in skillet and fry eggplant slices on each side until lightly browned. You will probably need to do this in several batches. (Since the first batch will absorb much of the oil, instead of setting the slices aside after cooking, lay them on top of the second batch. Some of the oil will drain onto the uncooked eggplant slices, eliminating or reducing the need to add more oil.) When eggplant is fork-tender, remove from skillet and set aside.

3. Sauté meat with onion, garlic, and spices, adding 1 tablespoon more oil if needed. Cook until meat loses its pinkness. Add 1 tablespoon yogurt and Harissa; cook a minute longer. Season with salt to taste.
4. Spread each eggplant slice with about 1 to 1½ tablespoons spiced meat mixture. To serve hot, place on cookie sheet and pop into 425° F. oven for 5 to 10 minutes, then serve immediately, topped with a spoonful of yogurt and a sprinkling of cilantro or mint. To serve at room temperature, eliminate the baking step.

Advance Preparation: Eggplant slices may be spread with meat, covered, and refrigerated several hours to a day in advance. Allow a few minutes longer in the oven to compensate for the chill from the refrigerator.

Variation: Instead of serving Keema atop eggplant slices, it may be simmered with 1 bunch cleaned, coarsely chopped spinach and 1 cup fresh, cooked (frozen are O.K.) lima beans. Serve with rice, yogurt and hot condiment of choice.

Note: Because eggplant can sometimes be bitter, many cookbooks suggest salting the eggplant slices, letting them stand until light brown beads of moisture appear on their surface, then rinsing and drying. For a long time, every eggplant I've used has been sweet-fleshed, so I've eliminated the salting step. One bitter eggplant (which, of course, ruins the dish) will send me back to salting, but meanwhile it doesn't seem necessary. Tasting a small bit of the raw eggplant can often tell you whether it is bitter.

Recommended Wine: Enjoy with a crisp, slightly sweet German Riesling or Gewürztraminer.

Bahmi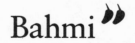

Curried Okra

India   Serves 4

Okra is one of those distinctive foods that elicits strong reactions. It has a unique flavor and consistency (like a viscous cooked bell pepper) that can put potential diners off. Bahmi is a good way of introducing anybody to okra because the sauce is so delicious it eases you into this individualistic vegetable. Enjoy with rice and Kofta Kabob and accompany with yogurt and hot sauce such as Piri-Piri; or for a more unorthodox but incredibly pleasing combination, serve the Bahmi with cooked Red Chile Pasta.

⅓ *cup vegetable oil*
12 *ounces fresh okra, whole, with stems removed*
 6 *shallots, chopped*
 2 *serranos, thinly sliced*
 4 *to 5 cloves garlic, coarsely chopped*
1 ½ *teaspoons Curry Powder*
 1 *teaspoon turmeric*
 ½ *teaspoon dry ginger*
 ¼ *teaspoon cloves*
    Pinch cumin
    Pinch cinnamon
 ⅓ *cup tomato sauce*
    Salt
    Squeeze of fresh lemon juice

1. Heat oil in skillet; add okra and cook over medium heat until okra feels soft to the fork, 3 to 4 minutes. Add shallots, serranos, and garlic. Lower heat and cook for a moment, until onion is translucent.
2. Add spices and cook a minute or two longer. Stir in tomato sauce and continue cooking for a minute to meld flavors. Season with salt to taste; squeeze lemon over okra and sauce. Serve immediately.

Causa a la Limon "

Lemon-Flavored Mashed Potatoes Garnished with Shrimp, Cheese, Olives, and Egg

Peru   *Serves 4*

Another example of a surprising combination—in this case, mashed potatoes with lots of lemon juice and onions—that somehow is perfect. I've been very conservative with the lemon juice; feel free to add up to ½ cup if you like your dish more lemony. After tasting this, I can't imagine the heavier, butter-laden mashed potatoes we grew up on.

Though this traditional Peruvian Indian dish is served as an appetizer, it also makes a nice side dish alongside simple meat or seafood. Authentically served hot, it's also good at room temperature, much like the Middle Eastern Tahina Dip. Accompany with Ají or other salsa of choice.

    4 to 8 medium-large shrimp in shells (about 6 ounces)
    1 slice lemon
    1 medium-sized sweet potato, peeled and sliced ½ to ¾ inch
       thick
    2 pounds baking potatoes (about 4 to 5 medium-large),
       peeled and quartered
    1 onion, finely chopped
    ¼ cup lemon juice (or more to taste)
    ¼ cup olive oil
    5 to 6 Tabasco peppers, pickled serranos, or 1 to 2 jalapeños,
       chopped
  1 ½ teaspoons red pepper flakes or to taste or 1 fresh jalapeño,
       thinly sliced
    ½ to 1 teaspoon salt
   15 Greek-style olives or 20 Niçoise olives
    4 ounces Monterey Jack cheese, cut into ½- to ¾-inch cubes
    2 hard-cooked eggs, quartered
    1 red chile, seeded and cut into strips for garnish, or several
       Thai Chile Flowers

1. Cover shrimp with water; add 1 slice lemon. Bring mixture to boil and cook 5 minutes. Remove from heat, cover, and let stand until room temperature. Drain and set aside.
2. Cover sweet potato slices with water and bring to boil. Cook for 5 to 10 minutes, or until tender but not mushy. Drain and set aside for garnish.
3. Cover baking potatoes with water and boil until tender, about 20 minutes. Drain and mash. Add onion, lemon juice, olive oil, Tabasco peppers or chiles of choice, red pepper flakes, and salt.
4. Garnish lemon-potato mixture with sweet potatoes, shrimp, olives, cheese, egg quarters, and chile strips or Thai Chile Flowers. Serve hot or at room temperature.

Advance Preparation: Potatoes may be made several hours ahead; assemble and heat (if desired) immediately before serving. If preparing ahead of time, be sure to taste for seasoning; the flavors can pale somewhat as the dish sits.

Gâteaux-Piments ""

Split-Pea Fritters with Hot Peppers

Mauritius   *Serves 4 to 6*

Deep-fried balls of soaked and ground legumes are eaten throughout Africa, India, and the Middle East. In Egypt they use fava beans for their *taamia,* and in Israel chick-peas are used for felafel. The fresh herbs in this African version provide an exciting change from everyday felafel. Serve as you would felafel, in a pita topped with salad, cilantro leaves, yogurt, and hot pepper sauce of choice.

  1 *cup yellow split peas*
  1 *teaspoon each turmeric, cumin, and Curry Powder*
  5 *cloves garlic, chopped*
  3 *to 4 green onions, chopped*
  ½ *cup fresh mint leaves*
  ½ *cup cilantro, chopped*
  3 *to 4 fresh serrano chiles (red if possible), thinly sliced*
  ½ *teaspoon salt*
  ¼ *teaspoon baking soda*
  2 *to 3 tablespoons dry felafel mix (or substitute finely milled*
     bulgur wheat plus 2 teaspoons extra cumin)
     Oil for deep frying

1. Soak the split peas overnight in water to cover.
2. Drain peas well. Puree in processor with spices, garlic, green onions, herbs, chiles, salt, soda, and felafel mix. Mixture should form a ball that holds together pretty firmly; if too loose, add a bit more felafel mix.
3. In heavy frying pan or wok, heat oil until very hot. Form mixture into ¾-inch balls and fry in the hot oil until golden brown; drain on paper towels. Serve hot.

Advance Preparation: May be mixed and fried an hour or two in advance and reheated on a cookie sheet in a 425° F. preheated oven.

Note: An easy way of determining when the oil is hot enough for frying is to drop a cube of bread into it. If the bread fries golden-brown immediately and the oil sizzles, it is ready.

Yataklete Kilkil 🖋

Vegetables Tossed in Spicy Butter

Ethiopia   *Serves 4*

An Ethiopian way with vegetables is to steam or boil them briefly, then toss with sautéed onion, garlic, chiles, and ginger. The vegetables should be crisp-tender, shiny from their spicy coating.

Serve this as a vegetable side dish accompanied by a squeeze of lemon or lime, alongside Chicken Moambe, Dag Ha Sfarim, or a curry of lentils, rice, and yogurt.

4 to 5 boiling potatoes (about ¾ pound)
2 medium-sized carrots, peeled and sliced ¼ inch thick
½ cabbage, cut into 1-inch chunks
½ cup cut green beans (about 1 ½-inch lengths)
½ red bell pepper, sliced
2 tablespoons butter
1 onion, chopped
5 cloves garlic, chopped
1 piece of ginger, 1 inch long (approximately 1 ½ tablespoons), chopped
1 poblano or Anaheim chile, seeded and sliced (roasting and peeling is not necessary)
1 to 2 serranos, sliced thinly
1 teaspoon Curry Powder
   Salt
   Lemon wedges for garnish

1. Steam or boil potatoes until almost tender; add carrots, cabbage, green beans, and bell pepper and continue cooking until all are crisp-tender. Drain vegetables and set aside; cut potatoes into quarters.
2. Gently sauté onion, garlic, ginger, poblano, serrano, and Curry Powder in 1 tablespoon butter until onion is limp. Add drained vegetables to onion mixture. Season with salt to taste, and add remaining tablespoon butter. Serve immediately, accompanied by lemon wedges.

Spicy Sephardic Simmered Cabbage 〃

Middle East, India   *Serves 4*

This recipe, from the now dispersed Jewish community of Cochin, India, is a typically Middle Eastern or Indian way of cooking vegetables: saucy, savory and hot! Meatballs may be sautéed and added to make a full meal. Serve the cabbage with a rice dish and Kofta Kabob and accompany with a bowl of Yemenite Zhoog.

1   onion, sliced
2   cloves garlic, chopped
1   green bell pepper, sliced
2   Anaheim chiles, seeded and sliced
1   teaspoon Curry Powder
½   teaspoon turmeric
½   teaspoon cumin
2   tablespoons olive oil
3   or 4 tomatoes, chopped, or ½ cup tomato sauce
1   head cabbage, thinly sliced
     Juice of ½ lemon
     Tabasco sauce or salsa
     Salt

1. Sauté onion, garlic, pepper, chiles, and spices in olive oil until vegetables are limp.
2. Add tomatoes and cook down a few minutes.
3. Add cabbage and cook until tender. Season with lemon juice and Tabasco and salt to taste.

Ethiopian Spiced Spinach 〃

Ethiopia   *Serves 4*

Ethiopian food is not only hot, it is a complex, spice-redolent cuisine. The traditional cooking medium is spiced butter, which Ethiopian cooks keep on hand for preparing nearly everything. Since this is impractical unless you cook large amounts of Ethiopian food, in this recipe sweet butter is spiced with turmeric and

Berberé; spinach is then added. The result is spinach not masked by spice but enhanced by it.

If you're eating this without another spicy sauced dish, increase the Berberé.

Serve with Chicken Moambe or Dag Ha Sfarim and steamed rice or crusty bread. A yam-and-red-onion salad is an authentic accompaniment.

> 1 *onion, chopped*
> 1 *tablespoon butter*
> 1 *teaspoon turmeric*
> 3 *or 4 small dried red chiles, or ½ to 1 teaspoon Berberé*
> 2 *bunches fresh spinach (or substitute 1 package frozen)*
>   *Salt*

1. Sauté onion in butter; add turmeric and chiles or Berberé and cook until onion is translucent.
2. Precook spinach for only 2 or 3 minutes. Drain and coarsely chop. (If using frozen spinach, just defrost, don't cook.)
3. Stir spinach into onion-spice mixture and cook a few minutes to meld flavors and evaporate any excess water. Salt to taste.

Dahl of Kidney Beans "

Spiced Kidney Beans

India   Serves 2 as a main course, 4 as a side dish

Dahl, the Indian lentil stew, may be any type of lentil or bean, stewed with a myriad of spices and aromatics. Dahl is eaten scooped up into flat breads such as *chappatis* or *puris,* ladled over rice, made into soup, or incorporated into a sauce for vegetables. High-protein dahl is especially appreciated by India's many vegetarians, for whom dahl, rice, and vegetables make up the basic diet.

Rich, flavorful kidney beans are particularly tasty in this spicy tomato sauce; I am reminded of an Indian-flavored chili. Accompany with steamed rice, yogurt, and any hot salsa or chutney, and chilled mango for dessert.

> 1 *onion, chopped*
> 5 *cloves garlic, chopped*
> 2 *serranos, thinly sliced*
> 1 *piece of ginger, about 1 inch long, peeled and chopped*

     2 *tablespoons vegetable oil*
     1 *teaspoon Curry Powder*
     1 *teaspoon turmeric*
     1 *teaspoon cayenne*
     ½ *teaspoon ground coriander*
     1 *cup chopped tomatoes*
     2 *cups cooked kidney beans (canned may be used)*
        Squeeze of lemon
        Salt

     ¼ *cup cilantro leaves, for garnish (optional)*

1. Sauté onion, garlic, serranos, and ginger in oil for several minutes, or until onion is softened; sprinkle in spices and cook a few moments longer to cook out any rawness. Be careful not to burn.
2. Add tomatoes and cook with the onions and spices for a few minutes. Stir in beans and cook a few minutes longer to blend flavors. Season with a squeeze of lemon and salt to taste, and garnish with cilantro leaves.

Spicy Black Beans "

Latin America, Caribbean, Southwestern United States   *Yield: 5 cups*

The Indians of the Southwest—the Zuni, Pueblo, and Hopi—cultivated a large selection of beans, cross-breeding to produce a rainbow array of colors. One ancient dish the Indians prepared was cooked beans, pounded to a paste, patted into cakes, then fried; much like the black-bean cakes made famous by Berkeley's Santa Fe Bar and Grill.

Black beans are beloved not only in Berkeley and the Southwest, but throughout Latin America. They have a distinctive flavor and are substantial without being overly starchy.

This tasty dish of ebony-colored beans is simmered with peppers, chile, and spices. Enjoy it wrapped up in a corn or flour tortilla, topped with melted cheese and salsa, or have a bowlful garnished with chopped raw onion, pickled jalapeños, cilantro, and a spoonful of sour cream. Leftovers are wonderful, too: make Black-Bean-Stuffed South-of-the-Border Pot-Stickers, or puree with an equal amount of broth for black bean soup; season to taste with salsa.

And don't forget the very typical Cuban meal of Moors and Christians— white rice topped with Spicy Black Beans, chopped green onions, charcoal-grilled pork slices, and butter-sautéed bananas in lengthwise slices, all accompanied by hot pickled peppers.

1   cup dried black beans
4   cups water
3   cups chicken or vegetable broth
2   cups tomato sauce
2   tablespoons olive oil
1   onion, chopped
5   to 8 cloves garlic, coarsely chopped
½   red bell pepper, sliced or chopped
½   poblano, Anaheim, or California chile, seeded and sliced
1   tablespoon cumin
2   teaspoons mild chile powder (optional)
1   teaspoon dried oregano
2   hot Italian sausages (casing removed), cut up
1   to 2 tablespoons salsa of choice
½   bunch (½ cup) cilantro, chopped

1. Sort through beans to remove any pebbles. Place beans in a large pot and add 4 cups water. Let soak overnight; or boil for 2 minutes, remove from heat, cover and let stand for 1 hour.
2. Add broth and tomato sauce to beans and soaking liquid. Simmer, covered, until beans are almost tender, about 1 to 1½ hours.
3. Heat olive oil in skillet and sauté onion, garlic, red bell pepper, chile, spices, and sausages until onion is limp. Add to beans with salsa and continue to simmer another 30 to 45 minutes. Boil over high heat for a few minutes if necessary to reduce liquid. Garnish with cilantro.

Advance Preparation: These beans are even better the next day (you may have to thin them a little).

Camp California Vegetables with Noodles ❯❯

United States   *Serves 4*

This whimsical name is the outcome of a California-style dinner party I once gave in New York. The guests, all having spent large amounts of time on the West Coast, were busy reminiscing, wondering why they were putting up with snow and slush. The children made name tags reading "Camp California" for everyone, with appropriate designations of social director, crafts instructor, and so on

(I, of course, was camp cook). There, on the 38th floor, overlooking the Hudson River in the most spectacular of Manhattan settings, we ate and drank this very California menu: baked goat cheese salad, whole roasted garlic, Tajine Msir Zeetoon, guacamole, and this vegetable-pasta dish. We drank Napa Valley Zinfandel and scooped up all the lovely bits of food with San Francisco sourdough bread.

½ *package won-ton skins (about 8 ounces)*
1 *to 2 tablespoons dark sesame oil*
1 *to 2 tablespoons soy sauce*
1 *to 2 tablespoons vegetable oil*
1 *piece fresh ginger, ½ inch long, chopped (1 ½ teaspoons)*
2 *cloves garlic, chopped*
1 *carrot, cut into matchstick pieces*
1 *red bell pepper, seeded and sliced*
1 *bunch broccoli, broken into small florets (you may also use the stems, but they must be peeled so as not to be tough)*
1 *teaspoon garlic-chile paste*
3 *to 4 green onions, chopped*
¼ *cup cilantro*

1. Boil the won-ton skins until barely tender, about 2 minutes. (Be careful that they stay separated during the cooking and don't clump together.) Drain, and toss with 1 tablespoon each sesame oil and soy sauce. Set aside.
2. Heat vegetable oil in wok or skillet and stir-fry the ginger, garlic, carrot, and red bell pepper for a minute. Add the broccoli and stir-fry until broccoli is bright green and crisp-tender. Toss the cooked won-ton skins in with the vegetables. Add garlic-chile paste and the remaining sesame oil and soy sauce.
3. Serve immediately, garnished with green onions and cilantro.

Curried Stuffed Potatoes ""

United States, India   *Serves 4*

When I was a child in the fifties, stuffed potatoes were all the vogue. As soon as I saw hollowed-out potato shells awaiting their stuffing, I knew there would be a party. Each Thanksgiving and national or religious holiday saw the emergence of these plump potato boats. Though they're not currently fashionable (and to be honest, they are a bit heavy), I still love them—only on holidays, of course.

The following is a zesty version of the potato dish I remember from my childhood. It is delicious with Chicken Sauté in Ancho-Vegetable Sauce or as an entrée accompanied by Borani Esfanaj and a bowl of cool yogurt. Mashed potatoes combine beautifully with the curry spices. This filling is similar to the filling of Khote, the Tibetan dumpling, and to the Indian savory pastry known as *samosa*.

2 or 3 medium baking potatoes, scrubbed
4 tablespoons (½ stick) butter
5 cloves garlic, chopped
2 or 3 fresh jalapeños, red or green, seeded and chopped
   Spear or two of broccoli, diced
⅓ carrot, diced
1 ½ teaspoons Curry Powder
½ teaspoon turmeric
½ teaspoon cumin
3 to 4 tablespoons plain yogurt
   Several tablespoons chopped cilantro (or to taste)
   Salt

1. Bake potatoes in 350° F. oven until easily pierced with fork, about 1 hour.
2. Halve potatoes lengthwise; scoop out flesh. Place shells on cookie sheet or in baking dish.
3. Mash potato flesh and set aside.
4. Melt 3 tablespoons butter in skillet. Add garlic, jalapeños, broccoli, carrot, and spices; cook a few minutes but don't brown. Add this mixture to potatoes, along with yogurt and cilantro and salt to taste.
5. Fill potato shells with the spiced mashed potatoes, then dot with remaining butter. Bake in preheated 400° F. oven until tops are browned a bit and potatoes are heated through, about 15 minutes.

Advance Preparation: May be stuffed in advance, then popped into the oven about 20 minutes before serving.

Variation: For a simpler vegetable curry, peel and quarter potatoes; boil, drain, and mash. Proceed as above with spices and garlic, adding ½ cup peas, 1 cup shredded cabbage, a few green beans, etc., to cook in vegetable mixture. Mix in mashed potatoes. Serve with Hatzilim Pilpel and yogurt seasoned with turmeric and garlic.

Hatzilim Pilpel ⁾⁾

Simmered Eggplant, Tomatoes, and Chiles

Israel   *Serves 4*

There is a saying in the Middle East that a cook's worth is judged by the number of eggplant dishes he or she can prepare—and the counting starts at 100!

One of the many eggplant dishes is this one, from Israel. It is equally good served hot or at room temperature. Make a big batch and keep it in the refrigerator to enjoy tucked into a pita, piled on top of crusty bread, stirred into scrambled eggs, with rice, or as a salad with yogurt on the side.

Though not painfully hot, this does linger on the tongue and lips.

1 *eggplant, peeled*
1 *onion, thinly sliced*
3 *large cloves garlic, chopped*
3 *Anaheim or California chiles, seeded and cut into strips*
1 *jalapeño, seeded and cut into strips*
2 *to 3 tablespoons olive oil*
2 *tomatoes, chopped*
1 *teaspoon turmeric*
   Salt
   Juice of ½ lemon
2 *tablespoons chopped cilantro*

1. Cut eggplant into 3-by-½-inch strips. Sprinkle generously with salt and let stand for 10 minutes to draw out any bitter juices.
2. Sauté onion, garlic, and chiles in 1 tablespoon oil over low heat. Add tomatoes, turmeric, and salt to taste. Cook 10 to 15 minutes, or until vegetables are limp. Remove from pan and set aside.
3. Rinse eggplant and pat dry. Sauté eggplant strips in remaining oil, adding more oil if necessary. When eggplant strips are cooked, return other vegetables to pan, toss together, and squeeze lemon over all. Transfer to bowl and serve garnished with cilantro leaves.

Green Beans, Malawi Style ⟫⟫⟫

Green Beans in Tomato-Peanut Sauce

Malawi   *Serves 4*

The large population of Indians throughout Africa contributed curry flavors to the diet of that vast continent. This dish combines the curry of India with the typical African style of stewing vegetables with tomatoes and peanuts. Accompany with rice steamed with shrimp, or soft flour tortillas. Whole roasted yams add an authentic touch to this simple yet deliciously uncommon meal.

   1 *onion, chopped*
   1 *tablespoon vegetable oil*
   5 *small, hot dried red chiles, coarsely crumbled*
 ½ *to 1 teaspoon Curry Powder*
   1 *pound green beans, cut into 2-inch lengths*
   1 *cup tomato sauce*
 ½ *cup peanut butter*
      Salt

1. Sauté onion in oil with chiles and Curry Powder until onion is limp.
2. Add green beans and cook a few minutes. Pour tomato sauce over beans and simmer until tender.
3. Stir in peanut butter and salt to taste. Serve hot.

Variation: Substitute 2 bunches of spinach, coarsely chopped, for the green beans.

Stir-Fried Green Beans in Hot Bean Sauce ⟫⟫⟫

China   *Serves 4*

The addition of serrano chiles and fermented chile paste transforms this simple green bean stir-fry into an unusual, fiery dish. Serve immediately or let cool to room temperature. Steamed rice or crusty bread may be served alongside, as a bland counterpoint to the heat. Roast chicken would be a delicious accompaniment.

1 *pound fresh green beans, cleaned, trimmed, and cut into 2-inch lengths*

3 *tablespoons vegetable oil*

¼ *cup water*

1 *piece firm tofu (approximately 4 ounces), cut into ½-inch cubes*

1 *slice fresh ginger, ½ inch thick, chopped (1½ tablespoons)*

1 *to 2 serranos, thinly sliced*

3 *tablespoons Chinese fermented black beans, soaked in water for a few minutes, then drained*

3 *tablespoons chicken broth mixed with 1 teaspoon cornstarch*

2 *tablespoons fermented chile paste with fermented beans*

1. In wok (or heavy skillet), stir-fry green beans in 2 tablespoons vegetable oil. Add ¼ cup water and cook until crisp-tender and bright green. Transfer beans to platter and set aside.
2. In remaining 1 tablespoon oil, stir-fry the tofu, ginger, and serranos; cook until tofu is slightly browned. Add fermented black beans chicken broth-cornstarch mixture and fermented chile paste. Return green beans to wok (or skillet) and combine with sauce. Serve immediately or at room temperature.

Eggs

Nothing approaches the egg for versatility. It may be poached, fried, cooked in the shell hard or soft, souffléed, or baked. Because of its blandness in each incarnation it takes readily to hot flavors.

The egg dishes in this chapter are intriguingly different from the standbys like *huevos rancheros*. A hearty Feta, Jalapeño, and Salami Omelette combines the heat of the chile with the salty tang of the cheese and the rich spice of salami. Huevos à la Flamenca nestles baked eggs into tomato sauce with an abundant garnish of asparagus and peas. Scrambled eggs go Indian when flavored with tomatoes, cilantro, chile, and curry in Ekuri. Brik à l'Oeuf and Poached Eggs with Tomato-Chile Sauce and Ancho Hollandaise are elegant enough for any brunch or supper. You don't need a recipe to dip shelled hard-cooked eggs into a mixture of cumin, cayenne pepper, and salt or to scramble eggs with cilantro and Jalapeños en Escabeche.

Eggs are featured in other recipes throughout this book as well. Nasi Kuning is garnished with thin strips of omelette; hard-cooked egg quarters accompany Lamb and Eggplant Tajine; while scrambled eggs are tossed into the sweet-hot-sour rice noodles of Pad Thai. Gado Gado includes egg quarters among its array of ingredients to be dipped into Indonesian Spicy Peanut Sauce. And, if you still yearn for *huevos rancheros,* you can spoon Salsa Ranchera (see the salsa chapter) over poached or fried eggs.

Poached Eggs with Tomato-Chile Sauce and Ancho Hollandaise ›

United States   *Serves 4*

Serve this spicy version of eggs Benedict for brunch on a lazy, sunny Sunday accompanied by orange juice mixed with tequila. Ancho Hollandaise is also good served with boned and flattened chicken breasts (paillards) marinated in olive oil and lemon juice, then quickly grilled, or with simple poached fish. A trick that I use to keep the hollandaise warm: pour it into a heated thermos; it stays warm for 30 to 45 minutes.

Tomato-Chile Sauce

- 2 *tablespoons olive oil*
- ½ *onion, chopped*
- 3 *cloves garlic, chopped*
- 1 *jalapeño, chopped*
- 1 *Anaheim chile, chopped*
- 1 *red bell pepper, chopped*
- 4 *tomatoes, chopped*
- ½ *teaspoon thyme*
  Salt

Ancho Hollandaise

- 8 *ounces sweet butter*
- 2 *egg yolks*
- 1½ *tablespoons water*
  Juice of ½ to 1 lemon
  Cayenne
- 2 *teaspoons to 1 tablespoon ancho chile powder*
  Salt
- 8 *ounces ham, cut into ¾-inch chunks*
- 2 *tablespoons olive oil*
- 4 *eggs*
- 2 *English muffins, halved*

1. To make Tomato-Chile Sauce: Heat olive oil and gently sauté onion, garlic, jalapeño, Anaheim chile, and red bell peppers until vegetables are soft. Add tomatoes, thyme, and salt to taste. Set aside and keep warm.
2. To make Ancho Hollandaise: Melt butter and set aside. Whisk egg yolks with water and place over very low heat or a double boiler. Continuing to whisk, gradually add melted butter, starting with a drop or two at a time and increasing it to a thin stream as the yolks accept the butter and the mixture thickens. Remove from heat when slightly thickened. Season with lemon juice, cayenne to taste, ancho chile, and salt to taste. Set aside and keep warm.
3. Sauté ham chunks in 2 tablespoons olive oil and set aside.
4. Poach eggs and toast muffins.
5. Onto each muffin, place several tablespoons Tomato-Chile Sauce; top with a poached egg. Pour Ancho Hollandaise over the egg and garnish with sautéed ham chunks. Serve immediately.

Advance Preparation: Tomato-Chile Sauce may be made the day before. The eggs may be poached an hour in advance, kept in cool water, and gently reheated in simmering water just before serving.

Variation: Instead of English muffins, use artichoke bottoms.

Ervilhas Guisadas a Portuguesa

Sausage and Pea Omelette

Portugal   *Serves 4*

Spicy sausages are much enjoyed in Portugal, by themselves or combined with other foods as in this dish. Authentically, this does not include jalapeños. In the classic version, the eggs are not beaten but are broken raw onto the peas and set to poach alongside them.

Serve with crusty bread and a hot sauce such as Piri-Piri and enjoy for Sunday breakfast, or for supper accompanying a bowl of steaming soup.

6 *to 8 ounces spicy hot sausage, sliced ¼ inch thick*
1 *tablespoon olive oil*
1 *onion, chopped*
3 *to 4 cloves garlic, chopped*
2 *to 3 jalapeños en escabeche, thinly sliced*
1 *cup fresh peas (or substitute frozen)*
¼ *cup chicken broth*

> 2 *to 4 ounces Monterey Jack, Fontina, or Lappi cheese, cut*
>   *into cubes*
> 6 *eggs, beaten*
> 1 *tablespoon butter*

1. Fry sausage in olive oil until browned; drain off all but about 1 tablespoon fat. Add onion, garlic, and chiles and cook over low heat until onion is soft.
2. Add peas and chicken broth. Cook until peas are tender and liquid evaporated.
3. Add cheese to beaten eggs. Melt butter in the pan with the peas, then pour in the eggs. Cook until bottom sets, then place under broiler and cook until top sets.

Feta, Jalapeño, and Salami Omelette

Mediterranean   *Serves 4*

This makes one large, flat omelette, much like an Italian frittata, which is usually layered with vegetables, cheese, or meats, baked and cut into wedges. It's great for brunches, and I've taken it to many a picnic. This is lusty, peasant-style food, but it's really not too hot. Accompany with crusty bread and a salad of thinly sliced fennel tossed with olive oil and lemon.

> 3 *to 4 large boiling potatoes, peeled and sliced*
>   *Several tablespoons olive oil*
> 1 *onion, sliced*
> 2 *ounces (approximately) spicy salami, cut into cubes of*
>   *½ to 1 inch*
> 3 *cloves garlic, chopped*
> 1 *to 2 jalapeños en escabeche*
> 1 *to 2 pickled sweet red peppers*
> 4 *to 5 ounces feta cheese, cut into cubes of ½ to 1 inch*
> 8 *eggs, lightly beaten*
> ½ *to 1 teaspoon dried oregano, crushed*

1. In heavy skillet, sauté potato slices in olive oil until tender but not mushy (some pieces should be golden and crisp, others soft and slightly translucent). Add onion and salami and continue cooking until onion loses its rawness, only a minute or two.

2. Add jalapeños, red peppers, and cheese to beaten eggs; pour over potato mixture, adding more oil if needed. Cook over medium heat until bottom turns golden brown.
3. Pop omelette under broiler to brown and cook top (unless you're extremely dexterous and can flip it right over in the skillet).
4. Sprinkle with crushed oregano and serve hot or at room temperature.

Brik à l'Oeuf

Deep-Fried Egg Pastries

Tunisia   *Serves 1*

The first bite of these golden, flaky, gossamer-thin layers of filo dough yields a burst of egg yolk. The contrast of the rich, soft egg, crisp pastry, and fiery dipping sauce is a sensual treat. Brik is sold on the street throughout the Middle East but is a specialty of Tunisia. It can contain a variety of fillings: spicy chopped lamb or brains, fillets of anchovy, or chunks of tuna, for example. Brik is eaten as a first course or snack, and it's great for brunch.

> *Vegetable oil for deep-frying*
> 1 *sheet of filo dough*
> 1 *teaspoon of chopped raw onion mixed with a pinch of chopped parsley*
> 1 *or 2 anchovy fillets, chopped, or approximately 1 teaspoon tuna*
> 1 *egg*

1. Heat oil for frying, about 4 inches deep (a wok is excellent for deep-frying).
2. Lay out a sheet of filo. Place the onion-parsley mixture and the anchovy or tuna in one corner and pat flat.
3. Break raw egg over filling; quickly and carefully fold filo into a triangle. (It's a good idea to practice this a few times with a piece of paper first; once you break the egg, it will run all over the place and you'll have to work fast. The important thing is that the egg be completely encased in pastry.)
4. Fry immediately in hot oil, a minute or two on each side (outside should be golden brown and crisp). Drain on paper towels and serve right away with Harissa Sauce (see recipe at the end of Couscous Fassi) or with salsa of choice.

Advance Preparation: Brik can be kept warm in 425° F. oven for 5 to 10 minutes while you prepare the remaining pastries.

Huevos a la Flamenca ""

Eggs Baked in a Spicy Sauce

Spain   *Serves 4*

This dish is as ubiquitous at tables in Spain as is paella. In Spain, the hearty, sausage-laden sauce would not have chiles, but I like it hot; otherwise this is an authentic recipe.

Huevos a la Flamenca is generally served as a first course; I think it makes a colorful and zesty brunch dish along with crusty bread, chilled pineapple, and a selection of cheeses, such as creamy French mountain cheese, goat cheese, and perhaps a dry California Jack.

2   *onions, chopped*
5   *cloves garlic, chopped*
1   *green pepper, chopped*
3   *or 4 small dried red chiles or 2 fresh red jalapeños,*
      stemmed and seeded
3   *medium potatoes, peeled and cut into ¾-inch cubes*
2   *tablespoons olive oil*
1   *piece of hot smoked sausage (4 to 6 ounces), sliced*
1   *piece ham (3 ounces), cut into ½-inch cubes*
2   *tomatoes, chopped*
¼   *cup tomato sauce*
8   *eggs*
⅓   *cup peas, boiled for 2 minutes, then drained (or substitute*
      frozen defrosted peas; do not parboil)
8   *spears of asparagus*
1   *red bell pepper, roasted, peeled, and sliced (canned*
      pimientos may be substituted)
2   *tablespoons dry sherry or vermouth.*

1. Preheat oven to 375° F.
2. Sauté onion, garlic, green pepper, chiles, and potatoes in olive oil until onion softens; add sausage, ham, and tomatoes. Reduce heat and cook until potatoes are tender, only a few minutes.
3. Stir tomato sauce into vegetable-sausage mixture. Spread in baking dish (any shape, but large enough to accommodate 8 eggs).
4. Break eggs separately into mixture. Garnish with peas, asparagus, and red bell pepper, then sprinkle with sherry or vermouth. Cover and bake in oven until eggs are set, about 10 to 15 minutes.

Ekuri ▶▶▶

Spiced Scrambled Eggs

India   *Serves 4*

Scrambled eggs become a spicy treat when prepared in the manner of India's Parsi community. The Parsis fled Persia 1,200 years ago to escape religious persecution and have retained much of their heritage through religion and culinary tradition. Theirs is a rich cuisine that includes a large array of brightly spiced egg dishes. Ekuri is probably the best known: chiles, tomatoes, onions, ginger, and cilantro bound together in creamy, soft scrambled egg. Authentic accompaniments are Indian flat breads such as *parathas* or *chappatis;* soft, warm flour tortillas are a good substitute.

2   *to 3 tablespoons butter*
6   *green onions, chopped*
6   *cloves garlic, chopped*
1   *piece fresh ginger, about 1 inch long, chopped (about 1 tablespoon)*
3   *or 4 serranos, chopped*
½   *to ¾ teaspoon turmeric*
¾   *teaspoon cumin*
½   *teaspoon Curry Powder*
2   *tomatoes, coarsely chopped*
6   *eggs*
2   *tablespoons water*
¼   *cup coarsely chopped cilantro*

1. Melt butter and sauté green onions, garlic, ginger, and serranos until softened, a minute or two.
2. Add turmeric, cumin, Curry Powder, and tomatoes, and cook a minute longer.
3. Beat eggs with water; add cilantro. Pour into pan along with the tomato-spice mixture. Cook as for scrambled eggs until just set. Serve immediately.

Egg Curry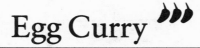

Many hot cuisines simmer hard-cooked eggs in a rich, spicy sauce. Lamb and Eggplant Tajine or Rendang are both delicious examples, as is this Egg Curry. This makes a nice dish for a summer brunch or supper. Accompany with Rosemary and Red Chile Focaccia (or flour tortillas) and Ethiopian Spiced Spinach.

    1 *onion, chopped*
    2 *cloves garlic, chopped*
    1 *piece (½ inch) fresh ginger, peeled and chopped*
    1 *to 2 serrano chiles, seeded and chopped*
    2 *tablespoons butter*
 1 ½ *teaspoons Curry Powder*
   ½ *teaspoon cumin*
   ½ *teaspoon turmeric*
    2 *cups coconut milk*
    1 *tablespoon mild to medium salsa*
       Salt
    6 *hard-cooked eggs, shelled and quartered*

1. Sauté onion, garlic, ginger, and chiles in butter until onion is soft. Add spices and cook a few minutes longer.
2. Stir in coconut milk and cook a few minutes, until slightly thickened.
3. Stir in salsa and salt to taste. Pour sauce onto serving platter and arrange egg quarters in a pleasant design over warm sauce.

Seafood and Fish

The light, delicate flesh of seafood and fish is a natural partner for hot flavors. The clearest example of this is raw clams dabbed with hot condiments, or any simple grilled fish served with salsa.

Most hot cuisines boast an array of fish dishes, especially Southeast Asia, Latin America, Portugal, and parts of India. An African specialty is Matata, an unlikely combination of peanut- and chile-spiced spinach cooked with clams, and the Curried Lemon Rice with Seafood hails from India. The Seafood and Dried Red Chile Stew with lime and salsa is one of the most exquisite dishes you may ever serve, and Moroccan Fish with Cumin Paste is one of those deceptively simple dishes that jolts your taste buds in a delicious way.

Fish and shellfish can be very elegant. Try the Daube des Langoustes aux Haricots Rouge, a subtle dish enlivened by one or two chopped serranos. Try also the Brazilian Vatapa, a shrimp and fish fillet dish of African descent that adds a Latin American garnish of cilantro-spiked salsa.

Start with the recipes in this book and see whether adding a little hot condiment doesn't invigorate nearly any fish dish.

Thai-Flavor Crab

Thailand   *Serves 4*

Sweet, succulent crab simmers in spicy broth for a light summer lunch. The distinctive flavors of lemon grass, fish sauce, and cilantro give the dish its character, but if you dislike cilantro, substitute chopped green onions. Shrimp, lobster tails, or clams are also delicious cooked in this simple broth, or try a combination of several types of seafood. Enjoy as a light meal with crusty bread to dip into the broth, or serve as a soup course and follow with roast chicken and Curried Lemon Rice with Seafood. Offer a bowl of Thai Chile Sauce on the side.

> 2 *stalks lemon grass, cut into 1½-inch lengths (or substitute sereh powder)*
> 1 *teaspoon laos powder*
> 2 *cups water*
> 3 *to 5 jalapeños, thinly sliced*
> 3 *cloves garlic, chopped*
> 1½ *tablespoons fish sauce*
> 1 *or 2 crab, cracked and cut into pieces (a crab will weigh about 1½ pounds; use 1 for a soup portion, 2 for a main dish portion)*
> *Juice of ½ lime*
> ¼ *to ½ cup cilantro for garnish*
> *Lime wedges for garnish*
> 4 *Thai Chile Flowers for garnish (or substitute sliced fresh red jalapeños)*

1. Place lemon grass and laos powder in large saucepan with water. Simmer for 5 minutes to draw out the lemony flavors.
2. Add chiles, garlic, fish sauce, and crab. Simmer another 5 to 8 minutes to let flavors permeate the seafood flesh.
3. Squeeze lime into soup and serve immediately, garnished with cilantro, lime wedges, and chiles.

Curried Lemon Rice with Seafood)

India   *Serves 4*

The combination of shapes, colors, and textures of the seafood and spices offers the visual pleasure of a still life. Accompany with Cilantro-Mint Fresh Chutney or salsa of choice, curried spinach, and yogurt seasoned with turmeric and garlic or coriander and diced bananas.

2　tablespoons butter
2　teaspoons mustard seeds
1　onion, chopped
3　cloves garlic, chopped
1　fresh red jalapeño, chopped
1　green jalapeño, chopped
1　teaspoon Curry Powder
1　piece of ginger (⅛ inch thick), chopped
1　cup rice
1　cup water
1　cup coconut milk
　　Lemon rind (grated from ½ lemon)
½　pound clams in their shells
4　to 6 ounces shrimp in their shells
　　Juice of 1 lemon
　　Salt (optional)

1. Melt butter and sauté mustard seeds until they begin to sputter and pop; add onion, garlic, and chiles and cook until onion is soft. Sprinkle Curry Powder and ginger over onions and cook a few minutes longer.
2. Add rice, 1 cup water, coconut milk, and lemon rind. Cook over medium low heat, covered, for 5 to 8 minutes. Add seafood and lemon juice to rice, cover, and continue cooking another 5 to 10 minutes, until rice is tender. Season with salt to taste if needed; serve immediately.

Variation: Omit seafood for a curried lemon rice.

Daube des Langoustes aux Haricots Rouges ›

Lobster Simmered with Red Beans

Guadeloupe　　　　　　　　　　　　　　　　　　　　　　　　Serves 4

The juxtaposition of humble bean and luxurious lobster is a visual enticement even before the first taste. While the combination seems new and perhaps trendy, seafood is traditionally prepared in a similar manner in the Caribbean. Flambéing the ouzo accents the sauce with an anise flavor that complements the earthiness of the bean and the sweetness of the lobster flesh. Shrimp or crawfish would also be delicious in this instead of the lobster.

Accompany with a salad of romaine lettuce cut into a chiffonade (thin strips) and dressed with a hazelnut oil vinaigrette.

> 1½   *tablespoons butter*
> ½   *cup chopped shallots*
> 3   *cloves garlic, chopped*
> 1   *serrano chile, thinly sliced*
> ½   *teaspoon Curry Powder*
> ½   *cup ouzo*
> ½   *cup chicken broth*
> 4   *lobster tails, in shells, with flesh slit lengthwise to let the sauce permeate the meat and to allow access for the diners*
> 1   *cup red kidney beans, cooked, drained, and rinsed with water*
> 2   *tablespoons chopped parsley*

1. Melt butter and sauté shallots, garlic, and serrano until they are softened. Add Curry Powder and cook a moment longer.
2. Pour in ouzo and ignite with a match. It may ignite by itself if the pan is hot enough, so be careful of your fingers. Be careful also that the pan is not near any curtains, cupboards, paper towels, or other things that could catch fire. When the flames die down, which they will do of their own accord, the alcohol will be burnt off completely, leaving behind a lingering scent of anise.
3. Add broth and lobster. Cook for 5 to 8 minutes, just until lobster is done. Add beans and serve immediately, garnished with chopped parsley.

Seafood and Dried Red Chile Stew

Mexico   *Serves 4*

The variety of chiles gives this dish richness; the more types used, the more complex the dish. This basic red chile sauce is made from steeping the dried peppers, adding onion, garlic, and other aromatic seasonings. An assortment of fish and shellfish is next added to the bubbling brew, along with green peas, sweet red pepper strips, and chunks of tender potato. As in other robust fish stews, such as Italian *burrida* or French bouillabaisse, there is no set requirement of types and amounts of fish; the recipe is merely a suggestion. Go to your fish market and see what is freshest and most delectable.

Serve this savory mixture in bowls, the deep flavor of the stew contrasting with its grassy cilantro garnish and a squeeze of tart lime. Accompany with crusty French bread or warm, soft corn or flour tortillas, and serve a little bowl of Pico de Gallo or Molho de Pimenta e Limao on the side. Fresh fruit or sorbet is the dessert of choice after this feast, but I wouldn't object to a simple butter cookie accompaniment to the sorbet.

> 4 *ancho chiles*
> 5 *New Mexico chiles*
> 2 *chiles negros or pasillas*
> 5 *cups boiling broth (use fish stock if you have it; if not, use half canned chicken stock and half bottled clam juice)*
> 1 *onion, chopped*
> 2 *tablespoons olive oil*
> 5 *cloves garlic, chopped*
> 4 *waxy boiling potatoes, peeled and diced*
> 1 *ripe red bell pepper, cut into strips (or substitute pimiento)*
> 1 *cup fresh peas (or frozen)*
> *Seafood assortment: choose 1 pound of any firm-fleshed white fish fillet, cut into 1-inch squares; clams in shells; shrimp in shells; a whole crab. Allow 1 or 2 clams, a shrimp or two, ¼ of a crab, and a few ounces of fish fillet per person.*
> *Juice of 1 lime*
> *Dash of cayenne pepper*
> *Cilantro leaves and lime wedges for garnish*

1. Remove stems from chiles; pour boiling broth over them. Let stand for 30 minutes to 1 hour, or until softened.
2. Drain and reserve broth. Puree soaked chiles in processor, adding enough broth to make a thin, saucelike consistency. Strain sauce to filter out the smaller bits of tough skin.
3. Sauté onion lightly in olive oil until softened; stir in garlic and strained chile sauce. Cook for 5 minutes over low heat, stirring frequently.
4. Add potatoes, red pepper, peas (if using frozen peas, add them at the last minute), and seafood according to cooking time: simmer crab for 10 minutes; simmer clams 10 minutes; simmer shrimp and white fish 5 to 7 minutes.
5. Squeeze lime into the stew and season with a dash of cayenne if needed. Garnish with lots of cilantro and a lime wedge.

Recommended Wine: Drink a slightly sweet California Riesling.

Garlic Scallops with Linguine*

Spain *Serves 4*

This recipe evolved from a description I read of a Spanish shrimp dish. I prepared it using delicate scallops sautéed with garlic and salsa, then thought that Cilantro Aïoli would be good on it. It was. As all my guests were licking their fingers and wiping the sauce up with bread, we decided it would even be better with pasta.

Serve this rich dish as a first course, and offer extra salsa to taste since it's very mild.

½ *pound linguine*
6 *cloves garlic, chopped*
½ *teaspoon dried thyme*
12 *ounces to 1 pound small scallops*
¼ *cup olive oil*
¼ *cup dry sherry*
1 *tablespoon medium-hot salsa*
½ *to* ⅔ *cup Cilantro Aïoli*
Salt
2 *tablespoons cilantro, as garnish*
Salsa of choice

1. Boil linguine *al dente.*
2. While pasta is cooking, sauté garlic, thyme, and scallops in the olive oil; cook a few minutes, until the scallops turn opaque. Stir in sherry, salsa, and salt to taste.
3. Drain pasta and arrange on plates; top each with one-quarter of the scallops and sauce, then top with a dollop of Cilantro Aïoli. Garnish with cilantro leaves and offer extra salsa.

Moroccan Fish with Cumin Paste"

Morocco *Serves 4*

A deceptively plain-looking dish, but watch out when the flavor hits your mouth! It's low in calories, simple to prepare, and economical. Enjoy accompanied by Salade Moroccaine or Pico de Gallo, and crusty French bread or warm, soft flour tortillas.

5   *cloves garlic*
2   *tablespoons cumin*
2   *tablespoons olive oil*
1   *tablespoon red pepper flakes*
2   *tablespoons cilantro, chopped*
    Juice of ½ lemon
    Salt
4   *fillets of red snapper*

1. Chop garlic in processor; add cumin, oil, red pepper flakes, cilantro, lemon juice, and salt to taste.
2. Place fish fillets in baking dish. Spread with cumin paste and cover tightly with foil.
3. Bake in preheated 350° F. oven for only 5 to 10 minutes, or until fish feels firm to the fork. Serve immediately.

Shrimp Etouffée))

Shrimp in Creole Sauce

United States   *Serves 4*

The word *etouffée* comes from the French word for smothered. In Louisiana it refers to a dish that is "smothered," with green onions. As with other traditional Cajun dishes, this begins with a roux, a cooked mixture of flour and fat. Take care to cook the roux over a medium heat, watching and stirring it continuously, as it can go from golden brown to burnt in just a moment.

Crayfish is another traditional fish to choose for this *etouffée;* try it sometime, or substitute lobster tails. Serve with steamed rice and icy beer.

⅓   *cup butter*
¼   *cup flour*
1   *onion, chopped*
3   *cloves garlic, chopped*
½   *to 1 green pepper, diced*
2   *ribs celery, leaves included, chopped*
2   *jalapeños, chopped*
2   *cups chopped tomatoes*
1   *cup clam juice*
1   *teaspoon tomato paste*
2   *teaspoons Worcestershire sauce*
½   *cup chopped green onions*

Juice of ½ lemon
2 *tablespoons chopped parsley*
Salt, freshly ground black pepper, and cayenne pepper to taste
1 *pound shrimp in shells*

1. Make roux: melt butter over medium heat and stir in flour. Cook, stirring continously, until mixture turns caramel colored.
2. Add onion, garlic, green pepper, celery, and jalapeños. Continue cooking and stirring for 5 minutes, then add tomatoes. Cook until tomatoes cook down into a saucelike consistency, then stir in clam juice and tomato paste.
3. Add rest of ingredients and bring to a boil. Simmer over low heat for 3 to 5 minutes, or until sauce thickens and shellfish turn pink. Serve hot, over rice.

Calamari Criolla ''

Squid Cooked in Spanish Sauce

Cuba   *Serves 4*

Hearty calamari can be prepared very simply, as in Greece, where it's served cold with only olive oil and lemon, or in Italy, where it's dipped in batter and deep-fried. Calamari—squid in English—are wonderfully versatile, however, and may also be sauced with vigorously flavored sauces such as this one. If you have access to pesticide-free nasturtiums, strew them across the dish as garnish. In addition to looking lush and colorful, they lend a peppery accent. Serve with steamed rice and offer a hot sauce as desired, perhaps Piri-Piri.

Traditionally prepared with lobster, the sauce is also good with shrimp. In fact, try it with whatever seafood or white-fleshed fish is available.

1 *onion, chopped*
6 *cloves garlic, chopped*
3 *tablespoons olive oil*
2 *Anaheim or California chiles, seeded and sliced thinly*
2 *jalapeños, thinly sliced*
12 *ounces smoky-flavored ham, cut into ¾-inch cubes*
2 *cups chopped tomatoes*
1 *cup tomato sauce*
1 *teaspoon thyme*
1½ *pounds calamari (squid)*
1 *cup white wine*
5 *or 6 unsprayed nasturtiums (or sprigs fresh parsley)*

1. Sauté onion and half of the garlic in 2 tablespoons olive oil until onion softens. Add Anaheim chiles, jalapeños, and ham; sauté a minute or two longer. Add tomatoes, tomato sauce, and thyme and simmer 5 minutes. Set aside.
2. Clean calamari: separate the tentacles from the body by holding the tentacles in one hand, the sac in the other, and pulling. Cut the head off right below the eyes and discard head and insides; squeeze out the bony beak. Remove thin bone from body tube and peel off the dark-colored outer skin. Rinse with water.
3. Slice body tube into ½-inch rings and tentacles into 2-inch lengths.
4. Heat remaining 1 tablespoon olive oil. Add remaining garlic and the cleaned, cut squid. Sauté over medium low heat for about 5 minutes. Remove from pan and set aside. Pour wine into pan. Over high heat, let it cook down to ¼ cup, then return squid to pan and add the reserved tomato-ham sauce. Simmer together 5 minutes or so to meld flavors. Serve immediately, garnished with nasturtiums or sprigs of fresh parsley. Accompany with steamed rice.

Matata

Spinach and Clams in Tomato-Peanut Sauce

Mozambique   *Serves 4*

Tomato-peanut sauce is typical of African flavors; here it is combined with juicy clams in their shells. When the clams pop open, their juices mingle with the spinach-peanut mixture. This is an interesting dish to serve alongside Couscous Fassi.

> ½ *onion, chopped*
> 2 *cloves garlic, chopped*
> 1 *tablespoon vegetable oil*
> 8 *dried small red chiles, crumbled*
> 1 *teaspoon Curry Powder*
> 2 *cups tomato sauce*
> 1 *bunch spinach, coarsely chopped, or ½ package frozen, defrosted*
> ½ *cup peanut butter*
> 1 *pound clams in shells*
> *Juice of ½ lemon*

1. Sauté onion and garlic in oil until soft; add chiles and Curry Powder and cook a minute or two longer.
2. Add tomato sauce and cook over high heat for 2 to 3 minutes. Stir in spinach and cook until it wilts. Stir in peanut butter and continue stirring until it melts into the sauce.

3. Pour sauce into baking dish; top with clams and sprinkle with lemon juice. Cover tightly with foil and bake in 375° F. preheated oven for 20 minutes, or until clams pop open. Serve immediately.

Advance Preparation: Spinach mixture may be prepared several hours to a day in advance.
Recommended Wine: Serve a slightly sweet California Riesling or Gewürztraminer, or a medium-bodied, sweet Sauternes.
Variation: This dish is also sensational without the clams as a vegetarian dish.

Spicy Baked Pork with Clams and Cilantro-Serrano Puree ▶▶▶

Portugal   *Serves 4*

Portugal's proximity to the sea accounts for the huge array of ocean creatures prepared in the country's cuisine. The Portuguese are particularly fond of combining meats with fish or shellfish in unique stews. This dish mixes the juices from clams with a spicy sauce of paprika-marinated pork; as if that were not flavorful enough, a puree of cilantro, serranos, and lime juice adds zest. While the Portuguese like cilantro almost as much as I do, they do not usually prepare this dish hot; I've spiced it with both chile paste and serranos. Serve with Munkaczina and steamed rice or warm corn tortillas.

1½   *pounds boneless pork, cut into 1½-inch cubes*
1   *tablespoon plus 1 teaspoon sweet paprika*
1   *tablespoon plus 1 teaspoon hot paprika (if not available, substitute 1 tablespoon sweet paprika plus ½ to 1 teaspoon cayenne)*
2½   *to 3 cups white wine*
1   *teaspoon salt*
1   *teaspoon Ají, Piri-Piri, or commercial garlic-chile paste*
1½   *pounds clams in shells*
8   *large cloves garlic, coarsely chopped*
4   *to 5 serranos*
2   *cups cilantro*
   Juice of 3 limes
   Salt

1. Combine pork with half the garlic, sweet and hot paprikas, white wine, and 1 teaspoon salt. Cover and let stand in refrigerator overnight.
2. Place meat, ají or chile paste, and marinade in shallow baking pan. Bake, uncovered, in a preheated 350° F. oven for 1½ to 2 hours, or until meat is tender.
3. Add clams. Return to oven and bake until clams pop open, about 20 minutes.
4. Chop remaining garlic and serranos in processor; add cilantro, lime juice, and salt to taste.
5. Just before serving, combine cilantro puree with meat, clams, and sauce. Serve immediately.

Advance Preparation: Meat may be cooked several hours to a day ahead of time, but clams must be added 20 minutes or so before serving, and cilantro puree must be prepared and added at the last minute.

Vatapa

Fish and Seafood in Thick Sauce

Brazil   *Serves 4*

I must admit that my interest in Brazilian foods was piqued by a Brazilian movie of several years ago about a cooking teacher whose no-good husband dies. In the scene that captured my attention, she is preparing a Vatapa. The camera comes in for a close-up of the colorful ingredients, and as she describes the preparation, she laments the fact that she will never again kiss her husband's lips, which always tasted of hot peppers after he ate this dish. I think of this scene each time I make Vatapa.

Vatapa is an intensely flavored Brazilian classic from the coastal state of Bahia, where the African influence is particularly strong, descending from the slaves brought over in colonial times. Bahian cooking is based on dêndé oil (palm oil), a subtly flavored orange colored oil from Africa.

Serve as a main course, accompanied by a green salad to which orange and red onion slices are added, or serve a smaller portion as a first course.

1½ *cups milk*
  1 *loaf (1 pound) French bread, crusts removed, torn up or sliced*
  2 *onions, chopped*
  5 *cloves garlic, chopped*

  1 *green bell pepper*
  5 *serranos, chopped*
  ¼ *cup dêndé oil (if unavailable, substitute olive oil mixed*
      with 1 teaspoon paprika)
2½ *cups chopped tomatoes (canned is O.K. if fresh ones are*
      mushy and pale)
1½ *cups coconut milk*
  ¼ *pound dried shrimp*
  1 *piece ginger, about 1½ inches long, chopped*
      (approximately 2 tablespoons)
  2 *teaspoons ground coriander*
  2 *cups crunchy peanut butter*
  1 *pound firm white fish, cut into 2-inch cubes*
  1 *pound shrimp, in shells*
  ¼ *cup chopped scallions*
  ¼ *cup chopped cilantro*
      Juice of ½ lemon
      Marlena's Salsa or salsa of choice

1. Pour milk into bowl; add bread and toss to coat; set aside.
2. Sauté onions, garlic, green pepper, and serranos in 2 tablespoons oil; cook until soft. Add tomatoes.
3. Stir in coconut milk, dried shrimp, ginger, and coriander and cook for 10 to 15 minutes, until tomato is cooked through.
4. Mash bread into a mush. Add to sauce mixture with the peanut butter and stir to a pastelike consistency.
5. Sauté fish and shrimp in remaining 2 tablespoons oil until opaque; do not overcook. Add reserved sauce and lemon juice to pan and heat through with the fish. Add more oil if needed. Serve immediately, garnished with scallions, cilantro, and salsa.

Curried Spinach and Clams ◗◗◗

India   *Serves 4*

A vibrant, unexpectedly good dish, this is a simple spinach curry topped with clams and spice mixture, then baked to open the clams. The secret is using a good, homemade Curry Powder. Enjoy with crusty bread to scoop up the spinach and clam juices.

    3 *tablespoons butter*
    2 *onions, chopped*
    6 *cloves garlic, chopped*
    4 *jalapeños, chopped*
    4 *teaspoons Curry Powder*
    1 *cup coconut milk*
    1 *bunch spinach, chopped (or 1 package frozen chopped
       spinach, defrosted)*
       Salt
  1½ *pounds clams in shells*
       Squeeze of lemon juice
    ¼ *cup chopped cilantro for garnish*

1. Melt butter; sauté onion, garlic, and jalapeños until onion is soft. Sprinkle Curry Powder over onion mixture and continue cooking a minute or two to cook out any raw spice flavor. Add coconut milk and set aside ¼ cup of mixture.
2. Add spinach and salt to taste. Pour into baking dish and top with clams. Squeeze lemon and reserved spiced coconut milk over the mixture. Cover tightly with foil and bake in preheated 375° F. degree oven for 20 minutes, or until clams pop open. Serve hot, garnished with chopped cilantro.

Dag Ha Sfarim ▶▶▶

Whole Fish Baked with Tomatoes and Sweet and Hot Pepper

Middle East   *Serves 4*

In this dish, a whole fish is marinated with lemon, topped with a pepper-and-tomato mixture, then baked. The combination of tomatoes, sweet and hot peppers, turmeric, and cilantro is typical of the foods eaten by Jews from the Middle East—Iran, Turkey, Yemen, Syria. This is similar to the Greek and Turkish fish *plaki,* as they are both prepared with olive oil, lemon, and tomatoes. Dag Ha Sfarim, however, is spicier and served hot, whereas *plaki*-style fish is generally not spice-hot and is served at room temperature.

Accompany with green bean pilaf and a hot sauce such as Yemenite Zhoog.

1 *whole fish such as red snapper, cleaned, with head and tail intact, weighing 2 ½ to 3 ½ pounds*
½ *teaspoon salt*
Juice of 2 lemons
1 *onion, sliced*
3 *cloves garlic, chopped*
¼ *cup olive oil*
1 *green bell pepper, seeded and sliced*
2 *to 3 Anaheim or California chiles, seeded and sliced*
1 *to 2 jalapeños, thinly sliced (seed if desired, for less heat)*
1 *teaspoon turmeric (or use ½ teaspoon turmeric and ½ teaspoon Middle Eastern Spice Mixture)*
2 *to 3 tomatoes, chopped*
¼ *cup tomato sauce*
½ *cup chopped cilantro or parsley*
½ *cup toasted pine nuts*
1 *lemon, cut into wedges, for garnish*

1. Rub fish with salt. Prick several times on each side with a fork, then place in bowl and squeeze lemon juice over it. Let stand for 2 hours.
2. Sauté onion and garlic lightly in olive oil until onion is soft. Add peppers, chiles, and turmeric and cook gently for several minutes. Stir in tomatoes, tomato sauce, and cilantro or parsley.
3. Scatter half of the pine nuts in bottom of baking pan. Top with half of the sauce, then add the fish and its marinade. Pour remaining sauce over fish, sprinkle with remaining pine nuts, and cover tightly with foil.
4. Bake in preheated 350° F. oven for 30 minutes. Remove foil and bake another 20 to 30 minutes, until fish feels firm to the touch or flakes easily with a fork. Serve hot.

Poultry

Chicken is particularly agreeable to spicing with hot flavors. Bland and fleshy, it may be roasted whole, cut up and stir-fried, marinated and grilled, and so on and will "yield" itself to each change of ingredient or method.

You can flavor chicken heartily or delicately. Chicken Moambe stews my favorite fowl in a robust peanutty sauce, and Szechuan Chicken with Eggplant stir-fries diced chicken breasts with eggplant and peanuts. The same chicken braised with olives, lemons, and chiles creates the tart-hot Moroccan dish Tajine Msir Zeetoon. Both Taxco Chicken Breasts in its creamy green chile sauce and Chicken Breasts with Cheese and Salsa are warmly flavored yet delicate. You could eat a different spicy chicken dish every day and not be bored.

Chicken's elegant cousin, the duck, is at home in the hot-foods kitchen as well. The rich, dark flesh of the duckling is enhanced by sharp spicing. The spice's heat seems to cut through the fatty or cloying flavor duck can sometimes have. The two duck dishes in this chapter are unusual—one with peas, the other spicy-sweet and served with steamed bread and herbs.

Chicken Breasts
with Cheese and Salsa

Italy, United States, Mexico   *Serves 4*

Despite the simple ingredients and preparation, this dish of boned, sautéed chicken breasts with melted cheese and salsa topping is especially good. A variation of the classic Italian dish *pollo alla Bolognese,* here the zip of salsa has replaced the salty tang of prosciutto, and Monterey Jack cheese has taken the place of Fontina. Serve with Aquacate Picante, crusty bread, and extra salsa as desired. For dessert, orange slices and strawberries sprinkled with sugar and orange flower water would be nice.

6 *chicken breast halves, skinned and boned*
Salt and freshly ground pepper
All-purpose flour for dusting chicken
½ *cup (1 stick) butter (approximately)*
2 *to 3 tablespoons (approximately) salsa (recipe follows) or substitute salsa of choice*
8 *to 10 ounces garlic-flavored or plain Monterey Jack, Lappi, or Jarlsberg cheese, cut into ¼-inch-thick slices*
2 *to 3 tablespoons freshly grated Parmesan cheese*
2 *to 3 tablespoons chicken broth*
8 *to 10 thin strips of red bell pepper (or pimientos), for garnish*

1. Preheat broiler.
2. Salt and pepper chicken breasts to taste; dust with flour. Melt butter in skillet and sauté chicken breasts over medium heat until golden but still under-cooked (they should still be pinkish inside, as they will cook a few minutes longer under the broiler).
3. Arrange chicken breasts in shallow baking pan. Spread each with a spoonful of salsa; top with cheese slices, a sprinkle of Parmesan, and a dribble of broth. Decorate with red bell pepper strips as desired.
4. Broil for several minutes, until bubbly and lightly browned. Serve immediately.

Salsa

4 *cloves garlic*
2 *or 3 jalapeños*
½ *bunch (½ cup) cilantro or ¼ cup parsley*
2 *tomatoes, chopped*
Salt
Cumin (optional)

In processor, chop garlic; add jalapeños, cilantro or parsley, tomatoes, and salt and cumin to taste. Process to slightly chunky sauce consistency. Serve any extra sauce at the table.

Advance Preparation: Chicken breasts may be sautéed, topped with salsa and cheese an hour or two before serving. Pop under the broiler when almost ready to serve.

Recommended Wine: Enjoy with a medium-bodied California Chardonnay or a crisp, slightly sweet German Spätlese.

Sautéed Chicken Paillards with Red Pepper Sauce ❥

Italy   *Serves 4*

I first tasted this in a restaurant specializing in the "new Italian cuisine." It has a delicate, sweet pepper flavor with a subtle hint of heat. Enjoy on an Indian summer evening when peppers are ripe and the air is fragrant with the scents of summer's end. Accompany with a salad of fennel drizzled with olive oil and lemon and studded with Greek or Italian-style olives. Fresh pasta, tossed with a little cream and freshly grated Parmesan cheese, would be good on the menu, too.

    The Red Pepper Sauce is also wonderful on sautéed scallops, or try it on plump Goat Cheese Ravioli peeking out from under a blanket of rosy sauce. It's ambrosial!

> 6 tablespoons butter
> ½ onion, chopped
> 3 to 5 cloves garlic, chopped
> 3 red bell peppers, roasted, peeled, and cut into strips
> 2 to 3 tomatoes, chopped
> ¼ cup flour
> ½ cup chicken broth
> ½ cup white wine
> ½ cup heavy cream
> 1 teaspoon medium-hot salsa, or 1 fresh red jalapeño, chopped
> 6 chicken breast halves, boned and skinned
>   Salt and pepper
> 4 sprigs cilantro or sweet basil

1. In 2 tablespoons butter, gently sauté onion, garlic, and peppers for a few minutes, until onions are limp. Add tomatoes and cook a few minutes longer to a saucelike consistency. Sprinkle in 2 tablespoons flour and cook, stirring, a few minutes longer.

2. Stir in broth and wine; cook until sauce thickens. (Don't worry about lumps; sauce will be pureed.)
3. Puree sauce with cream and salsa in blender or processor. Transfer to saucepan and taste for salt.
4. Pound chicken breasts lightly until even in thickness. Dredge with remaining flour and sauté in remaining butter until golden. Add more butter if needed. Salt and pepper to taste.
5. Gently reheat sauce and serve with chicken breasts; garnish with a sprig of cilantro or sweet basil and serve immediately.

Yucatecan Marinated Grilled Chicken

Mexico   *Serves 4*

The Yucatecan method of marinating with lemon, lime, and orange produces a tender, succulent chicken, at its best grilled over mesquite charcoal but also good broiled in the oven or even pan-fried. Serve with warm, soft corn tortillas and a selection of several salsas ranging from mild to hot, smooth to chunky. Avocado and tomato slices or guacamole would be a good salad accompaniment.

Juice of 2 oranges, 2 limes, 2 lemons
3 *cloves garlic, chopped*
1 *serrano or jalapeño, thinly sliced*
1 *tablespoon New Mexico or pasilla chile powder*
1 *teaspoon cumin*
½ *to 1 teaspoon cayenne pepper*
½ *teaspoon oregano*
1 *teaspoon salt*
1 *chicken, cut into serving pieces (2½ to 3 pounds)*

1. Combine all ingredients except chicken. Pour over chicken and marinate overnight in refrigerator.
2. Remove chicken from marinade. Barbecue over mesquite charcoal or broil in oven (will be cooked through when juices run clear, not pink, when pricked deeply with a fork). Serve immediately.

Variation: Boned chicken breasts are fabulous in this marinade. Since they're delicate, and the marinade is intense, decrease the marinating time to 1 to 2 hours. They cook very quickly, only a few minutes on each side. Accompany with crusty French bread, a favorite salsa and Salade Moroccaine.

Asian-Style Roast Duck ♪

China, Southeast Asia | *Serves 3 to 4*

Simple roast duck is transformed by a coating of Chinese sweet-hot basting sauce. The accompaniment of fresh mint leaves and cilantro is a Southeast Asian accent to this simplified version of the classic Peking roast duck. The steamed French bread is a reminder of Vietnam's French occupation, and an interesting variation from the thin Mandarin pancakes that traditionally accompany the Chinese dish.

The duck is roasted *au naturel* for the first part of its cooking, then painted with a hoisin-based hot sauce. The duck is carved into slices; each diner takes a slice of steamed bread, wraps up a piece of duck and fresh herbs, then pops it into his or her mouth. Offer a hot condiment such as Piri-Piri if desired.

1 *whole duckling, about 3 to 4 pounds, insides removed*
  Salt and pepper
1 *piece fresh ginger (about 2 inches long), left whole*
1 *cup hoisin sauce*
2 *teaspoons sugar*
1 *tablespoon commercial garlic-chile paste or homemade Ají*
1 *tablespoon vinegar*
  About ½ loaf French bread, sliced approximately ½ to
  ¾ inch thick
3 *green onions, cut into 2-inch lengths*
⅔ *cup fresh mint leaves*
⅔ *cup cilantro*

1. Place duck in large baking dish. Sprinkle duck inside and out with salt and pepper to taste, then place ginger inside its cavity. Roast in a preheated 400° F. oven until almost done, about 50 minutes. Baste once or twice with the hot drippings from the bottom of the pan; this will encourage the fat to render itself more completely.
2. Reduce heat to 325° F. Pour off fat from bottom of pan, but save any drippings from the duck. Mix hoisin sauce with the sugar, garlic-chile paste, and vinegar; take several tablespoons of the mixture and brush or smear it all over duck. Return duck to oven for about 10 minutes, then repeat the brushing of sauce and return it to the oven for a final 10 minutes.
3. While the duck is in the oven for its final bake, place the bread in a steamer, overlapping to make room for all the slices but allowing space for the steam to circulate, warming and moistening the bread. The bread should steam for 5 minutes, beginning when the duck is done; this will give you time to carve the

duck while the bread is steaming. Bring bread to table in steamer or covered in a towel, so it won't dry out.
4. Place the remaining hoisin sauce mixture, green onions, mint, and cilantro in separate bowls. Diners make small sandwiches of the bread, duck, and herbs, spread with the remaining hoisin sauce mix.

Pato con Guisadas

Duck with Peas

Portugal   *Serves 2*

A deceptively simple treatment of roast duck, inspired by the cuisine of Portugal. In classical treatment, the duck is braised and not hot; but duck is so delicious roasted, and a little chile-heat lifts it to out-of-the-ordinary.

One duck generally serves two people; double the recipe for four. Serve accompanied by rice tinted yellow with a little turmeric, or crusty peasant bread to scoop up the sauce and peas.

1 *whole duckling (approximately 3 to 4 pounds), internal*
  organs removed
  Salt and freshly ground pepper
1 *piece ginger (approximately 1 or 2 inches long), left whole*
1 *onion, cut in half*
1 *onion, chopped*
⅔ *cup chopped tomatoes*
1 *poblano chile, seeded and cut into strips*
1 *serrano, chopped*
2 *tablespoons cilantro or parsley, chopped*
1 *cup dry sherry*
1 *cup briefly cooked peas (frozen O.K.)*
1 *cup drained pimiento-stuffed green olives*

1. Place duck in large baking dish; sprinkle inside and out with salt and pepper to taste. Place ginger and the two onion halves inside duck. Roast in pre-heated 400° F. oven until almost done, about 50 minutes. During roasting, baste duck once or twice with the drippings. (The hot fat will actually draw more fat from the duck.)
2. Reduce heat to 325° F. Pour off fat from bottom of pan and remove ginger and onion halves, and discard. To the pan, add chopped onion, tomatoes, poblano, serrano, cilantro, sherry, peas, and olives. Return duck and vegetables to oven and continue cooking for another 20 minutes or so. Serve immediately, accompanied by a medium-hot salsa or Pico de Gallo.

Taxco Chicken Breasts

Sautéed Chicken Breasts in Cream and Green Chiles

Mexico   *Serves 4*

This dish of succulent chicken breasts in creamy chile-scented sauce will please even those who cannot take much heat. In Mexico, any dish made with cream is given the name "Swiss," since the Swiss are so fond of dairy foods. This is the "Swiss" sauce that I once encountered in Taxco, Mexico. It is delicious with plump boned chicken breasts.

> 4   *chicken breast halves, boned and skinned*
>   *Salt and freshly ground pepper*
> 1   *tablespoon cumin*
> 2   *tablespoons all-purpose flour*
> 3   *tablespoons butter*
> 2   *cloves garlic, chopped*
> ½   *cup chicken broth*
> 3   *Anaheim or California chiles, roasted, peeled, and*
>   *chopped, or small can (3 ounces) mild green chiles*
> 1   *cup sour cream*
> ½   *cup shredded cheese (combination Monterey Jack and*
>   *Parmesan)*

1. Season chicken with salt and pepper to taste and 1 teaspoon cumin. Dredge in flour. Melt butter in skillet, then sauté chicken over medium-low heat a few minutes on each side; do not overcook. Remove from skillet.
2. Add garlic to skillet and sauté a moment. Add broth, chiles, and remaining cumin. Cook until liquid has almost evaporated. Reduce heat, then stir in sour cream and cheese and cook over low heat until cheese has melted. Return chicken to pan and heat through, being careful not to let sour cream sauce boil. Serve immediately.

Chicken Breasts in Avocado Sauce

Italy, Mexico   *Serves 4*

This elegant dish is simple to prepare, yet delicate and unusual. The tender boned chicken breasts are sautéed, then surrounded with pale green avocado puree. Be sure to choose the black Haas avocado, as it has the richest flavor and smoothest consistency.

Accompany this rich, subtle dish with the lively crunch of Pico de Gallo and warm corn tortillas.

> 4 *chicken breast halves, boned*
> *Salt and freshly ground black pepper*
> *All-purpose flour for dusting chicken*
> ¼ *cup butter*
> ½ *onion, chopped*
> 2 *cloves garlic, chopped*
> ¼ *teaspoon cumin*
> 1 *teaspoon New Mexico chile powder*
> ½ *cup chicken broth*
> 2 *ripe avocados, peeled and seeded*
> 1 *to 2 tablespoons medium salsa such as Salsa Verde*

1. Season chicken breasts with salt and pepper to taste. Dust with flour; shake off excess.
2. Heat half the butter in skillet until bubbly; do not let brown. Sauté chicken lightly several minutes on each side; undercook slightly. Remove from pan and set aside.
3. Add rest of butter to pan and sauté onion and garlic until onion is limp. Sprinkle with cumin and chile powder. Pour broth into pan and boil down until it is reduced one-half in volume.
4. Puree avocado with salsa. Add reduced broth.
5. Place chicken in pan, gently heat, and pour the sauce around chicken to warm it. Serve immediately, accompanied by Pico de Gallo.

Chicken Sauté
in Ancho-Vegetable Sauce⁾

Mexico   *Serves 4*

This is as much vegetable and sauce as it is chicken. The tender medallions of chicken are served on a bed of potatoes, onions, peas, green olives, and pimiento, all cloaked in a spicy and suave mahogany-colored sauce. Actually, the vegetables and sauce are so delicious and substantial, you can eliminate the chicken entirely for a satisfying vegetarian meal.

Accompany with soft corn tortillas, Abala, or crusty bread, a vinaigrette-laced salad, and a bowl of Pico de Gallo.

> 4   *chicken breast halves, boned but not skinned*
> 2   *tablespoons ancho chile powder (or substitute New Mexico or pasilla chile powder)*
> 1   *tablespoon olive oil*
>   *Juice of ½ lemon*
> 2   *cloves garlic, chopped*
> 2   *onions, chopped*
> 5   *cloves garlic, coarsely chopped*
> 2   *fresh California, Anaheim, or poblano chiles (or combination), cut into ¼-inch strips*
> ½   *red bell pepper, cut into ½-inch strips (or substitute canned pimiento)*
> 2   *tablespoons olive oil*
> 1   *to 2 teaspoons cumin*
> 1   *teaspoon cinnamon*
> 2   *boiling potatoes, peeled and cut into ¾-inch cubes*
> ½   *cup white wine*
> ¾   *cup tomato sauce*
> ¾   *cup red chile sauce (or substitute canned enchilada sauce)*
> 1   *cup fresh peas, briefly cooked (or substitute frozen)*
> ½   *cup stuffed green olives*
> 1   *pint sour cream for garnish*

1. Marinate chicken breasts in chile powder, olive oil, lemon juice, and 2 cloves chopped garlic.
2. Sauté onion, remaining garlic, green chiles, and red bell pepper in olive oil until onion softens; sprinkle with cumin and cinnamon. Add potatoes and cook over medium heat until tender, tossing occasionally to prevent burning.
3. When potatoes are tender, remove from pan and sauté chicken breasts a few minutes on each side (undercook chicken, as it will continue to cook in sauce). Remove chicken breasts from pan and pour off grease.
4. Return potato mixture to pan and increase heat to high. Add wine and cook down for a minute or two. Stir in tomato sauce, chile sauce, peas, and olives. Return chicken to pan and heat through to mingle flavors.
5. Serve with a dollop of sour cream on top and soft tortillas or crusty bread to soak up the bits of vegetable and sauce.

Chicken with Chiles in Peanut Sauce ”

Indonesia   *Serves 4*

This is a smooth, subtle dish of chicken breasts simmered in coconut milk, chiles, and peanut butter. Typically Indonesian in its ingredients, it's milder than most Indonesian curries. Enjoy with plain steamed rice, Curried Spinach and Clams, and Sambal Ketjap.

> 1   *onion, chopped*
> 4   *cloves garlic, chopped*
> 2   *tablespoons vegetable oil*
> 1   *teaspoon coriander*
> ½   *teaspoon sereh, or 1 stalk lemon grass*
> 1   *poblano, cut into strips*
> 1   *jalapeño, thinly sliced*
> 4   *boned chicken breasts, skinned and cut into 2-inch cubes*
> 2   *cups coconut milk*
> 2   *tablespoons sugar*
> 2   *tablespoons soy sauce or fish sauce*
> ¼   *cup peanut butter*
>   *Squeeze of ½ lemon*
>   *Salt*

1. Sauté onion and garlic in oil; add coriander, sereh, and chiles. Cook gently a few minutes until chiles are soft.
2. Add chicken and sauté in onion-chile mixture until slightly opaque. Pour in coconut milk, sugar, soy sauce, and peanut butter and simmer until sauce thickens, about 5 to 10 minutes.
3. Season with a squeeze of lemon and salt to taste.

Chicken Breasts and Broccoli in Curry-Yogurt Sauce ”

India   *Serves 4*

This is one of my comfort dishes—I make it when I'm a little down and the world seems not quite right. Boned chicken and broccoli are cooked in a spicy-tart sauce. In addition to being tasty and nourishing, it has the bonus of being very low-calorie. Serve with plain, steamed rice and a hot condiment on the side.

½ *onion, chopped*
5 *cloves garlic, chopped*
1 *piece (¾ inch long) fresh ginger, chopped (1 tablespoon)*
1 *jalapeño, chopped*
1 *tablespoon butter*
1 *teaspoon Curry Powder*
½ *teaspoon cumin*
   Seeds of 6 cardamom pods
6 *chicken breast halves, boned*
¾ *cup chicken broth*
2 *stalks of broccoli, cut into 1-inch lengths*
1 *tablespoon chopped cilantro*
¾ *cup plain yogurt*
   Juice of ½ lemon

1. Sauté onion, garlic, ginger, and jalapeño in butter until onion is soft. Add Curry Powder, cumin, and cardamom.
2. Add chicken breasts and broth. Cover and reduce the heat. Cook over low heat for about 5 minutes on each side, or until opaque. Do not overcook; they should still be slightly pink inside. Remove from pan, set aside, and keep warm.
3. To remaining broth in pan add the broccoli and cilantro. Cover and cook over high heat briefly until crisp-tender. Remove and set aside with chicken. Bring cooking liquid (broth, spices, and juices from the broccoli and chicken) to a boil and cook down until almost evaporated. Remove from heat and stir in yogurt. Pour sauce over chicken and broccoli, squeeze lemon over mixture, and serve immediately.

Chicken and Shrimp Gumbo 〞

United States   *Serves 4*

The name gumbo comes from an African word, *gombo,* which means "okra." There are as many versions of gumbo as there are cooks on the bayou. Some gumbos do not use okra at all. They are thickened by filé, dried sassafras root, first used by the Native Americans. Do not use both okra and filé powder, or your gumbo will be unpleasantly stringy. Gumbo is a freewheeling dish; throw in any seafood you like, in addition to or instead of the shrimp. If you'd like it hotter, add more cayenne. Serve over steamed rice.

⅓ *cup vegetable oil*
⅓ *cup all-purpose flour*
1 *onion, chopped*
1 *green bell pepper, chopped*
2 *stalks celery, chopped*
4 *cloves garlic, chopped*
2 *tablespoons vegetable oil*
1 *teaspoon thyme*
1 *teaspoon paprika*
1 *bay leaf*
  Salt and freshly ground black pepper
8 *ounces fresh okra, sliced ¼ inch thick*
4 *cups boiling chicken broth*
4 *ounces spicy sausage such as Cajun andouille or kielbasa, Polish garlic sausage, sliced*
3 *dried small red chiles*
1 *cup cooked tomatoes (canned is fine)*
1 *pound shrimp in shells*
1 *cup cooked, shredded chicken*
  Cayenne pepper to taste
½ *cup chopped parsley*

1. First make that savory Cajun sauce base, the roux: heat oil in heavy skillet (it must be heavy to prevent roux from burning) and add the flour. Stir constantly over medium-low heat until mixture is dark caramel color; do not burn, as that will give a bitter taste. Set roux aside.
2. Sauté onion, green pepper, celery, and garlic in 2 tablespoons oil. Cook until onion is soft, then add thyme, paprika, bay leaf, salt and pepper to taste, and okra. Continue cooking until okra is soft to the fork, 3 to 5 minutes.
3. In large pot, combine roux and vegetable mixture. Stir in broth, sausage, dried red chiles, and tomatoes. Simmer 20 minutes or so.
4. A few minutes before serving, add shrimp and cook just until pink. Add cooked chicken, season with cayenne pepper and heat through. Garnish with chopped parsley.

Advance Preparation: May be made several hours to a day ahead and reheated before serving.

Chicken Moambe »»

Chicken with Peanut Sauce

Zaire   *Serves 4*

Peanuts are a typical ingredient in Western, Central, and East African cooking. Often they are pounded into a paste and used to thicken sauces and soups or to flavor stews.

Chicken Moambe is the national dish of Zaire, though variations are eaten throughout much of Africa. In Ghana the dish is not as spicy, and in Ethiopia it is torrid from the hot chile mixture, Berberé. Meats, vegetables, and fish—fresh as well as smoked and dried—are also simmered in tomato sauce and peanut butter. Sometimes they are prepared in combination with other vegetables, legumes, meats, and so on.

Sprinkle this saucy, sturdy dish with sliced green onions and accompany with Ethiopian Spiced Spinach and crusty bread for scooping up bits of chicken and sauce. Millet would also be an authentic accompaniment.

1   *chicken, 2 ½ to 3 pounds, cut into serving pieces*
    Salt and freshly ground black pepper
2   *to 3 tablespoons peanut oil*
2   *onions, coarsely chopped*
3   *bay leaves*
1   *cup broth*
2   *cups water*
3   *ounces (½ a 6-ounce can) tomato paste*
2   *teaspoons commercial garlic-chile paste, or homemade*
    Berberé or Harissa
3   *to 4 tablespoons peanut butter*

1. Season chicken with salt and pepper to taste. Sauté in oil until golden. Add onions and bay leaves and continue browning for a few more minutes.
2. Stir in broth, water, tomato paste, and chile paste. Simmer until chicken is tender, about 45 minutes to an hour. Spoon excess fat from top of sauce.
3. Stir in peanut butter and adjust seasoning to taste.

Tajine Msir Zeetoon ⟩⟩

Chicken with Olives and Lemon

Morocco   *Serves 4*

There are as many versions of this classic dish as there are types of olives in the
souk (marketplace). Traditionally it is prepared with a light-fleshed black olive
such as Kalamata or with unripe green ones, but I am fond of using pimiento-
stuffed green ones, for aesthetics as well as taste. Tajine Msir Zeetoon is authentically spicy, not hot, but I like to season it with cayenne or salsa; hot flavors
combine beautifully with the tart lemon.

This may well be my favorite recipe. The scent of lemon permeates the flesh of
the chicken while the olives are salty accents to the mildly *picante* sauce. Serve
with steamed rice or couscous tossed with cumin and peas, and Salade Moroccaine.

  1 *chicken, 2 ½ to 3 pounds, cut into serving pieces*
  1 *tablespoon cumin*
  2 *teaspoons paprika*
  ½ *to 1 teaspoon dried ginger*
  ½ *to 1 teaspoon turmeric*
  2 *tablespoons medium salsa or 1 teaspoon cayenne pepper*
  4 *cloves garlic, chopped*
  ½ *bunch cilantro, chopped (½ cup)*
     Juice of 2 lemons (see note)
  ½ *cup all-purpose flour*
  1 *cup green olives, imported Italian or Greek, or pimiento-*
     stuffed
  1 *lemon, cut into 6 wedges*
  1 *cup chicken broth*

1. Preheat oven to 325° F. Coat chicken with spices, salsa, garlic, and cilantro.
   Place in baking dish and pour lemon juice over it.
2. Sprinkle chicken with flour; mix to coat chicken pieces.
3. Add olives, lemon wedges, and broth to dish. Bake uncovered for about 1
   hour, until chicken is tender and a delicious sauce has formed.

Note: Moroccans use salt-preserved lemons, which contribute a distinctive,
slightly pickled flavor. I use fresh lemons, and though the dish is not the same, it

tastes wonderful. Salt-preserved lemons are not readily available commercially; Paul Wolfert offers excellent directions for preparing them in *Couscous and Other Good Things from Morocco,* Harper and Row.

Ají de Gallina 》

Shredded Chicken in a Hearty Peanut Sauce

Peru   *Serves 4*

Believed to have been first cultivated high in the Andes, peanuts soon spread to become part of the diet of the Indians in such far-off places as Brazil and Chile. After the discovery of the New World, peanuts found their way into Chinese, Southeast Asian, and (especially) African cooking. Peanuts have made a large contribution to many of the world's great cuisines; another example of the American Indians' agricultural gifts to the world, a huge list that includes chile, tomato, corn, chocolate, avocado, and pineapple.

Ají de Gallina is a rustic dish, one I can imagine the Indians preparing for the Spanish settlers. In this very typical Peruvian dish, the shredded chicken is served in a sauce thickened with soaked bread, spiced with hot peppers, and enriched with peanut butter. Serve garnished with hard-cooked egg slices, Greek-style olives, cilantro leaves, and thin strips of red chile. Accompany with corn on the cob, sweet potato slices, and a green salad with vinaigrette. Offer Ají or Piri-Piri on the side.

2 *onions, chopped*
4 *cloves garlic, chopped*
1 *tablespoon olive oil*
2 *thick slices French bread, soaked in milk, squeezed dry, and torn into pieces*
¾ *cup chicken broth*
3 *tablespoons salsa, or 2 jalapeños, chopped*
⅔ *cup peanut butter, preferably crunchy*
   Squeeze of lime
   Salt
1 *chicken, about 2½ pounds, poached or boiled in water to which several bay leaves, peppercorns, and allspice berries have been added; shredded.*
2 *hard-cooked eggs, sliced or cut into wedges*
5 *to 8 Greek-style olives*

2 *tablespoons cilantro leaves*
2 *fresh red jalapeños, seeded and thinly cut into long strips*

1. Sauté onion and garlic in olive oil until onion is limp. Add bread, chicken broth, and salsa or jalapeños. Cook until bread breaks up and sauce thickens a little, about 5 minutes.
2. Stir in peanut butter and lime juice; taste for seasoning; salt to taste.
3. Add shredded chicken and warm through. Serve immediately, garnished with egg slices, olives, cilantro, and red pepper strips.

Szechuan Chicken with Eggplant ▸▸▸

China   *Serves 4 as part of a multicourse Chinese meal*

It is said that the Szechuanese lavish chiles on all their dishes because they believe them to have aphrodisiac qualities. The chiles may not inflame other desires, but they do arouse the passion to eat. This is a rich dish of stir-fried eggplant and chicken, crunchy with peanuts and aromatic with chopped green onions. The basis of the sauce is a purchased Chinese preparation, fermented chile paste with fermented soy beans; if it is unavailable, garlic-chile paste can be substituted. The flavor will be different, but it will still be delicious and hot. Serve with steamed spinach to balance the richness of the dish, and crusty bread to scoop up the saucy bits.

2 *tablespoons soy sauce*
2 *tablespoons chicken broth*
2 *tablespoons sherry or brandy*
1 *tablespoon cornstarch or flour*
2 *large chicken breasts, boned, skinned, and cut into ½- to 1-inch diced pieces*
1 *tablespoon distilled white vinegar*
1 *tablespoon sugar*
¼ *cup vegetable oil*
2 *cloves garlic, chopped*
1 *piece ginger (½ inch), chopped (about 1 tablespoon)*
2 *tablespoons sesame oil*
½ *large eggplant, cut into strips ½ inch thick, ½ inch wide*
2 *tablespoons fermented chile paste with fermented beans*
½ *to ¾ cup dry roasted peanuts (preferably unsalted)*
3 *green onions, chopped*

1. Mix 1 tablespoon soy sauce, chicken broth, 1 tablespoon sherry, and corn-starch in a bowl. Add chicken; toss to coat. Set aside.
2. Combine remaining 1 tablespoon soy sauce and sherry with vinegar and sugar. Set aside.
3. Heat vegetable oil in wok or skillet. Drain chicken, then stir-fry with garlic and ginger until chicken is opaque. Remove with slotted spoon and set aside. Add 2 tablespoons sesame oil to wok and stir-fry eggplant strips.
4. Return chicken to wok; add soy sauce mixture, chile paste, and peanuts. Cook a minute or two longer, then turn out onto platter and garnish with green onions.

Variation: Use broccoli instead of eggplant.

Yassa Chicken 〉〉〉

Marinated, Baked Chicken

Africa   *Serves 4*

This African dish is really quite different from any other chicken dish I've found. The chicken is first marinated with a large amount of onions, lemon juice, and red chile, then broiled or grilled while the onions and marinade cook separately. The two are then combined for 10 minutes at the end of cooking to remarry their flavors. This is tart, hot, and very good.

Serve with rice and sliced yams and a green salad with Picante Vinaigrette.

> 1 *chicken, cut into serving pieces (about 2½ to 3 pounds)*
> 2 *onions, thinly sliced*
>   *Juice of 2 or 3 lemons*
> 2 *teaspoons (or more) hot red chile flakes*
> 1 *teaspoon salt*

1. Arrange chicken in bowl or pan; cover with onions, lemon juice, chile flakes, and salt. Mix together, cover and refrigerate overnight.
2. Broil or grill the chicken until almost done. At the same time, cook the onions and marinade over the grill in a pan or bake them in the oven (it will be hot from the broiler).
3. When chicken is almost done (about 20 minutes), combine it with the cooked onions and marinade and let them finish cooking together.

Thai Chicken
with Basil and Mint ▶▶▶

Thailand   *Serves 4*

I've always adored basil in all its traditional guises—in pesto, with sun-dried tomatoes, as a pizza topping, in *soupe au pistou*. In Thai food, however, it shows a different dimension—as in this dish, where the herb is paired with its cousin mint. The basil echoes the mint's sweetness but offers depth of flavor. This simple stir-fry has the bite and sweet-sour balance representative of Thai food.

Serve garnished with lime wedges and Thai Chile Flowers and accompanied by steamed rice or rice noodles (¼-inch-wide ones).

> 1 ½ *tablespoons flour*
>   2 *or 3 chicken breast halves, (about 6 to 8 ounces each)*
>   *boned, skinned, and cut into ½- to ¾-inch cubes*
>   2 *tablespoons brandy*
>   2 *tablespoons soy sauce*
>   2 *to 3 red jalapeños, chopped*
>   1 *tablespoon vinegar*
>   1 *tablespoon sugar*
> ½ *teaspoon sereh powder (powdered lemon grass)*
>   2 *tablespoons vegetable oil*
>   4 *to 5 shallots*
>   *Juice of ½ lime*
> ¼ *cup chopped basil leaves*
> ¼ *cup fresh mint leaves*
> ¼ *cup cilantro leaves*
>   2 *to 3 tablespoons coarsely chopped peanuts*
>   4 *lime wedges as garnish*
>   *Thai Chile Flowers*

1. Sprinkle flour over chicken; toss with brandy and 1 tablespoon soy sauce. Set aside.
2. For sauce mixture, combine chiles, vinegar, sugar, sereh powder, and remaining soy sauce. Set aside.
3. Stir-fry chicken and shallots in oil just until chicken turns white but is not cooked through.

4. Pour sauce mixture over chicken and cook over high heat for a moment or two until sauce thickens. Squeeze lime over chicken and sauce.
5. Top with basil, mint, cilantro, and chopped peanuts. Garnish with lime wedges and Thai Chile Flowers.

Recommended Wine: Enjoy a slightly sweet Gewürztraminer from California or Washington state or a dry Alsatian Gewürztraminer.

Meat

We're tending to eat less meat these days, and when we do include it in our diet, we want interesting, zesty dishes. A large, unadorned steak with potatoes is less appealing, to me at least, than a small steak accompanied by a fresh hot salsa and warm, soft tortillas.

Meat both supports and requires more hot spicing than do poultry or vegetables. Where more delicate foods are overwhelmed by fiery flavors, meat is only enhanced. Unlike poultry, eggs, or vegetables, different meats have different affinities for spices—lamb and curry blend, or beef and paprika, for example.

For many reasons—religious, aesthetic, agricultural—not all cuisines eat all meats. Lamb is beloved in the Middle East, not only because sheep are easier to raise in the arid desert than cows, but also because of the Moslems' and Jews' dietary proscription against the flesh of the pig. Beef is seldom found in an Indian curry because of the Hindu adoration of the cow. In Mexico and the Caribbean, goat is a popular meat—one most North Americans are not eager to try.

Whatever your favorite meat, try spicing it liberally with chiles, mustard, or horseradish, and you'll find yourself eating smaller amounts and enjoying it more.

Braised Lamb and Vine Leaves in Tomato Sauce ♪

Balkans, Middle East   *Serves 4*

I once lived next to eight acres of wild grapes. In the summer and fall we gorged on grape sweets of all kinds, put up jam and preserves, and even produced a little homemade wine. In early spring, before the budding of fruit, the young leaves were extremely tender and perfect for cooking or preserving in brine. I filled large baskets to overflowing with the tangy leaves from the uncultivated vineyard. In addition to stuffing the leaves at least fifty different ways, I found that they added an unusual flavor to soups and stews. The idea was not as original as it was delicious; grape leaves are occasionally simmered with lamb and tomatoes throughout the Balkans and Middle East.

Since this recipe is highly seasoned, serve with simple steamed rice and a bowl of cool yogurt. Accompany with a plate of cucumber wedges, green onions, and leaves of butter lettuce. Don't forget to offer some pickled chiles or other hot condiment.

3	to 4 ounces shelled pine nuts
1½	pounds boned lamb shoulder, cut into 1-inch cubes
1	tablespoon olive oil
6	cloves garlic, chopped
3	small dried red chiles
10	to 15 fresh grape leaves (or use about ⅓ of an 8-ounce jar; be sure to rinse well to rid the leaves of salty brine)
1½	teaspoons cinnamon
1	teaspoon cumin
¾	teaspoon Curry Powder or Middle Eastern Spice Mixture
½	cup raisins
2	cups tomato sauce
1	onion, sliced
	Pinch of sugar
	Squeeze of ½ lemon
	Salt to taste (omit if using brined leaves)

1. Toast pine nuts in an ungreased skillet until lightly browned. Set aside.
2. Sauté lamb in olive oil; add garlic and chiles and cook a minute or two longer.
3. Add the rest of the ingredients as well as the reserved pine nuts. Cover and simmer for about 1½ hours, or until meat is very tender. Serve with steamed rice.

Advance Preparation: This may be prepared a day or two in advance and reheated to serve. A little extra water may be added if the sauce has become too thick.

Recommended Wine: Drink a medium- to full-bodied rich and fruity Cabernet, or a slightly sweet Gewürztraminer or California Riesling.

Dubu Jjim

Stuffed Tofu

Korea

Serves 4 as an appetizer,
or 2 as a main course

Korean cuisine is hearty and very spicy. The basis of the diet—rice, bean sprouts, cabbage, seafood, and beef—is liberally seasoned with sesame oil, garlic, and chile. The number one condiment is kimchee, a pickle of cabbage and other seasonal vegetables fired with a hefty amount of cayenne. Kimchee is eaten at almost every meal and sometimes combined with other foods, as in *bab kimchee:* cooked rice with shredded pork, chopped garlic, green onions, and lots of kimchee. It's available bottled in Oriental groceries and in many supermarkets.

The Koreans also eat quite a bit of tofu. This dish is a delicious example of the creamy tofu absorbing the lively flavors of the other ingredients. Makes a zesty first course, or serve as a main course with steamed rice and kimchee.

> 2 *tablespoons sesame seeds*
> 6 *ounces lean ground beef*
> ¼ *cup chopped cilantro*
> 2 *green onions, chopped*
> 2 *cloves garlic, chopped*
> 4 *tablespoons sesame oil*
> 3 *tablespoons soy sauce*
> 1 *piece ginger (½ inch), grated*
> 1 *teaspoon cayenne*
> ½ *pound firm tofu*
> 1 *tablespoon water*
> 1 *tablespoon sugar*

1. Toast sesame seeds in ungreased skillet until golden brown. Set aside.
2. Mix ground beef with cilantro, green onions, garlic, 1 tablespoon sesame oil, 1 tablespoon soy sauce, ginger, and cayenne. Set aside.
3. Cut tofu into 8 slices, 3-by-5 inches, ½ inch thick. Sauté in 3 tablespoons sesame oil, taking care not to break apart tofu.
4. Spread meat mixture over tofu. Turn the small parcels over so that they are meat side down in the pan. Cook for 5 minutes.
5. Mix together 2 tablespoons soy sauce, 1 tablespoon water, and 1 tablespoon sugar. Pour over meat and tofu; cook until sauce evaporates. Serve sprinkled with toasted sesame seeds.

Variation:

Gochu Jeon (Korean stuffed peppers or chiles)

4   *whole California or Anaheim chiles, stems intact, but slit and seeds removed*
    Meat mixture from above recipe
3   *tablespoons flour*
2   *eggs, beaten*
3   *tablespoons sesame oil*
2   *tablespoons soy sauce*
1   *tablespoon vinegar*

Stuff each chile with one-fourth of the meat mixture. Dredge edges where the meat shows in flour, then in egg. Fry in sesame oil. Dip in sauce made of the soy sauce and vinegar.

Variation: Gaji Jjim
Substitute ½-inch-thick eggplant slices for the tofu.

Lamb and Eggplant Tajine ♪

Casserole of Sautéed Eggplant Slices with Roasted Lamb

Morocco   *Serves 4*

The creamy richness of eggplant pairs with tender, spicy lamb in this Marrakesh-inspired dish. Crunchy almonds, hard-cooked egg, and pungent cilantro (you could substitute parsley) add textural interest and accent the lamb and eggplant's smooth flavor.

Serve with Rudjak, Couscous Fassi, and accompany with a small bowl of Harissa for extra heat.

2   *onions, thinly sliced*
5   *cloves garlic, chopped*
3   *tablespoons olive oil*
1½   *teaspoons cumin*
1   *teaspoon paprika*
½   *teaspoon Ras Al Hanout*
1   *slice (¼ inch thick) ginger, chopped (or use ¼ teaspoon dried)*

½ cup cilantro, chopped
½ to 1 teaspoon Harissa or commercial garlic-chile paste
¼ teaspoon powdered saffron (or a pinch saffron threads)
dissolved in 2 tablespoons warm water
2 pounds boneless shoulder of lamb, cut into 1-inch chunks
1½ cups beef broth
Juice of 1 large or 2 small lemons
1 medium-sized eggplant
¼ to ½ cup vegetable oil, olive oil, or mixture
Salt
¼ cup toasted almonds (if salted, rub off excess salt)
2 hard-cooked eggs, peeled and quartered

1. Sauté onion and garlic in olive oil until softened; add cumin, paprika, Ras Al Hanout, ginger, ¼ cup cilantro, Harissa, and saffron. Remove from heat and set aside.
2. Place meat in baking dish (about 3 quarts in size). Pour onion mixture over meat, along with broth and half the lemon juice. Cover and place in 350° F. oven for 1 to 1½ hours, or until meat is very tender. Liquid should be saucy; add a little water if all liquid has evaporated. Skim off fat.
3. Slice eggplants ¼ to ½ inch thick (see note at end of Eggplant with Keema recipe). Brown in skillet in ¼ to ½ cup oil.
4. Arrange cooked eggplant slices in wide, shallow casserole or baking dish. Top with lamb so that half the eggplant is covered by the meat and sauce, half the eggplant uncovered. (This gives a nice contrast of texture of the eggplant.) Turn heat up to 400° F. and return to oven to brown meat and meld flavors, about 15 to 20 minutes. Squeeze remaining lemon juice over meat to taste, and season with salt to taste if needed. Serve immediately, garnished with almonds, hard-cooked eggs, and remaining cilantro.

Advance Preparation: Lamb may be baked, eggplant fried and the two combined several hours to 1 day ahead of time. Heat in 375° F. oven for 30 minutes or so, then season with lemon juice, garnish, and serve immediately.

Ma Ho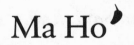

Spicy Ground Meat Presented on Pineapple Slices

Thailand   *Serves 4 as part of a larger meal*

The English name for Ma Ho is "Galloping Horses." Why it's called this I do not know, but the idea of combining fresh fruit with spicy fried meat is as intriguing to me as the name. While the recipe calls for serving the meat mixture atop small wedges of fresh pineapple, for a festive presentation try serving each person half a pineapple shell, hollowed out with the fronds left on, filled with spicy meat, pineapple chunks, and steamed rice. Garnish with fresh mint leaves. Traditionally, the topping for Ma Ho is simpler: ground pork cooked with garlic, chiles, fish sauce, and sugar. I like the way the more complex sauce binds together the sweet, tart, and hot flavors of the dish.

½ *(approximately) medium-sized, sweet pineapple, peeled*
1 *tablespoon sesame oil*
8 *ounces ground pork*
5 *cloves garlic, chopped*
1 *yellow wax pepper or jalapeño, thinly sliced*
1 *serrano, thinly sliced*
2 *tablespoons hoisin sauce*
2 *tablespoons sugar*
1 *tablespoon white distilled vinegar*
 Cayenne pepper to taste
¼ *cup toasted peanuts*
½ *cup cilantro, chopped*
¼ *fresh mint leaves, chopped*

1. Cut pineapple crosswise into about 4 slices, each about ½ to ¾ inches thick. Cut each slice into 4 to 6 wedges. Set aside.
2. Heat sesame oil in wok; add pork, garlic, and peppers and sauté until meat loses its pink color. Stir in hoisin sauce, sugar, vinegar, cayenne, and peanuts. Cook about 5 minutes; remove from heat and stir in half the cilantro.
3. Mound a tablespoon or so of filling onto each pineapple wedge; garnish with remaining cilantro and mint. Serve immediately.

Gulasz Wieprzowy ❯

Pork and Sauerkraut Goulash

Poland   *Serves 4*

This Eastern European stew is flavored with hot paprika and sauerkraut; it's rich and tangy, with just enough gustatory heat to warm your lips. Enjoy on a blustery winter's evening instead of turning up the thermostat. This Polish dish of Hungarian extraction is usually not so spicy, but my version turns a tasty dish into an exciting one. Accompany with noodles, a salad of chopped onion, green pepper, and cucumber, and hearty black bread.

1 ½   *pounds pork butt or shoulder, cut into ¾-inch cubes*
½   *cup flour for dredging*
¼   *cup vegetable oil*
4   *onions, coarsely chopped*
5   *to 6 cloves garlic, coarsely chopped*
½   *green pepper, chopped*
2   *tablespoons sweet paprika (use Hungarian if possible)*
2   *tablespoons hot paprika (if not available, substitute*
   1 tablespoon sweet paprika mixed with ¾ teaspoon
   cayenne pepper, or to taste)
2 ½   *cups chicken broth*
¾   *cups chopped tomatoes (canned is O.K.)*
4   *cups sauerkraut, rinsed with water and squeezed dry*
1   *celery root (about 1 ¼ pounds), peeled and diced*
   Tiny pinch of sugar
1   *or 2 bay leaves*
   Salt and freshly ground black pepper
1   *pint sour cream, for garnish*
2   *to 3 tablespoons chopped parsley, for garnish*

1. Dredge meat with flour. Heat oil in skillet or wok; when hot, brown the meat over medium-high heat. Remove with slotted spoon and set aside.
2. In pan with oil from cooking the meat, sauté onion, garlic, and green pepper until onion is soft. Add both sweet and hot paprikas; cook for a minute or two longer.
3. Combine meat with onion mixture in large saucepan; add broth, tomatoes, sauerkraut, celery root, pinch sugar, bay leaves, and salt and pepper to taste. Cover and simmer gently for 1½ to 2 hours, or until meat is tender. Serve hot, garnished with a dollop of sour cream to help put out the fire, and a sprinkling of fresh parsley.

Advance Preparation: A great dish to make the day before!

Braised Veal and Sweetbreads in Chile Sauce 🌶

Mexico   *Serves 4*

Both veal and sweetbreads are light, delicate meats, so it is surprising how delicious they are braised in chile sauce. The sauce is elegant and understated, but distinctly chile-accented. While the dish is easy to prepare, the sweetbreads do need a little attention: they must be soaked, blanched, and pressed to be tender.

Serve accompanied by crusty bread and Pico de Gallo or salsa of choice; to drink, a Sauvignon Blanc.

> 1   *pound sweetbreads*
> 1   *onion, chopped*
> 4   *cloves garlic, chopped*
> 2   *tablespoons olive oil*
> 1 ½ *pounds veal, cut into 1- to 2-inch chunks*
> 1   *to 2 poblanos, roasted, peeled, and cut into strips*
> 1 ½ *cups white wine such as Pinot Blanc or white Burgundy*
> 1 ½ *to 2 cups Basic Chile Sauce (containing at least half*
>   *anchos)*
>   *Salt*
> ¼   *cup cilantro leaves as garnish*
>   *Squeeze of lime juice (optional)*

1. Several hours to a day ahead of time: Soak sweetbreads in cold water for 1 to 2 hours; transfer to saucepan and boil for a minute or two. Rinse with cold running water. Pull off the tough, rubbery membranes that surround and cling to the sweetbreads.
2. Place a clean towel on a cutting board or cookie sheet. Lay out sweetbreads and cover with another towel. Place another board or cookie sheet on top and a heavy weight on top of that. Let stand for at least 2 hours, overnight if desired.
3. Sauté onion and garlic in olive oil until onion is limp. Add veal and poblanos and cook a few more minutes. Pour in wine and chile sauce.
4. Simmer on top of stove (or braise, covered, in 350° F. preheated oven) for 1½ hours, or until meat is tender and sauce is rich and complex.
5. Slice pressed sweetbreads into pieces the size of the veal and add to the veal-chile mixture. Return to stovetop or oven and cook another 20 to 30 minutes; season with salt to taste. Garnish with a few leaves of cilantro and a squeeze of lime if desired. Serve immediately.

Zuni Lamb,
Green Chile, and Hominy Stew ❱❱

United States   *Serves 4*

The Zuni Indians of the Southwest were cultivating crops a thousand years before the arrival of the Europeans. From them comes this unusual dish. It's easy to imagine this stew simmering in a clay pot over an open fire. The combination of chiles gives complexity and depth; each chile creates a slightly different layer of flavor.

Serve with Sopaipillas or with soft flour tortillas, breaking off pieces for dipping into the stew or wrapping up bits of meat. For an authentic regional flavor, serve with blue corn tortillas.

1 *yellow onion, coarsely chopped*
4 *or 5 cloves garlic, chopped*
2 *tablespoons vegetable oil*
1 *teaspoon oregano*
1½ *teaspoons cumin*
1 *pound lamb shoulder chops or stew meat, cut into 1½-inch chunks*
  Flour for dredging
3 *large chiles (choose either California, poblano, or combination; I usually use 1 poblano, 1 green bell, and 1 roasted jalapeño)*
3 *cups beef or chicken broth*
2½ *cups canned white hominy*
¼ *cup chopped cilantro*
2 *tablespoons New Mexico chile powder, or other medium-mild chile powder (or substitute ½ cup Basic Chile Sauce)*
4 *or 5 California chiles, roasted, seeded, and peeled, coarsely chopped (or substitute 6-ounce can diced mild green chiles)*
  Salt and freshly ground black pepper

1. Sauté onion and garlic in oil; add oregano and cumin.
2. Dust lamb with flour, then add to pot with onions and brown lightly.
3. Add 3 large chiles, broth, hominy, cilantro, and chile powder or sauce; simmer for 1½ to 2 hours, or until meat is fork-tender. A few minutes before

serving, add the diced green chiles and salt and pepper to taste. Since lamb can be fatty, skim the surface of any grease.

Advance Preparation: As with most stews, this is even better made a day ahead of time.

Lamb and Cashews with Orzo »

India/Mediterranean   *Serves 4*

I concocted this dish one day when there were several leftover rare lamb chops languishing in the refrigerator, as well as a bowl of cold cooked orzo, the Italian rice-shaped pasta. I tossed Indian spices into the Mediterranean orzo, added the lamb, and as an afterthought stirred in some chutney, as an English cook might. Somehow this blend of heterogeneous ingredients works, making a warming, colorful, delicious dish.

Serve with salsa of choice for more heat, and a cooling mixed green salad.

½ to ⅔ *cup raw cashew nuts*
1 ½ *tablespoons olive oil*
1 *tablespoon cumin*
3 *cooked lamb chops (on the rare side, if possible), boned and cut into chunks or slices*
3 *cloves garlic, chopped*
Salt
½ *to 1 teaspoon turmeric*
1 *piece ginger (¼ inch thick), chopped*
2 *cups cooked orzo*
3 *tablespoons mango chutney*
1 *to 2 tablespoons raisins or currants*
3 *tablespoons plain yogurt*
2 *tablespoons medium-hot salsa*

1. Sauté cashews in ½ tablespoon olive oil until lightly browned. Add 2 teaspoons cumin and cook a few moments longer, until cumin and cashews are toasted and fragrant. Set aside.
2. In 2 teaspoons of oil, sauté lamb chunks with garlic and rest of cumin. Sprinkle with salt to taste and set aside.

3. Pour the remaining teaspoon of oil into pan and add turmeric and ginger. Toss in orzo, combining with the spice mixture. Return lamb and cashews to pan and stir in chutney, raisins, yogurt, and salsa. Serve immediately.

Estofado "

Braised Beef and Peppers

Mexico   *Serves 4 to 6*

Meat and peppers braise together in this south-of-the-border pot roast of tender, savory meat. Enjoy shreds wrapped up in flour on corn tortillas with salsa and/or Pico de Gallo, avocado and tomato slices, and sour cream. Or try the Estofado served alongside steamed rice and firm, sliced bananas sautéed in butter.

> 1 *green bell pepper, sliced*
> 1 *red bell pepper, sliced (optional)*
> 2 *poblanos, seeded and sliced*
> 2 *tomatoes, chopped*
> 5 *to 6 jalapeños, sliced*
> 1 *cup cilantro, chopped*
> 5 *cloves garlic, chopped*
> 1 *onion, chopped*
> 2 *bay leaves*
> 1½ *teaspoons cumin*
> *Salt to taste*
> 1 *chuck roast (about 2½ pounds)*
> 1 *cup beef broth*
> *Hot salsa of choice*

Place half the vegetables and seasonings in bottom of baking pan; top with chuck roast, then top with rest of vegetables and broth. Cover with foil and bake in 350° F. preheated oven for about 2 hours, or until very tender, adding more liquid if needed to keep meat from burning. Remove foil and bake 30 minutes longer. Serve immediately, with salsa on the side.

Advance Preparation: May be made a day or two ahead of time.

Fajitas "

Grilled Steak Strips Wrapped in Tortillas

Texas, Northern Mexico   *Serves 4 to 6*

The name Fajitas means "little belts." This refers to the cut of meat used, the skirt steak, which "belts" the belly of the cow.

Fajitas originated on the cattle ranches near the Texas-Mexico border and soon spread to the cities, where it has become very popular. Lately, every Texan I meet wants to share his or her secret of Fajitas with me. There is no secret, however; this simple Tex-Mex dish derives its flavor from fresh ingredients rather than any special technique. Much like the Greek *souvlaki* or Middle Eastern *shwarma*, in which grilled meats are tucked into pita bread, Fajitas consists of thin strips of grilled meat wrapped in a soft flour tortilla. It is then topped with crunchy Pico de Gallo and creamy guacamole, doused with fiery salsa, and rolled up. That's all there is to it. By the time you've finished one, another piece of meat is sizzling on the grill, ready to eat.

You could accompany this with corn in its husks cooked on top of the grill, Mexican-style beans or *frijoles refritos*, and lots of icy beer.

       1 *beef skirt steak, 1 to 1½ pounds*
          Juice of 3 limes (about ½ cup)
      ¼ *cup tequila*
       6 *cloves garlic, chopped*
       2 *serrano chiles, thinly sliced*
      ¼ *cup cilantro, finely chopped*
       1 *teaspoon salt*
     12 *flour tortillas*
       1 *recipe Pico de Gallo*
          Salsa of choice
          Guacamole (recipe follows)

1. Cut steak into 3- to 4-inch pieces. (This is for marinating; they will be grilled in these pieces and sliced as desired after cooking.)
2. Combine steak with lime juice, tequila, garlic, serranos, cilantro, and salt. Cover tightly and let marinate in the refrigerator for at least 2 hours.
3. Drain; discard marinade. Grill meat over hot coals (mesquite is authentic) 3 to 4 minutes per side. Slice as desired and wrap up in tortillas. Offer bowls of Pico de Gallo, salsa, and guacamole for each person to add as desired.

Variation: Tougher yet flavorful cuts such as flank steak may be used. The meat should be sliced thinly first, then pounded to break down connective tissues, much like scallopini. The thin, pounded pieces are then grilled over the barbecue.

Guacamole

 2 avocados
½ onion, finely chopped
  Juice of ½ to 1 lemon or lime
½ tomato, chopped
 1 jalapeño, chopped or thinly sliced
  Salt

Peel avocado; coarsely mash with fork. Add other ingredients and season with salt to taste.

Rendang *))*

Southeast Asian Curried Meat

Malaysia   *Serves 4*

This simply prepared Malaysian curry simmers meat in spiced coconut milk, which is then boiled down at the end of cooking time to form a thick sauce. If eaten while the sauce is still soupy, it is called *kalio*. Occasionally, hard-cooked eggs will be added to a *kalio* during the last 15 minutes of simmering. Rendang or *kalio* should be served with steamed rice; accompany with a saucy vegetable and fiery Sambal Olek or Sambal Trassi.

  1 onion, chopped
  6 cloves garlic, chopped
  3 or 4 jalapeños, seeded and thinly sliced
  1 piece ginger (1 inch long), peeled and chopped
  2 tablespoons vegetable oil
  2 tablespoons ground coriander
  1 teaspoon turmeric
  1 bay leaf
1½ pounds beef stew meat, cut into 1-inch cubes
  3 cups coconut milk
  2 bouillon cubes

1. Sauté onion, garlic, chiles, and ginger in oil until onion is softened. Add spices and meat, raising heat for a few minutes to brown the meat.
2. Add coconut milk and bouillon; simmer over low heat until meat is fork-tender, about 2 hours.
3. Turn heat to high and cook sauce down to a thick pastelike coating on the meat. This may take 15 to 20 minutes, depending on sauce consistency.

Advance Preparation: This may be prepared a day ahead; in fact, I think it's better.

Texas Chili Con Carne ""

United States   *Serves 6*

Texas chili always contains coarsely ground or cut beef, garlic, cumin, and onions; it even allows tomatoes and occasionally beans, something their neighbors in New Mexico frown upon. (In New Mexico, chili means beef or pork stewed in either fresh green or dried red chile sauce.) Texans claim to have originated chili, sometime toward the end of the nineteenth century, by including the wild-growing chile pepper in the fill-the-stomach stews prepared for the cowboys.

Chile devotees are a pretty dedicated bunch. Each chili lover is convinced that his or her bowl of red is the best. Often the recipes contain some rather unorthodox ingredients, some of which can be alarming: consider armadillo meat, dried red ants, or even cigarette ashes. There are no exotic ingredients in this great chili, however; just good quality basics, a generous hand with the seasonings, and a nice long simmer.

    2   cups boiling beef broth
    3   New Mexico chiles
    3   ancho chiles
    3   pounds beef chuck, coarsely ground or cut into ½-inch
        cubes
    3   tablespoons oil (a true chili aficionado would use lard or
        beef suet)
    2   onions, chopped
    5   to 8 cloves garlic, chopped
    2   tablespoons cumin
    1   tablespoon oregano leaves
    ½   teaspoon cinnamon
    5   serrano chiles, thinly sliced

2 large (16-ounce) cans tomato sauce
3½ to 4 cups chopped tomatoes
2 cups beer
Salt
Cayenne pepper
4 cups cooked pinto or red kidney beans (canned is fine)

Garnishes:
Salsa of choice
1 onion, chopped
5 to 10 pickled jalapeños
1 cup shredded cheddar cheese
2 cups shredded lettuce
2 cups sour cream
1 avocado, peeled, pitted, and diced
Crisp fried tortillas or tortilla chips

1. Pour boiling broth over ancho and New Mexico chiles. Cover and let stand for 1 hour. Remove stems, tear chiles into 1-inch pieces, and puree in blender or processor to a smooth paste, adding broth gradually to make a sauce. (Any unused broth should go into chili.) Set chile puree aside.
2. Brown meat on all sides in oil. Add onions, garlic, and spices and cook until onion is translucent.
3. Add chile puree, serranos, tomato sauce, tomatoes, and beer. Simmer uncovered for 1½ to 2 hours, then taste for seasonings. Add salt and cayenne to taste.
4. Serve alongside beans and an assortment of garnishes: salsa, chopped onion, pickled jalapeños, cheddar cheese, lettuce, sour cream, avocado, and tortilla chips, so that each diner can choose his or her own accompaniments.

Pork and Poblano Sauté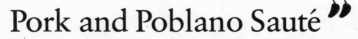

Caribbean   *Serves 4*

This Caribbean-inspired dish underscores the old saying, simplest is best. What could be simpler than a sauté of meat and peppers? It's a special combination, though: the richness of the meat next to the fresh kick of poblano, accented by cumin, dried chile powder, and a generous squeeze of lime. Serve with Spicy Black Beans, rice, and a hot sauce such as Molho de Pimenta e Limao or Mango Hot Condiment.

    2 *tablespoons olive oil*
    1 *pound pork tenderloin, thinly sliced (⅛ inch thick)*
    1 *teaspoon New Mexico chile powder*
    1 *teaspoon cumin*
   ½ *teaspoon oregano leaves*
    3 *poblano chiles, roasted, peeled, and cut thinly*
    4 *cloves garlic, chopped*
       Salt and pepper
    1 *lime, cut into wedges*
   ¼ *cup cilantro (optional)*

1. Sprinkle pork with chile powder and cumin. Heat oil in large skillet or wok; sauté pork in severed small batches until lightly browned and no longer pink inside.
2. Return cooked meat to pan, then add poblano strips and garlic and cook together a minute or so. Season with salt and pepper to taste and a squeeze of half the lime. Garnish with cilantro and remaining lime wedges. Serve immediately.

Variation: Beef may be used instead of pork.

Shawarbit "

Lamb and Red Lentil Stew with Spinach

Middle East   *Serves 4*

This is one of those hearty, sustaining dishes; tender lamb simmers in a thick sauce of spinach and pureed lentils fragrant with spice and tart from lemon juice. In addition to a stew, Shawarbit may also be prepared as a soup by adding several cups more broth.

    A typical Arabian dish, Shawarbit is one I can imagine a tribe of Bedouins sharing underneath the desert night sky. Lamb is the favored meat throughout much of the Middle East, where sheep are the easiest animals to raise in the arid, often rocky, landscape. Instead of spinach, other greens such as chard or wild nettles could be added. While masoor dahl (red lentils) are my favorite for this dish because of their creamy, hearty, smooth flavor, any lentil (such as the familiar brown lentils, or any of the more exotic colored dahl available in Indian food stores) may be used. Allow long cooking time for the larger, tougher legumes.

    Serve topped with a spoonful of yogurt and accompanied by steamed rice, Yemenite Zhoog or hot sauce of choice.

   1 *pound lamb stew meat, cut into 1- or 2-inch chunks*
   3 *cups beef broth*
1 ½ *cups masoor dahl (red lentils)*
   4 *to 6 small dried red chiles, crumbled*
   2 *bunches fresh spinach, coarsely chopped (or substitute*
      1 package frozen)
   1 *onion, coarsely chopped*
   3 *or 4 cloves garlic, coarsely chopped*
   3 *tablespoons olive oil*
   1 *tablespoon Ras al Hanout (or substitute Curry Powder)*
  ¼ *cup lemon juice*
      Salt
   1 *cup yogurt*

1. Simmer lamb in broth for 1½ hours, or until meat is tender.
2. Pick over masoor dahl to check for any small stones (occasionally found in Middle Eastern lentils and rice). Add masoor dahl and red chiles to lamb stew and simmer another 40 minutes, until dahl forms a thick sauce.
3. Add spinach to lamb and lentils; continue to simmer.
4. Sauté onion and garlic in olive oil until onion is soft. Sprinkle Ras al Hanout over onion and garlic, cook a few minutes, then add to lamb-spinach-lentil mixture.
5. Stir in lemon juice and season to taste with salt if needed. Top each portion with a spoonful of yogurt and offer hot sauce of choice.

Advance Preparation: Any stage of this may be prepared a day or two in advance, as may the whole dish. In fact, the stew is best the second day.

Rawalpindi-Style Lamb ''

Pakistan   *Serves 4 generously*

The inhabitants of Pakistan are mostly Muslims, and there lamb is the favored meat. It is often spiced and roasted in a special oven called a tandoor from which it emerges tender and juicy. At other times it is simmered with spices. This dish incorporates both simmering and roasting; it is much like curry-flavored *carnitas,* the Mexican fork-tender chunks of spiced pork. The secret to the tenderness lies in simmering the meat, then roasting it in a spicy coating. You must choose a meat that has enough fat in its flesh to stay moist during the arduous cooking. It's an adaptable dish, dependent on the seasoning: spice pork with cumin and oregano for Mexican *carnitas,* flavor beef with peppers and paprika for Hungarian flavor, or choose this recipe for a taste of India. Serve with Borani Esfanaj and steamed rice. Offer Roasted Green Jalapeño Salsa as desired.

> 2 *pounds boneless lamb, cut into 1½-inch chunks*
> 1 *onion, chopped*
> 5 *whole cloves garlic*
> 1 *bay leaf*
> 5 *cloves garlic, chopped*
> 3 *jalapeños, sliced*
> 2 *tablespoons yogurt*
> 2 *teaspoons paprika*
> 2 *teaspoons cumin*
> 1 *teaspoon turmeric*
> ½ *teaspoon ground ginger, or 1 slice (¼ inch thick), chopped*
> ½ *teaspoon cinnamon*
> ½ *teaspoon hot chile paste such as Ají or Berberé, or cayenne pepper*
> *Salt*
> 1½ *tablespoons vegetable oil*

1. Place lamb in pot with enough water to cover. Add onion, 5 whole cloves garlic, and bay leaf and simmer until tender, 2½ hours or so. Remove lamb from liquid (save cooking liquid to use later in soup).
2. Toss cooked, drained lamb chunks with chopped garlic, jalapeños, yogurt, spices, chile paste, and salt to taste. Dribble with vegetable oil. Bake in preheated 400° F. oven until crispy and fork-tender, about 30 to 45 minutes.

Kofta Kabob ❯❯

Seasoned Ground Meat Patties

Middle East, India   *Serves 4*

Ground meat, strongly seasoned with aromatic spices and formed into patties, is enjoyed throughout India and the Middle East. It is known as Kofta, Kefta, or Kufta, depending upon geographical location. Either lamb or beef may be used, and the patties may be fried, grilled, or simmered in a rich, fragrant sauce.

It's a wonderful alternative to hamburger—just as easy to put together but hot, spicy, and exciting. I vary Kofta Kabob each time I prepare it: leftovers such as cooked rice or thick dahl are likely to find their way in, and sometimes I add raisins and/or freshly chopped mint. Serve with steamed rice, tuck into soft pita bread, and dress with a spoonful of yogurt and a salad of chopped tomato, cucumber, and raw onion. Accompany with Yemenite Zhoog or Roasted Green Jalapeño Salsa.

> 1 *pound ground lamb or beef*
> 1 *to 2 slices of bread, soaked in water and squeezed dry (or*
>   *½ cups fresh bread crumbs or cooked rice)*
> 3 *to 5 cloves garlic, chopped*
> ¼ *cup chopped cilantro or parsley*
> 2 *tablespoons plain yogurt*
> 1 *teaspoon cumin*
> 1 *teaspoon paprika*
> 1 *teaspoon Middle Eastern Spice Mixture (or Curry Powder)*
>   *Pinch cardamom powder or turmeric*
> 1 *teaspoon tomato paste*
> 1 *tablespoon hot salsa or to taste*
>   *Salt and freshly ground pepper*

1. Combine all ingredients and form into 6 loaf-shaped patties. Sprinkle with salt and pepper to taste.
2. Broil or fry patties to desired doneness, turning once. Serve immediately. Mixture may be a bit soft when shaping patties or removing them from pan; if so, just handle with care.

Advance Preparation: Meat mixture may be put together several hours before cooking.

Variation: This is an unusual method of preparing stuffed potatoes that I first tasted in the Arab quarter of the Old City of Jerusalem, at a courtyard table under a grape arbor. Allow 1 to 2 medium-sized boiling potatoes per person, boiled or steamed until tender yet firm. Hollow out the insides in a tunnel-like fashion, leaving about ¾ inch wall. (There is a tool available for hollowing out vegetables; it's long and sharp like a knife, but the blade is arched into a semitubular shape. A long, thick knife may also be used.) Fill the hollow in each potato with several tablespoons Kofta Kabob mixture; pack tightly. Place stuffed potatoes in shallow baking dish, drizzle with olive oil, and bake in 375° F. oven for 25 to 35 minutes, until potatoes are roasted golden brown and meat is cooked through.

Mediterranean Mini-Grill ▶▶▶

Mediterranean	*Serves 4*

Most nationalities have a variation of marinated, grilled meats. In Russia, *shashlik* is fragrant and tart from pomegranate juice; in Greece, *souvlaki* is marinated in olive oil and lemon, then grilled and served rolled up with salad in soft pita bread. In Indonesia, meat or chicken *saté* is grilled and served along with a spicy peanut sauce and cool cucumber chunks to put out the fire. The Turks skewer marinated halibut cubes, alternating the fish with whole bay leaves. Whatever you choose to grill, marinating in garlic, olive oil, lemon, and a healthy dash of cayenne gives a juicy, sizzling kabob.

Serve accompanied by crusty bread and a salad of shredded cabbage, sliced cucumber, tomatoes, and chunks of feta cheese, sprinkled with oregano and dressed with olive oil and lemon juice.

> 2 *hot Italian sausages*
> 1 *tender steak such as rib or sirloin (about 8 ounces)*
> 2 *chicken breasts, boned (8 to 10 ounces total)*
> ⅔ *cup olive oil*
> ⅔ *cup lemon juice (or juice of 2 to 3 lemons)*
> 2½ *teaspoons cayenne pepper*
> 6 *cloves garlic, chopped*
> 1 *green bell pepper*
> 1 *red bell pepper*
> ½ *red onion*
> 12 *to 16 bamboo skewers*
> *Salt to taste*
> *Lemon wedges*

1. Simmer sausages in water for 7 to 10 minutes, or until slightly undercooked (cut into one to see if it's still slightly pink inside). Drain, slice ¾ inch thick, place in bowl, and set aside.
2. Cut steak and chicken into ¾-inch chunks and place each in separate bowl. Pour one-third of the olive oil into each of the three bowls. Add lemon juice, cayenne pepper, and garlic equally to each bowl. Cover bowls with plastic wrap and set in refrigerator to marinate overnight.
3. Cut vegetables into approximately ¾-inch chunks. Thread a piece of red pepper onto each skewer, then follow with a piece of chicken, a chunk of onion, a slice of sausage, and so on until all ingredients are used up.

4. Grill over an open fire if possible, or broil in broiler. Sprinkle with salt to taste and serve immediately, garnished with lemon wedges.

Burmese Pork, Potato, and Pea Curry ▶▶▶

Burma   *Serves 4*

Burmese curries are distinguished by their method of preparing curry paste: onion, garlic, ginger, chile, and turmeric (occasionally other spices as well) are pounded together (or ground in a blender or food processor, for westerners), then slowly fried in sesame oil until all moisture has evaporated from the mixture. The vegetable, meat, or fish is then added (along with broth or coconut milk if gravy is desired).

    Serve with steamed rice or rice noodles, a hot relish, and Thai Cabbage Salad.

1 onion, cut into quarters
5 cloves garlic
1 piece ginger (¾ inch thick), peeled and chopped
6 small dried red chiles, coarsely crumbled
1 teaspoon turmeric
1 teaspoon cumin
2 tablespoons sesame oil
2 stalks lemon grass, cut into 2-inch lengths
1 pound pork tenderloin, cut into 1-inch cubes
3 raw medium-sized boiling potatoes, peeled and cut into
   ¾-inch cubes
2 tablespoons soy sauce (or for authenticity, use fish sauce,
   Nuoc Nam)
1 cup fresh peas (or substitute frozen)
   Juice of ½ lemon

1. Puree onion, garlic, ginger, chiles, turmeric, and cumin in processor or blender.
2. Heat sesame oil in wok or heavy skillet. Add onion-spice mixture, reduce heat and cook slowly for 15 minutes, or until the oil separates from the solids. Stir in lemon grass, pork, potatoes, and soy sauce and continue cooking until potatoes are tender and pork no longer pink (about 15 to 20 minutes). Add peas and lemon juice and cook until peas are tender. Serve immediately.

Michoacan
Meat with Nopales ◢◢◢

Mexico   *Serves 4*

Tender chunks of beef simmer with slightly astringent nopales (cactus leaf) in this smoky chipotle-flavored stew. Michoacan is a lush region of central Mexico. Its cuisine reflects the abundant fresh produce. Cactus grows in profusion in this region, and the flesh of its leaves is eaten in salads, stews of all kinds, or scrambled with eggs. I find the unusual taste and texture of these cactus strips can be addictive.

Serve this stew in a bowl along with a stack of warm, soft tortillas to make tacos with, a bowl of freshly grated dry Monterey Jack or Parmesan cheese for sprinkling, and a side plate of jalapeño strips.

1½   *pounds round steak, cut into 1½-inch cubes*
      All-purpose flour, for dredging
  2   *tablespoons vegetable oil*
  2   *large onions, chopped*
  5   *cloves garlic, chopped*
  2   *tomatoes, chopped*
  3   *or 4 canned chipotle chiles, chopped (you can use a little of*
       the sauce from the can for extra heat and smoky flavor)
  1   *large nopale leaf, peeled and sliced ½ inch wide, boiled and*
       rinsed to rid it of its "slimy" juice (or use canned, about 10
       to 12 ounces, drained)
  3   *cups beef broth*

1. Dredge meat in flour, then brown in oil. Add onion and garlic and cook a few minutes longer.
2. Add tomatoes, chiles, nopale, and broth. Cover and simmer over a low heat for 2½ hours, or until meat is very tender. Skim off any fat that rises to the surface.

Breads and Pastries

Bread is the perfect accompaniment to hot foods. The starchy substance absorbs the chiles' volatile oils, bringing a sense of relief. Warm, soft corn or flour tortillas and crusty bread are several of the store-bought breads that are both delicious and efficacious, but I've included two other breads popular in the Southwestern United States: Navajo Fry Bread, made from fried bread dough, and Sopaipillas, similar cloudlike puffs of fried bread, dipped in honey and often eaten hot as a dessert.

In addition to being a bland counterpoint to hot cuisine, baked goods may be spicy themselves. Consider my variation on an Italian classic, Rosemary and Red Chile Focaccia with Garlic-Olive Oil Dipping Sauce; its heat emanates from crumbled small, hot chiles scattered throughout the dough. New Mexican Chile Bread spreads French bread with rich and spicy New Mexican chile-flavored butter. Pizza lovers should be sure to taste the Chèvre and Poblano Calzone, as well as the Indian version of spicy pizza called Keema Naan. They are both unusual, delicious versions of the familiar dough-based snack.

My recipe for empanadas uses filo dough, an unorthodox method but one that yields flaky, crisp pastry. Try filling it instead with finely chopped curried vegetables or with Keema and a fresh chutney for dipping.

In hot and spicy cuisines, breads and pastries are elevated to a status of their own.

Navajo Fry Bread and Sopaipillas

United States   *Yield: 4 to 6 rounds*

Fried discs of bread dough are one of the Navajos' culinary gifts to us. Though these are not hot at all, they are eaten throughout New Mexico accompanying chile stews, or smeared with chile paste as a snack. When the same bread is cut into triangles or squares, it is called Sopaipillas and dipped in honey, as a heat-quencher.

    1 ½ *cups unbleached flour*
      2 *teaspoons baking powder*
      1 *teaspoon salt*
      2 *tablespoons butter or shortening*
     ¼ *cup hot water (plus another 1 to 2 tablespoons if dough*
         seems dry)
         Vegetable oil for frying

1. Stir together flour, baking powder, and salt. Add butter and work into flour with a fork until the mixture resembles coarse meal.
2. Add water and knead for 5 minutes or so (adding another tablespoon or two if dough seems dry), then cover dough and let rest 15 minutes.
3. Heat oil in wok or deep skillet.
4. Roll out dough into 4 to 6 rounds, each about 4 inches in diameter and ¼ inch thick. Cut 3 slits in the center of each dough round and fry for 2 or 3 minutes on each side, until golden brown. Drain on paper towels and serve immediately. I like to serve these accompanied by Pico de Gallo.

Variation 1: For Sopaipillas, roll the dough out and, instead of rounds, cut into triangles measuring 3 inches at the widest part. Serve with salsa or honey.

Variation 2: For a New Mexico-style tostada, use Navajo Fry Bread and spread with hot refried beans topped with cheese and meat cooked in red chile sauce. Add shredded lettuce, jalapeños, cilantro, chopped onion, tomatoes, salsa, and sour cream.

Variation 3: Instead of a baking powder dough I sometimes use yeast dough, either left over from baking or commercial frozen (and defrosted). It has a fluffy, slightly chewy quality.

Chèvre and Poblano Calzone

Goat-Cheese-Filled Turnovers

Italy   *Serves 6*

Calzone is simply pizza dough folded into a turnover shape, then baked. The filling is inside instead of on top. The sophisticated flavor of chèvre elevates commonplace pizza to culinary heights, and the addition of thyme mixed into the dough is delicious and unusual. The strips of poblano chiles add a subtly warm accent; sprinkle with hot pepper flakes for an extra kick.

Dough

  1 *envelope dry yeast*
  1 *cup warm water*
  2 *tablespoons thyme (or ¼ cup fresh rosemary leaves, chopped)*
  3 *tablespoons olive oil*
  1 *teaspoon salt*
2½ *cups flour*

Sauce

  1 *onion, chopped*
  5 *cloves garlic, chopped*
 ½ *poblano chile, roasted, peeled, and sliced*
  2 *tablespoons olive oil*
 ½ *teaspoon thyme*
  3 *cups tomato sauce*
     Salt

Filling

  6 *to 8 ounces goat cheese (Montrachet, Lezay, California chèvre), sliced into ½-inch pieces*
  3 *to 5 cloves garlic, chopped*
  2 *poblano or Anaheim chiles, roasted, peeled, and sliced*
 10 *Greek-style or Moroccan Spiced Olives, pitted and halved*
  4 *to 6 ounces mozzarella, Monterey Jack, or Lappi cheese, sliced thinly*
  2 *to 3 tablespoons olive oil*

¼ to ½ cup freshly grated Parmesan
Red pepper flakes as desired

1. For dough, sprinkle yeast over warm water and let stand until dissolved. Add thyme, oil, and salt; gradually add 3 cups flour and combine until it holds together.
2. Knead on floured board until smooth, elastic, and no longer sticky. Cover with plastic wrap and leave in a warm place to rise for about 1 hour.
3. For sauce, sauté onion, garlic, and poblano in olive oil until onion is soft, then add thyme and tomato sauce. Season with salt to taste.
4. Punch down dough. Divide in half and shape each into a ball. Roll out into flat discs about 11 or 12 inches in diameter.
5. Place about half the goat cheese over half of each circle; top with garlic, chile slices, olives, mozzarella or other cheese, and drizzle with the olive oil. Fold over into a turnover shape and seal edges. Spread the top of each calzone with one-fourth of the sauce, then sprinkle on Parmesan cheese and the remaining olive oil. Bake in preheated 450° F. oven until dough is lightly browned, about 20 minutes. Cut into wedges and serve with extra sauce and red pepper flakes as desired.

Variation 1: Make into 6 individual calzones instead of 2 large ones.

Variation 2: For pizza, roll out dough and place on an oiled baking or cookie sheet. Top with sauce, then goat cheese, then garlic, poblano slices, thyme, and mozzarella or other cheese. Drizzle with olive oil, Parmesan, and red pepper flakes. Bake 15 to 25 minutes, or until crust is lightly browned and crispy.

Keema Naan

Indian-Style Pizza

India   *Serves 6*

Naan is the bread traditionally baked in the *tandoor*, or Indian oven. Keema is the Indian name for ground, spiced meat. Keema Naan is much like an Indian version of pizza, topped not with Parmesan cheese or dried chiles, but smeared with a relish of fresh, fragrant mint, cilantro, and jalapeño. Serve as part of an Indian-style buffet or as a first course.

1 pound purchased frozen bread dough, defrosted, or homemade Focaccia dough (omit the rosemary and chiles)
1 onion, chopped
4 cloves garlic, chopped
1 tablespoon vegetable oil

    1 *pound ground lamb or beef*
    2 *tablespoons paprika*
 1 ½ *teaspoons cumin*
   ½ *teaspoon cinnamon*
   ½ *teaspoon turmeric*
   ½ *teaspoon dried ginger*
   ½ *teaspoon Curry Powder*
    1 *tablespoon yogurt*
   ½ *to 1 teaspoon Ají or commercial garlic-chile paste*
   ½ *cup cilantro, chopped (substitute mint if desired)*
       Salt

1. Let bread dough rise in warm place until doubled, about 40 minutes.
2. Sauté onion and garlic in oil. Add meat and spices and cook until browned. Stir in yogurt, chile paste, and cilantro. Season with salt to taste.
3. Pinch off walnut-sized balls of dough and flatten into ½-inch-thick circles. Top each with a tablespoon or two of ground meat mixture. Arrange on greased baking sheet and bake in preheated 400° F. oven for 10 to 15 minutes, or until bread rounds are fully baked. Serve immediately, accompanied by fresh Mint Relish.

Fresh Mint Relish ▶▶▶

   ½ *cup mint leaves*
   ½ *cup cilantro leaves (or another ½ cup mint leaves)*
    1 *clove garlic, chopped*
    1 *fresh jalapeño, chopped*
   ½ *teaspoon sugar*
   ½ *teaspoon salt*
       Juice of ½ lime

Blend all ingredients in blender or processor.

New Mexican Chile Bread ▶

New Mexico   Serves 4 to 6

Despite any resemblance to ordinary garlic bread, this is a delicious, savory accompaniment to almost anything. The garlic, chile, and other flavorings melt into the warm bread, and the edges are crispy. The last time I prepared it, it was meant as an hors d'oeuvre, but we ate so much it became dinner—along with a bottle of Sauvignon Blanc!

> 3   cloves garlic
> ½   cup cilantro or parsley
> 1   green onion, chopped
> 2   to 3 tablespoons New Mexican Chile Powder (or combination with ancho)
> ½   cup (1 stick) unsalted butter
> 2   to 3 tablespoons olive oil
>   Salt
> 1   (1 pound) loaf French bread
> ½   cup freshly grated Parmesan cheese

1. Puree garlic in processor or blender. Add cilantro, green onion, and chile powder and process until finely chopped.
2. Add butter, olive oil, and salt to taste. Blend until smooth.
3. Split loaf of French bread in half lengthwise. Spread with chile butter; sprinkle with Parmesan cheese. Bake in preheated 400° F. oven for 10 to 15 minutes, or until edges are crisp and butter has melted into bread. Serve hot.

Variation: Instead of spreading on bread, spread the chile butter on corn that has been roasted over an open grill.

Gorditas

Tortilla Dough Cups Filled with Beans and Meat

Mexico   *Yield: 12 to 15*

Literally translated, Gorditas means "little fat ones." These are little bowls made from tortilla dough, deep-fried and filled with mashed beans, shredded meat, and fresh garnishes. Gorditas are only one of Mexico's snack foods called *antojitos,* or "little whims." Tacos, tostadas, and burritos are familiar *antojitos,* but there is an unlimited variety of these snacks, varying in shape, size, thickness of dough, type of filling, and so on. *Chalupas* are little boats of fried tortilla dough, filled with beans, meat, and salad. Quesadillas are made from tortillas or tortilla dough, folded over to enclose a slice of cheese. *Garnachas* are a variation of Gorditas from the Yucatan, where they are stuffed with black beans and garnished with onion. Serve these hot, accompanied by cold Mexican beer, and offer extra salsa.

1 ½ cups masa harina
2 ½ tablespoons shortening (lard is traditionally used)
1 ½ teaspoons New Mexico chile powder
 ½ teaspoon salt
 ¾ cup cold water
     Oil for deep-frying
 1 to 1 ½ cups refried beans (canned is O.K.)
 ¾ to 1 cup (approximately) shredded cooked chicken or other
     savory meat (or 1 or 2 chorizo sausages, fried and
     crumbled)
     Several pickled jalapeños, sliced
     Freshly grated Parmesan cheese
     Shredded lettuce
     Salsa of choice
     Sour cream
     Several radishes, sliced (optional)
     Thin raw onion slices (optional)
 1 to 2 tablespoons cilantro (optional)

1. Combine masa, shortening, chile powder, and salt using fork or food processor. Blend to make fine crumbs. Add water and work together to make dough.
2. Working one piece at a time, pull off large walnut-sized pieces of dough and shape each one with your fingers to make a bowl 2 to 3 inches in diameter and about ¼ to ½ inch thick, with a flat bottom. (These can also be formed in tiny tartlet pans; you can drop the whole little shell, tin and all, into the hot oil.) Cover shells with a damp cloth to keep them from becoming brittle. If masa becomes too dry as you are working with it, add a small amount of water.
3. Heat oil in wok or heavy skillet. Fry shells in hot oil several at a time until shells are lightly browned and crisp. Fill and serve immediately, or make a whole batch and keep hot in oven while you're preparing the rest.
4. If serving immediately, have the beans and meat warm. Place a spoonful of the beans into fried shell; top with a spoonful of meat, then several slices of jalapeño, a sprinkle of Parmesan cheese, a little shredded lettuce, salsa of choice, and a dollop of sour cream (plus radishes, onions, and cilantro if desired).

Advance Preparation: Make shells several hours to a day ahead of time. Fill with beans and meat and heat in 400° F. to 425° F. preheated oven. The advance preparation makes this a good dish for entertaining.

Variation 1: For a vegetarian Gordita, eliminate meat.

Variation 2: Substitute Spicy Black Beans for refried beans, and garnish with Cebollas en Escabeche.

Variation 3: Garnish with strip of smoky chipotle chile.

Filo-Dough Empanadas ❞

Pastries Filled with Spicy Ground Meat

Latin America, Spain   *Yield: approximately 40 pastries*

Empanadas are individual pastries enjoyed in Spain as well as Latin American countries. They are filled with meat combined with spices and chile. Though traditionally made with a piecrust-type dough, empanadas of filo dough are unusual and crispy rather than chewy.

I love filo dough. Once you get the feel of it, it becomes easy to work with quickly, and you can keep it in your freezer for instant availability. Best of all, it produces the flakiest, lightest, most delicious crust to encase almost anything.

The filling in this recipe is called Picadillo. It is a complex combination of spicy, sweet, fragrant, and hot. Try serving Picadillo nestled into the hollow of a small baked pumpkin or acorn squash, or stuffed inside a roasted, peeled poblano.

Empanadas make exceedingly good hors d'oeuvres, as well as a delicious accompaniment to soup or salad. They freeze extremely well. To bake, just place, still frozen, on a cookie sheet (do not defrost, or they will become limp). Bake as directed, allowing a few extra minutes.

   1   onion, chopped
   3   cloves garlic, chopped
   1   pound ground beef
   1   tablespoon olive oil
   1   teaspoon cinnamon
   1   teaspoon cumin
   ½   teaspoon ground cloves
   1   medium-sized raw baking potato, peeled and shredded
   ⅓   cup sherry or red wine
   ½   cup coarsely chopped toasted almonds
   ½   cup raisins
   2   jalapeños, chopped
   ½   cup tomato sauce (or 3 tablespoons tomato paste)
   1   to 2 tablespoons sugar
   1   to 2 tablespoons wine vinegar
       Salt to taste

½ cup cilantro, chopped (or substitute parsley)
½ pound filo dough
1 stick (½ cup) butter, or more as needed

1. Sauté onion and garlic with ground beef in olive oil until meat is no longer pink.
2. Add all remaining ingredients except cilantro, filo dough, and butter. Simmer for 5 minutes, then taste for salt and seasonings (mixture should be quite spicy and aromatic; add more cumin and cinnamon if needed). Stir in cilantro.
3. Make two crosswise cuts through the roll of filo dough—one about 3 inches from end, the other 3 inches below that. This will give approximately 40 strips of dough.
4. Melt butter. Working with several strips of dough at a time, brush each strip with melted butter. At end of each strip, place about 1 to 2 teaspoons of filling in corner, then fold over corner to enclose filling. Continue folding, as if you were rolling up a flag (see illustration). Bake in 400° F. preheated oven 10 minutes or until golden brown.

Variation 1: Use Keema filling from Eggplant with Keema; you will need double the recipe, about 1 pound of meat.

Variation 2: Use filling from Curried Stuffed Potatoes or Khotes. Serve with yogurt and Cilantro-Mint Fresh Chutney for dipping.

Variation 3: This Anglo-Indian filling is simple, sweet, and spicy.

½ roast chicken
⅔ cup (approximately) mango chutney or green tomato
    chutney
1 tablespoon medium-hot to hot salsa

Skin chicken, remove meat from the bones, and shred. Combine with chutney and salsa.

Rosemary and Red Chile Focaccia »

South of France, Italy   *Yield: 1 large loaf*

This herb-scented, flat leaf-shaped loaf is enjoyed in many variations throughout the south of France and Italy. Focaccia may be flavored with olives, marjoram, sage, or sun-dried tomatoes. Here it is flavored with rosemary and studded with chiles, an unorthodox yet perfect combination, especially with the Garlic-Olive Oil Dipping Sauce. You may vary the amount of chiles used, as some are hotter than others.

> 2 teaspoons dry yeast (1 package)
> 1 cup warm (not hot) water
> 1 tablespoon olive oil
> 2½ cups flour
> 1 teaspoon salt
> ¼ cup fresh rosemary leaves, coarsely chopped (if you must use dried, use 2 tablespoons, but it will not have as much flavor)
> 5 or more small hot dried red chiles, seeded and crumbled
>   Glaze made from 1 egg yolk and 2 tablespoons water
>   Garlic-Olive Oil Dipping Sauce (recipe follows)

1. Dissolve yeast in water; stir in flour, salt, olive oil, rosemary, and chiles. Knead for 7 to 10 minutes or until dough is shiny and no longer sticky.
2. Place dough in oiled bowl covered with a damp cloth. Put in a warm place and let rise until doubled in bulk.
3. Flatten dough with hands to about ¾ to 1 inch thick; make large gashes in dough, leaving enough space in center of cuts so that dough doesn't swell during the rising and baking to close the holes. It should have a ladder- or leaflike appearance. Place on oiled cookie sheet; brush with yolk-and-water glaze.
4. Bake in 375° F. preheated oven for about 40 to 50 minutes. Serve with butter or with the following sauce.

Garlic-Olive Oil Dipping Sauce

> ¼ cup olive oil
> 5 to 6 cloves garlic, coarsely chopped

Heat olive oil gently for a minute or two. Remove from heat and add garlic. Use as dipping sauce for bread, and offer a small bowl of coarse salt for sprinkling.

On Pairing
Food and Beverages

by Ronn Wiegand

Hot, spicy foods present more of a challenge in matching with suitable mealtime beverages than other foods. On the face of it, the incendiary nature of hot dishes would seem to rule out entire groups of traditional drinks that are not perceived as palate soothing and/or flame resistant. For example, hot tea is out (it's too warm already); so are sake and dark beer. Wine is too fragile; unmixed spirits are too strong. But milk, soft drinks, fruit juices, light-colored beers, and mixed drinks (well chilled or over ice), on the other hand, appear refreshing and therefore quite appealing. But virtually all types of chilled beverages are enjoyable with the majority of hot foods and condiments mentioned in this book.

Nevertheless, hot foods are so varied in character, texture, and temperature that even hot tea should not be omitted completely from your list of potential beverages. Nor should wine. While it is true that many wines are engulfed by heat-intensive dishes, many are not. It may come as a surprise to wine traditionalists and to the "cold-beer-only" crowd that wine is often a better accompaniment to hotly spiced foods than other alcoholic beverages. In my experience, only apple cider (still or sparkling) comes close to wine in its ability to partner up consistently with a wide variety of these dishes.

What cider and wine have in common is a ripe fruit flavor, crisp acidity, and (sometimes) some sweetness. Generally, beverages that fall into this category are the most successful with spicy-to-hot foods. Among wine types, slightly sweet Rieslings, Gewürtztraminers, and Chenin Blancs (domestic, German, and French) are very good drinks with these dishes. The cool liquid is refreshing by itself, and the wines' sweetness and acidity tend to awaken and excite the front part of the palate, while the back part of it is given over to the lingering effects of heat or spiciness. For the most part, these wines have moderate to low alcohol levels; levels above 13 percent by volume seem to add fuel to the fire among white wines and are not as successful as those in the 9 percent to 12 percent range. For the same reason, fortified wines such as sherry and Madeira have a hard time complementing most hot foods. They are also quite heavy and sometimes too thick or viscous to quench the thirst.

Dry white wines, such as Chardonnay, Sauvignon Blanc, and Pinot Blanc, and the scores of established European types (Gavi, Orvieto, white Rioja, etc.) are best with only mildly spiced and/or lukewarm dishes. Thus, for some of the milder dishes in this book, these wines are appropriate beverages. If hot sauces, salsas, or condiments are added, however, these dry white wines will invariably wilt under the heat intensity. One example: a crisp California Chardonnay is excellent with Chicken Breasts with Cheese and Salsa. But when additional salsa is eaten with the dish, thereby raising its temperature, a much more enjoyable accompaniment would be a slightly sweet German Riesling Spätlese or a supple, herbal, ripely flavored California Cabernet Sauvignon.

Red wines with hot foods? Yes. Red wines of depth and substance with ripe fruit flavors and moderate to high tannin levels perform surprisingly well along-side "heated" dishes, especially those involving cumin, mustard, ginger, horse-radish, and/or cinnamon in addition to pepper and chile. Slightly sweet wines are usually devastated by a combination of spices and chiles in a recipe; red wines, particularly youthful, fleshy, oak-flavored ones, rise above them. Braised Lamb and Vine Leaves in Tomato Sauce, simmered with dried red chiles and cinnamon, is wonderful with a rich California Zinfandel, Merlot, Cabernet Sauvignon, or Petite Sirah. Light, fruity, quaffing red wines (Valpolicella, Beaujolais, and California Gamays) usually can't overcome the spiciness or heat above one chile on our heat-rating guide. Most rosés and Blanc de Noirs (white red wines), whether dry or sweet, also reach their food-enhancing limitations at the one- to two-chile level.

One word of red wine caution, however. When chile is the main spice in a dish, the tannin content of most young red wines can actually magnify the heat. In this case, it is back to a crisp, off-dry Mosel Spätlese, cider, or a very hoppy lager beer for liquid satisfaction.

When selecting a beverage for hot foods, also bear in mind the occasion, the time of day, the taste preferences of the people you are with, and your budget. It is customary but hardly mandatory to serve local or regional beverages to match the menu; Mexican beer or tequila with Mexican foods, for example. Too, lighter beverages are normally consumed early in the day, heavier ones later on. The ambient temperature also affects beverage preferences—darker, heavier bodied, and fuller-flavored drinks are more satisfying in cool or cold environments than in warm or hot ones. As for your budget, drink what you can comfortably afford. Fine and rare wines are not ideal beverages with hot foods—their flavor nuances are overshadowed by strongly spiced dishes—but there are occasions when no other drink will do. At such times, simply upgrade the quality of the wine you would normally serve with a given dish, and enjoy the inevitable fireworks.

Some Simple Suggestions and Menu Ideas

Part of the delight of hot foods is their ability to transform a dull, everyday food into a spicy treat. Here are a few of my favorite simple suggestions and menu ideas.

One or two poached eggs atop plain steamed rice. Top with salsa of choice and garnish with cilantro.

Believe it or not, this is delicious: salsa on matzo balls!

A corn tortilla topped with several juicy, cooked shrimp, shredded Monterey Jack cheese, then broiled until bubbly. Douse with salsa and thinly sliced onions.

Nasturtiums arranged in salads, floated in soups, or tossed into pasta dishes add a pretty, peppery accent.

Quick salsa: pickled or canned hot chiles such as jalapeño or serrano, stemmed and coarsely chopped in blender or food processor.

Add a hefty amount of Salsa Verde to chicken or fish broth, then poach clams or mussels in this mixture until they pop open. Garnish with cilantro and lime.

Thai shrimp and orange salad: arrange juicy cooked shrimp and orange slices on a plate; dress with lemon juice, sugar, and Thai Chile Sauce. Garnish with cilantro and/or fresh mint leaves.

Serve raw seafood in the open shell with a dab of cilantro pesto, Molho de Pimenta e Limao, or salsa of choice.

Hot, homemade potato chips with fresh salsa for dipping.

Slice avocado onto a piece of buttered whole wheat bread, dribble with salsa and lemon juice, and garnish with thinly sliced onion.

Sopa de Ajo (Garlic Soup)
Roasted and Marinated Peppers
Tajine Msir Zeetoon
(Chicken with Olives and Lemon)
Rice tossed with cumin and peas
Marlena's Salsa

Borani Esfanaj
(Spinach-Yogurt Salad or Dip)
Soft flour tortillas
Zuni Lamb, Green Chile, and Hominy Stew
Roasted Green Jalapeño Salsa

Vietnamese Noodles
with Peanut Sauce and Salad
Thai Chicken
with Basil and Mint
Hot and Sweet Cabbage Salad

Spiced Zucchini-Lime Soup
Braised Veal and Sweetbreads
in Chile Sauce
Blue corn tortillas
Salsa Fresca (Fresh Table Sauce)

Curry Lemon Rice with Seafood
Pato con Guisadas (Duck with Peas)
Green salad with Picante Vinaigrette
Piri-Piri (Fresh Red Jalapeño Relish)

Middle Eastern Black-Eyed-Pea Soup
Bahmi (Curried Okra) with Red Chile Pasta
Cilantro-Mint Fresh Chutney or salsa of choice

Baba Ghanoush (Pureed Eggplant with Tahina)
Dag Ha Sfarim (Whole Fish Baked
with Tomatoes and Sweet and Hot Pepper)
Abala (Steamed Packages of Curry Spiced Rice Puree)
with yogurt raita to dip into
Yemenite Zhoog (Hot Sauce/Relish
with Middle Eastern flavor)

Salade Moroccaine
(Diced Pepper, Cucumber, and Tomato Salad)
Causa a la Limon
(Lemon-Flavored Mashed Potatoes
Garnished with Shrimp, Cheese, Olives, and Egg)
Moroccan Fish with Cumin Paste
Horef (Sautéed Chile and Tomato Appetizer)

Chicken Breasts with Cheese and Salsa
Spicy Black Beans
Aguacate Picante (Diced Avocado
in Tomato-Chile Sauce)
Marlena's Salsa

Matata (Spinach and Clams in Tomato-Peanut Sauce)
Nasi Kuning (Garnished Turmeric Rice Platter)
Rudjak
Sambal Olek (Red-Chile Condiment)

Mail Order Sources

If an ingredient is not available locally, it may usually be purchased by mail order from the following stores. Those that issue catalogs are so noted.

Antone's
Box 3352
Houston, TX 77001
(713) 526-1046
Indonesian, Indian
Catalog

Albuquerque Traders
Box 10171
Albuquerque, NM 87114
(505) 897-1650
Complete selection of New Mexico regional specialities
Catalog

Cardullos Gourmet
6 Brattle St.
Cambridge, MA 02138
(617) 491-8888
Indian, Indonesian

Casa Moneo
210 W. 14th St.
New York, NY 10011
(212) 929-1644
Complete selection of Latin American and Spanish groceries

Casa Pena
1636 17th St. NW
Washington, DC 20009
(202) 462-2222
Latin American and Spanish

Delmar and Co.
501 Monroe Ave.
Detroit, MI 48226
(313) 961-5504
Indonesian, Indian

Haig's Delicacies
642 Clement St.
San Francisco, CA 94118
(415) 752-6283
*Complete selection of Indian, Indo-
nesian, and Middle Eastern foods as
well as coffees, teas, books*

**Kalustyan Orient Export Trading
Corp.**
123 Lexington Ave.
New York, NY 10016
(212) 685-3416
Indonesian, Indian
Catalog

Kam/Man
200 Canal St.
New York, NY 10013
(212) 571-0330
Chinese, Southeast Asian

La Palma
2884 24th St.
San Francisco, CA 94110
(415) 647-1500
*Mexican spices, complete selection of
Latin American and Spanish groceries*

Leong/Jung Co. Ltd.
99 Clark
Montreal, Canada
(514) 861-9747
Chinese, Southeast Asian

Ratto's International Grocery
821 Market St.
Oakland, CA 94607
(415) 832-6503
Indian, Indonesian, Middle Eastern
Catalog

Star Market
3349 N. Clark St.
Chicago, IL 60657
(312) 472-0599
Chinese, Southeast Asian

Zabar's
85th and Broadway
New York, NY 10024
(212) 787-2000
Middle Eastern, international
Catalog

Index